# PRIMER ON WAGE & HOUR LAWS

## Second Edition

# PRIMER ON
# WAGE & HOUR LAWS

## Second Edition

## Joseph E. Kalet

The Bureau of National Affairs, Inc., Washington, D.C.

Copyright © 1990
The Bureau of National Affairs, Inc.


**Library of Congress Cataloging-in-Publication Data**

Kalet, Joseph E., 1951–
  Primer on wage & hour laws / Joseph E. Kalet. —2nd ed.
    p.  cm.
  Includes index.
  ISBN 0-87179-662-7
  1. Wages—Law and legislation—United States.   2. Hours of labor—
Law and legislation—United States.   I. Title.   II. Title: Primer
on wage and hour laws.
  KF3489.K35   1990
  344.73'0121—dc20
  [347.304121]                                                      90-41729
                                                                        CIP


.  Authorization to photocopy items for internal or personal use, or
   the internal or personal use of specific clients, is granted by BNA
   Books for libraries and other users registered with the Copyright
   Clearance Center (CCC) Transactional Reporting Service, provided
   that $0.50 per page is paid directly to CCC, 21 Congress St., Salem,
   MA 01970. 0-87179-662-7/90/$0 + .50.


Published by BNA Books
1231 25th St., N.W., Washington, D.C. 20037


Printed in the United States of America
International Standard Book Number: 0-87179-662-7

# PREFACE

Legal developments in the field of wages and hours have accelerated in the past few years, making this area of the law turbulent where it once was quiescent. The change was abrupt rather than gradual: Early in 1985, the U.S. Supreme Court in *Garcia v. San Antonio Metropolitan Transit Authority* decided that there was no constitutional bar to applying the Fair Labor Standards Act (FLSA) to state and local governments. This decision had the explosive impact of another Supreme Court decision from 1946, *Anderson v. Mt. Clemens Pottery Co.*, wherein the Court held that employers must compensate their employees for time spent in pre- and postshift activities, if these activities are a "necessary prerequisite" to their principal work activity. The intricate network of federal laws and regulations governing wages and hours of work has grown increasingly complex in recent years. This book represents a broad canvas on which the outlines of each of the major statutes have been drawn, with a general idea of the individual profiles of each law and how each law interacts with other laws within the network.

Other wage-hour laws existed prior to the FLSA, but Congress intended the FLSA to be the most comprehensive and pervasive federal statute in this area. The Act has been amended several times, most recently in the FLSA Amendments of 1989, which raised the minimum wage (for the first time in a decade), introduced a subminimum training wage for teenage workers, increased the amount of "tip" credit that may be applied toward a tipped employee's minimum wage, and set a new "annual dollar sales" volume threshold for determining which businesses meet the minimum for FLSA enterprise coverage.

In addition, the FLSA Amendments of 1985 have created a number of disputes involving coverage, retaliation, and compensatory time eligibility, which are addressed in the *Primer*. The dust kicked up by these legislative, judicial, and regulatory actions may not settle for years.

Regulations interpreting and applying the wage-hour laws are the responsibility of the U.S. Department of Labor. The Wage-Hour Division and the Equal Employment Opportunity Commission (EEOC) are the two main enforcement agencies within the Labor Department's wage-hour mandate. The Division historically has had responsibility for ensuring compliance with these statutes. The EEOC was delegated authority to enforce the Equal Pay Act under the 1977 Reorganization Act. Together, these agencies constitute a comprehensive adjudicatory process that will enable the wage and hour laws to develop along consistent and predictable lines.

Employees are granted the right to bring a private lawsuit under several, but not all, wage-hour laws. Congress has determined that, in many instances, allowing employees to operate as "private attorneys-general" would enhance the policies underlying a particular statute, and to that end have granted employees the right to sue. Generally, where an act grants such a right, it also subordinates that right to the federal government's right to sue, on the theory of the greater good. That is, a lawsuit by the Secretary of Labor will create a greater benefit to the public as a whole than will an action by a private individual. Different remedies are available to the party instituting the action, depending on whether it is a private individual or a government official.

The Fair Labor Standards Act, the Walsh-Healey Act, the Davis-Bacon Act, and the McNamara-O'Hara Service Contract Act comprise the bulk of the wage-hour statutes discussed in this *Primer*. They are the primary statutes that govern wages and hours in the United States today. These laws were created during specific historic periods, with specific goals. They have withstood the test of time and continue to play a very important part in the federal statutory apparatus, despite amendments and putative changes. Conflicts in the area of wages and hours appear to be proliferating beyond traditional battlegrounds and into new arenas of combat. For this reason, these laws must be clearly understood to ensure faithful compliance and fair enforcement.

Throughout the *Primer*, abbreviations have been used to designate various sources. In addition to abbreviations in the text, several abbreviations appear without explanation. These abbreviations include references to such publications of The Bureau of National Affairs, Inc. (BNA) as: "LRX" (Labor Relations Expediter); "WHM" (Wages and Hours Manual); "WH Cases" (Wage and Hour Cases); "LRRM" (Labor Relations Reference Manual); and "FEP Cases" (Fair Employment Practice Cases). BNA is the exclusive publisher of the source material that is cited in the *Primer*, unless otherwise noted. Where no source for a particular document or decision is provided, none was available.

Although many people contributed indirectly to the book, Anne Scott and Tim Darby must be singled out for their concern for quality and attention to detail. Kurt Dargis of the University of Notre Dame provided invaluable assistance with proofreading and indexing. Finally, I wish to thank Edward S. Faggen, Legal Counsel of the Metropolitan Washington Airports Authority, for his guidance.

*Joseph E. Kalet*

*Washington, D.C.*
*July 1990*

# CONTENTS

**Preface**     v

**1: THE FEDERAL SCHEME OF WAGE
  AND HOUR LEGISLATION     1**
Fair Labor Standards Act     2
Portal-to-Portal Pay Act     6
Equal Pay Act     7
Walsh-Healey Act     8
McNamara-O'Hara Service Contract Act     9
Davis-Bacon Act     9
Contract Work Hours and Safety Standards Act     10
Consumer Credit Protection Act     11
Child Support Enforcement Act     12

**2: FAIR LABOR STANDARDS ACT     13**
Amendments     14
Interstate Commerce Requirement     17
Employer Coverage     18
"Enterprise" Coverage     20
Employee Coverage     22
Employee Exemptions     25
Hours of Work     33
Minimum Wages     34
Overtime     40
State and Local Government Employees     43
Recordkeeping     47
Child Labor     48
Enforcement     49
Statute of Limitations     50
Liquidated Damages     51

## 3: PORTAL-TO-PORTAL PAY ACT  53
Preliminary and Postliminary Activities  54
Basic Purpose  55
Willful Violations  56
Other Provisions  59
Good-Faith Defense  60

## 4: EQUAL PAY ACT  64
Major Provisions  65
Enforcement  66
Coverage  67
Exceptions to Coverage  70
Penalties  74
Remedies  74

## 5: WALSH-HEALEY PUBLIC CONTRACTS ACT  75
Requirements  76
Covered Contracts  78
Covered Contractors  79
Personal Liability  80
Exemptions  80
Recordkeeping  84
Enforcement  84
Safety and Health Standards  85

## 6: McNAMARA-O'HARA SERVICE CONTRACT ACT  87
Coverage  88
Prevailing Wage Standard  91
Successors  92
Variance Proceedings  93
Wage Payments and Deductions  94
Fringe Benefits  95
Fringe Offsets and Payments  96
Enforcement  97
Limitations Period  98
Blacklist Penalty  98
Attorney's Fees  100

**7: DAVIS-BACON ACT    102**
Coverage    102
Conflict With Other Laws    106
Prevailing Wages    107
Fringe Benefits    112
Enforcement    113
Debarment    116

**8: CONTRACT WORK HOURS
AND SAFETY STANDARDS ACT    118**
Coverage    119
Health and Safety Standards    120
Enforcement    121
Liquidated Damages    122
Debarment Penalty    124
Other Laws    125

**9: OTHER FEDERAL LAWS    126**
Anti-Kickback Law (Copeland Act)    126
Title III, Consumer Credit Protection Act    126
Child Support Enforcement Act    128
Occupational Safety and Health Act    128
Miscellaneous Statutes    130

**APPENDICES**
A.    Directory of U.S. Department of Labor
        Administrative and Regional Offices    133
B.    Chart of FLSA White-Collar Exemption Tests    139
C.    Chart of FLSA Exemptions From
        Minimum Wage and Overtime    143
D.    Directory of U.S. Department of Labor
        Employment Standards Administration,
        Administrative and Regional Offices    149
E.    Chart of State Minimum Wages    157
F.    Coefficient Table for Computing Overtime    181
G.    Chart of State Maximum Hours-Overtime    185
H.    Chart of Overtime Compensation Rules
        for State and Local Government Employees
        (Part 553, 29 C.F.R.)    209

I.      Directory of U.S. Equal Employment Opportunity
        Commission Administrative and
        District Area Offices     213

J.      Directory of U.S. Department of Defense, Defense
        Contract Administration Services,
        Regional Offices     219

K.      Training Wage Regulations     223

**TABLE OF CASES     241**

**INDEX     247**

# 1
# THE FEDERAL SCHEME OF WAGE AND HOUR LEGISLATION

The federal law governing the payment of wages and the regulation of hours worked had its roots in the Hours of Work Laws enacted between 1892 and 1913. The most important piece of legislation enacted, however, is the Fair Labor Standards Act of 1938 (FLSA), because of its broad sweep. Currently, the federal statutory scheme for regulating wages and hours in the United States consists of the FLSA, the Portal-to-Portal Pay Act (Portal Act), five narrower statutes (Equal Pay Act, Walsh-Healey Public Contracts Act, McNamara-O'Hara Service Contract Act, Davis-Bacon Act, and Contract Work Hours and Safety Standards Act), and two laws directed at protecting specific classes of individuals through employer practices involving payroll deductions (Consumer Credit Protection Act and Child Support Enforcement Act).

These laws can be categorized under three classes of federal wage-hour statutes: the first class consists of the FLSA, the Portal Act, and the Equal Pay Act. These statutes are designed to reach most employees in the nation and to ensure fair compensation in terms of minimum wages, overtime pay, and equal pay for equal work.

The second class of federal laws consists of the Walsh-Healey Public Contracts Act (WHA), the McNamara-O'Hara Service Contract Act (SCA), the Davis-Bacon Act (DBA), and the Contract Work Hours and Safety Standards Act (CWHSSA). These statutes establish "prevailing" wage rates for certain

1

classes of employees performing work for a contractor which has a contract to provide material or services to the federal government.

The third class of statutes consists of, among others, the Consumer Credit Protection Act (CCPA) and the Child Support Enforcement Act (CSEA). These laws are designed to protect specific classes of individuals. The CCPA limits the amount of wages that can be garnished from an employee's paycheck and establishes the conditions under which an employee may be discharged for having his wages garnisheed excessively. The CSEA requires employers to withhold from employees' wages any amounts determined to be due under support orders issued by a court or an administrative body. This law also protects employees from employer retaliation as a result of having wages withheld pursuant to the CSEA.

This *Primer* discusses the federal statutory scheme governing wages and hours according to the three classes previously mentioned, and in that sequence.

In addition to the federal laws, it should be pointed out that most states have adopted their own versions of some of the federal laws. Under principles established in the U.S. Constitution, states may pass laws that are stricter, but not less stringent, than the federal apparatus. As a consequence, many states have enacted "little" Davis-Bacon laws, and "little" Walsh-Healey acts, and so on. These state statutes coexist with the federal apparatus, and employers and contractors may be liable for wage violations under either or both statutes simultaneously. For further information, contact the U.S. Department of Labor (see Appendix A), or the appropriate state agency.

## FAIR LABOR STANDARDS ACT

Prior to passing the Fair Labor Standards Act (FLSA) in 1938 (WHM 90:51), Congress attempted to establish fair minimum and overtime wage standards with limited success. These efforts to regulate wages and hours had been limited to workers employed either by the federal government or by specific industries in the private sector. Between 1892 and 1913, for example, Congress passed a series of statutes governing public works employees that became known collectively as the Eight-Hour Law, since the legislative purpose of these enactments was to establish a standard eight-hour work day for these workers. Once this limit had been exceeded, overtime pay was mandatory, to be calculated at the rate of one-and-one-half times (or time-and-one-half) the employee's basic rate of pay. This overtime rate was payable for all overtime hours worked.

When the onset of the Great Depression led to widespread unemployment, the scarcity of jobs was perceived as an invitation to wage abuses by employers who knew that it was a "buyer's market" for labor, particularly since many industries were not covered by either state or federal wage-hour laws. In 1937, for example, the employer in *West Coast Hotel v. Parrish*, contended that the state's Minimum Wage Law violated the Due Process Clause of the Fifth Amendment to the U.S. Constitution. But the Supreme Court affirmed the validity of a Washington State law setting minimum wages for women, reasoning that the statute was a legitimate and reasonable exercise of the state's police power to protect the health of women, to guard them against unscrupulous employers, and to correct the abuse of casting a direct burden upon the community for the support of women who are denied a living wage. This decision created the impetus for the federal government to establish wage and hours of work standards for industries not covered by state law.

The FLSA regulates employment practices in the areas of minimum wage, overtime pay, equal pay, recordkeeping, and child labor. The Act specifically requires employers to maintain adequate records reflecting employees' hours of work and pay for all hours worked. It covers employees who are "engaged in interstate commerce," or in the "production" of goods for travel in interstate commerce, or employed in "an enterprise engaged in commerce or the production of goods for commerce."

Coverage was extended to certain federal government employees and to state and local hospitals and educational institutions by the 1966 amendments to the Act. The 1974 amendments extended coverage to household domestic service workers and to most federal employees and to employees of any "state, political subdivision of a state" and interstate government agencies. However, this latter aspect of the 1974 amendments was overturned by the Supreme Court in 1976 when it decided in *National League of Cities v. Usery* that the amendments "operated to directly displace the States' freedom to structure integral operations in areas of traditional governmental functions."

In February 1985, however, the Supreme Court decided that the FLSA applies to state and local government employees, notwithstanding the principle of state sovereignty under the Tenth Amendment to the U.S. Constitution. (*Garcia v. San Antonio Metropolitan Transit Auth.* overruling *National League of Cities v. Usery*) The extention of the FLSA to cover these governmental entities created a chaotic situation, and soon Congress was forced to act. In November 1985, Congress passed and President Ronald Reagan signed into law the Fair Labor Standards Amendments of 1985, effective April 15, 1986.

The 1985 amendments govern the wage and hour practices of state and local government employers. They provide for the payment of compensatory (comp) time in lieu of cash payments for overtime work; the comp time is calculated at the rate of time-and-one-half of the employee's regular rate of pay for each hour of overtime worked. The amendments provide limits on the amount of comp time that may be accrued, a higher ceiling being allowed for safety, emergency, and seasonal personnel than is allowed for other public employees. They also provide special rules for firefighters and police personnel concerning tour-of-duty practices. (The FLSA is discussed in greater detail in Chapter 2.)

In 1989, Congress finally addressed several important issues that had surfaced years earlier. For example, the most recent increase in the federal minimum wage had been implemented in 1980. There was strong support for, and substantial opposition to, increasing the minimum wage. In addition, there was a perception that an increased minimum wage would create serious financial burdens on employers while overcompensating young, unskilled employees. Finally, a consensus developed that FLSA coverage of businesses should not depend on the type of business, but on the amount of business done. Therefore, after much wrangling, Congress passed the FLSA Amendments of 1989, which:

- Raised the minimum wage in increments, from $3.35 per hour to $4.25 per hour;
- Introduced a subminimum training wage for teenage workers, aged 16–19;
- Increased the amount of "tip" credit that may be applied toward a tipped employee's minimum wage; and
- Set a new, uniform "annual dollar sales" volume threshold for determining which businesses meet the minimum for FLSA enterprise coverage. (See Chapter 2 for more detailed information on these changes.)

Employers are covered under the Act if they meet a minimum threshold dollar-volume-of-business test of $500,000 per annum. If the employer takes in this much money per year, then the next step is to determine whether the employer is an "employer" within the meaning of the Act. For this determination, the courts apply the "economic realities" test to the employer's relationship with the employee: Do the *economic realities* of the relationship indicate that the employer in fact controls the employee in the payment of wages and performance of work? The test is complex and is addressed in greater detail in Chapter 2. An employer may also be covered under the Act by virtue of the "enterprise" concept, which means that the employer's total business operations, taken as a single enterprise, may bring the employer within the Act's coverage under the dollar-volume test. FLSA case law also indicates that an employer may be covered if it is a "joint employer" with another entity; in such situations all individual businesses that make up the "joint employer" can be liable for wage violations.

The Act provides numerous exemptions from coverage for certain classes of employees, along with "tests" to determine whether individuals fall within these classes. Executive, administrative, and professional employees fall within the so-called "white-collar" exemptions. An individual may qualify for more than one exemption, but the effect is not cumulative. Finally, the Act provides a list of employees involved in certain industries who are exempt from FLSA coverage.

The Act states that an employer who *willfully* violates the minimum wage or overtime requirements is liable for liquidated damages in an amount equal to the back pay due the employee. A two-year statute of limitations is established for filing a timely action under the Act. (The FLSA is discussed in greater detail in Chapter 2.)

## PORTAL-TO-PORTAL PAY ACT

The 1947 Portal-to-Portal Pay Act (Portal Act; WHM 90:121) was enacted to rectify a situation that arose after the U.S. Supreme Court decided in *Anderson v. Mt. Clemens Pottery Co.* that employees were entitled to compensation for time spent in preliminary and postliminary activities ("from portal to portal"). The Portal Act also amends the Davis-Bacon and Walsh-Healey Public Contracts acts, which govern the construction of public buildings for the federal government and the manufacture or supply of goods for the government, in the same way it affects the FLSA.

The Portal Act, which is discussed in Chapter 3, provides a "good-faith" defense to the otherwise mandatory provision of the FLSA which imposes liquidated damages liability on employers who *willfully* violate the wage provisions of the FLSA. If an employer can demonstrate that it acted in good faith with a reasonable belief that its actions did not violate the Act, then the Portal Act gives the court discretion to reduce or deny any liquidated damages award. The U.S. Department of Labor's Wage-Hour Division has participated in the development of regulations applying this difficult aspect of the Portal Act; a more detailed discussion of this area of the law is provided in Chapter 3.

The Portal Act also provides a two-year limitations period for actions brought under the FLSA and the Walsh-Healey and Davis Bacon acts; this period will be extended to three years upon a finding that the employer's violations were willful. Since Congress did not define "willfulness," the courts were left to give meaning to this very important phrase. For almost two decades, the courts applied a standard known as "in the picture," which meant that if the employer knew or had reason to know that the FLSA was "in the picture," then the employer was presumed to have acted willfully. (*Coleman v. Jiffy June Farms*)

In 1988, the Supreme Court rejected the "in the picture" standard, and determined that, for purposes of the three-year statute of limitations, a "willful" violation requires a showing that the employer either "knew or had reckless disregard" for whether its conduct was prohibited. (*McLaughlin v. Richland Shoe Co.*) (See Chapter 3 for a more detailed discussion of this area.)

The Portal Act also banned actions brought by unions or other representatives of employees, but allowed employees to sue on behalf of themselves and similarly situated employees. In these actions, each participant is required to give his or her consent in writing, that is, affirmatively to "opt in" to the action.

## EQUAL PAY ACT

In June 1963, President John F. Kennedy signed into law the Equal Pay Act of 1963 (EPA; WHM 90:131). The EPA requires employers to pay equal pay to men and women performing work requiring equal skill, effort, and responsibility and performed under similar working conditions. The Act amended the FLSA and was incorporated into the Title VII of the Civil Rights Act of 1964; it may be enforced in an action initiated under either amended statute.

Congress specified that the EPA would cover employers who are covered under the FLSA. However, Congress removed the "enterprise" concept from EPA coverage, thus restricting the number of employers (and hence, employees) who were covered under the EPA. Although the FLSA provides for enterprise coverage, any EPA action is limited to the employer's individual "establishment" and may not extend to the employer's enterprise.

While the EPA requires equal pay for work of equal skill, effort, and responsibility, it provides an exception where such payment is made pursuant to a seniority system, a merit system, a system that measures earnings by quantity or quality of production, or a differential based on any factor other than sex. (The EPA was inadvertently drafted with the phrase "any *other* factor other than sex.") The EPA, perhaps anticipating employer intransigence in complying, precludes employers from reducing the wage rate of any employee to comply with the requirement to pay equal wages for equal work.

The EPA is essentially enforced, as is the FLSA, by private actions, class actions, or actions by the Secretary of Labor. However, the EPA also provides an administrative route to enforcement under Title VII through the Equal Employment Opportunity Commission, which is specifically authorized to enforce the EPA. Any amounts owing under the EPA are treated as if they were owed under the FLSA, including the imposition of liquidated damages and attorney's fees liability, where appropriate. (The EPA is discussed in greater detail in Chapter 4.)

## WALSH-HEALEY ACT

The Walsh-Healey Public Contracts Act (WHA; WHM 90:201) was enacted in June 1936 to regulate employment conditions under government contracts. In addition to regulating hours of work and wages, the Act deals with the problems of child labor, convict labor, and hazardous working conditions. It covers all government contracts for the manufacture or furnishing of materials, supplies, articles, and equipment in any amount exceeding $10,000. Any contract covered by the WHA must provide that all workers will be paid not less than the prevailing minimum wage rate determined by the Secretary of Labor for similar work in the locality. Employees are entitled to overtime pay for any work in excess of 40 hours per week. Prior to the passage of the Department of Defense Authorization Act of 1986 (DOD Act), which amended the WHA, employees who worked on a contract that was covered by the WHA were entitled to overtime for any work in excess of 8 hours per day, but the DOD Act removed the 8-hour limit, while maintaining the 40-hour per week overtime limit. As with most other wage-hour laws, overtime under the WHA is calculated on the basis of time-and-one-half the employee's regular rate of pay.

The Secretary of Labor is authorized to investigate and decide cases involving alleged violations of the WHA. Liquidated damages found due in such proceedings may be obtained by the government through a lawsuit, or may be deducted by the government from amounts due the contractor under another contract.

The most significant sanction for violating the WHA is the rarely used debarment ("blacklist") penalty, under which contractors who are serious and willful violators of the Act are barred from receipt of government contracts for a period of three years. (The WHA is discussed in greater detail in Chapter 5.)

## McNAMARA-O'HARA SERVICE CONTRACT ACT

The McNamara-O'Hara Service Contract Act (SCA; WHM 90:225), commonly known as the Service Contract Act, was enacted in 1965 to complement the WHA in regulating labor standards for employees who work under contracts let by the federal government.

Whereas the WHA covers the manufacture or furnishing of materials and supplies which exceed $10,000, the SCA covers contracts for the performance of services for the federal government which exceed $2,500. (Attempts were made in 1986 to raise the minimum dollar amount, but they were unsuccessful. In light of government efforts to reduce federal spending, additional attempts to raise the threshold may be expected.)

The SCA requires the payment of wages and fringe benefits found to be prevailing locally or as found in a previous existing contract, but in no event less than the federal minimum wages under the FLSA. The same enforcement provisions as apply in the WHA—the withholding of payments to a contractor to correct underpayments to its employees—applies in the SCA, including the three-year debarment penalty. (The SCA is discussed in greater detail in Chapter 6.)

## DAVIS-BACON ACT

The Davis-Bacon Act of 1931 (DBA; WHM 90:251) regulates the rate of wages for laborers and mechanics employed in the construction of public buildings for the federal government by contractors and subcontractors, where the contract calls for an expenditure of more than $2,000. (Attempts were made to raise the minimum amount in Congress in 1986, but they were unsuccessful.) The Act also applies to work performed under certain other laws, such as the Federal Aid Highway Act and the Area Redevelopment Act of 1961. Under the DBA, the Secretary of Labor is required to establish prevailing minimum wage rates to be incorporated into contracts covered by the Act. The Comptroller General, however, is the official authorized to withhold payments to the contractor if necessary to make good any underpayments to employees; employees may sue the contractor for back pay owing to them if the amount withheld by the Comptroller General is insufficient to reimburse them.

The DBA provides a three-year debarment of blacklist penalty which bars *willful* violators of the Act from obtaining a contract under the DBA. (The DBA is discussed in greater detail in Chapter 7.)

## CONTRACT WORK HOURS AND SAFETY STANDARDS ACT

The Contract Work Hours and Safety Standards Act (CWHSSA; WHM 90:271) was enacted in 1962 to regulate employer practices in the area of contracts calling for the performance of services for the federal government. The Work Hours Act, as it is commonly called, covers mechanics and laborers employed on any public work for the federal government and employees performing services similar to those of mechanics and laborers in connection with dredging or rock excavation in any river or harbor of the United States or the District of Columbia. The CWHSSA also requires the payment of overtime at the rate of time-and-one-half the employee's regular rate of pay for all hours worked in excess of 40 per week. Prior to the enactment of the Department of Defense Authorization Act of 1986 (DOD Act), the Work Hours Act required overtime pay when an employee exceeded 8 hours per day or 40 hours per week. The DOD Act eliminated the

8-hour day limit for overtime so that only the 40-hour per week limit now applies.

The enforcement mechanism for the CWHSSA is different from most of the federal labor standards acts in that inspectors must report to the contracting officer any violations of the Act they find. The officer may then withhold from the contractor any amounts due the employees, including penalties, as a result of such violation. Decisions made by the contracting officer can be appealed to the head of the contracting agency and then to the U.S. Court of Claims. Willful violations of the Act are punishable by a fine of up to $1,000 and/or imprisonment of up to six months. (The CWHSSA is discussed in greater detail in Chapter 8.)

## CONSUMER CREDIT PROTECTION ACT

The Consumer Credit Protection Act (CCPA; WHM 90:141), enacted in 1968, limits the amount of an employee's wages that can be subjected to garnishment to not more than 25 percent of the employee's "disposable earnings" for any workweek; or to the amount by which his disposable earnings are greater than 30 times the federal minimum hourly wage, whichever is greater. It covers all employees, regardless of the size of the employer's business. Under the Act, the Secretary of Labor is authorized to bring enforcement proceedings, however, proceedings are carried out by the Wage-Hour Division which is the Department of Labor's enforcement arm. The Act's restrictions on the amount of an employee's wages that are subject to garnishment do not apply in cases of wage deductions based on a court order for the payment of support, or on an order from a bankruptcy court, or to a wage deduction for any debt due on any state or federal tax.

Under the Act, employers are precluded from discharging employees solely because of a single wage garnishment. This relatively straightforward language had led to much litigation over whether the issuance of consecutive, but not concurrent, garnishment orders constitutes a "single" order for purposes of the protection afforded the employee under the Act. Employers who violate this prohibition are subject to criminal penalties of a $1,000 fine and/or one year imprisonment.

One important aspect of the Act concerns state sovereignty under the Tenth Amendment to the U.S. Constitution. The CCPA purports to set standards in areas that have traditionally been controlled by the states. In view of the constitutional protections retained by the states, the Act does not prohibit states from applying their own garnishment laws where they prescribe stricter garnishment restrictions than federal law. The Act also does not affect or alter state laws which prohibit an employer from discharging an employee because the employee had more than one wage garnishment. Any state may have garnishments that are issued under its own laws exempted from the Act, where the state laws provide for restrictions that are substantially similar to the Act. The state must apply to the Secretary of Labor for this exemption. (The CCPA is discussed in greater detail in Chapter 9.)

## CHILD SUPPORT ENFORCEMENT ACT

The Child Support Enforcement Act of 1984 (CSEA: WHM 90:143) requires employers to withhold from employees' wages any amounts determined to be due under support orders issued by a court or administrative body.

Employers are prohibited from disciplining, discharging, or refusing to hire an individual because of a withholding order for support. Employees are entitled to advance notice and a hearing before the order becomes effective. Employers who fail to comply with the Act may be subject to penalties. (The CSEA is discussed in greater detail in Chapter 9.)

# 2
# FAIR LABOR STANDARDS ACT

The Fair Labor Standards Act of 1938 (FLSA; WHM 90:51) was enacted to meet the economic and social problems existing during the Great Depression. Low wages, long working hours, and high unemployment were rampant during this time, and Congress sought a way to establish minimum wage standards while encouraging the spread of employment. The policy of the FLSA was to correct and, as rapidly as practicable, to eliminate labor conditions detrimental to the Act's goals of establishing minimum wage standards.

The Act, as amended, sets general standards for minimum wages, overtime compensation, equal pay, and child labor for all employees who are not specifically exempted under the Act. All covered employees include those who are:

- Engaged in interstate commerce. "Commerce," under the Act and case law developed under it, includes both incoming and outgoing foreign transportation of goods, as well as such trade between the states; or
- Engaged in the production of goods for commerce. This production of goods includes not only the actual production operations, but also "any closely related process or occupation directly essential" to the production; or
- Employed in an "enterprise engaged in commerce or in the production of goods for commerce." This standard relates directly to the "enterprise" coverage for employers, all of whose emloyees in a particular business unit may be covered, regardless of how their individual duties

13

relate to commerce or the production of goods for commerce. In 1966, the Act was amended to bring state and local hospitals and educational institutions within the definition of an "enterprise engaged in commerce."

## AMENDMENTS

In 1963, Congress passed the Equal Pay Act (EPA; WHM 90:131) which amended the FLSA in several important respects. The EPA requires that male and female workers receive equal pay for work requiring equal skill, effort, and responsibility, where the work is performed under similar working conditions. Since EPA coverage is the same as that for the minimum wage provisions of the FLSA, an employer covered by the minimum wage provisions of the FLSA is therefore also covered by the EPA.

The EPA does not exempt from coverage those categories of executive, administrative, and professional employees and outside salesmen who are exempt from FLSA minimum wage and overtime provisions. The EPA provides specific exemptions from liability when wage differentials are:

- Based on any factor other than sex;
- Paid pursuant to a bona fide seniority system;
- Paid pursuant to a bona fide merit system; and
- Paid pursuant to a system which measures earnings by quantity or quality of production.

In equalizing past wage disparity based on sex, an employer may not lower the wages of the higher-paid worker to those of the lower-paid worker.

As with the FLSA, unpaid wages may expose an employer to liquidated damages liability for willful violations, and to attorneys' fees and costs. The EPA is enforced by private actions and by the Equal Employment Opportunity Commission for agency actions, unlike the FLSA, which is enforced by private actions and by the Secretary of Labor through the U.S. Department of Labor's Wage-Hour Division. (For further information on the EPA, see Chapter 4).

In 1966, the Act was amended to bring state and local hospitals and educational institutions within the definition of enterprises engaged in commerce, the third prong of the coverage test discussed earlier in this chapter. At that time, Congress also extended coverage of the FLSA to certain federal employees, without regard to the three prongs of the coverage test.

In 1974, Congress amended the Act to cover most federal employees; to employees of states, political subdivisions of states, and interstate agencies; and to private household domestic service workers.

In 1976, the U.S. Supreme Court ruled in *National League of Cities v. Usery* that the 1974 FLSA amendments extending the Act's coverage to state and local government employees were unconstitutional, insofar as the amendments operate "directly to displace the States' freedom to structure integral operations in areas of traditional governmental functions." The Court said that the Commerce Clause of the U.S. Constitution, which authorizes Congress to regulate in areas involving interstate commerce, did not provide a sufficient basis for Congress to interfere with states' relationship with their employees in such areas as fire prevention, police protection, sanitation, and public health.

In 1985, the Supreme Court overruled the *National League of Cities* decision, stating that the extension of the FLSA to state and local government employees did not violate any affirmative limit placed on Congress under the Commerce Clause. (*Garcia v. San Antonio Metropolitan Transit Auth.*) The effect of this decision was to impose FLSA overtime requirements and the Act's general ban against using compensatory time to most state and local government employees.

Following a storm of criticism from public sector employers, who said the decision would wreak havoc on state and local budgets and services, Congress passed the Fair Labor Standards Amendments of 1985, (WHM 90:89), which became effective on April 15, 1986.

The 1985 amendments allow for the payment of compensatory (comp) time in lieu of cash payments to certain employees, establish limits on how much comp time an employee may accrue before cash overtime payments become mandatory, and set standards for determining payment for comp time upon termination of employment. They also establish methods for the treatment of "volunteers," and those employees involved in sporadic and substitute employment in a public agency. The amendments also provide protection against discrimination or adverse action by an employer in retaliation for an employee's assertion of coverage under the FLSA overtime provisions.

Finally, the amendments treat the accrual of comp time by public safety, emergency, and seasonal personnel different from accrual by all other public employees, by allowing a higher ceiling for the former group to accrue comp time than is available for the latter group. The amendments also provide special rules for firefighters and police personnel concerning tour-of-duty practices. (These issues are discussed in greater detail later in this chapter under State and Local Government Employees.)

In 1989, Congress responded to a changing economic climate by passing the "Fair Labor Standards Amendments of 1989," which President George Bush signed into law on November 17, 1989 (Pub. Law 101-157). The legislative history of these amendments indicates that the public was concerned over several related issues. These issues included the fact that the minimum wage had not been increased since 1981, and concern that such an increase could adversely affect employment opportunities for new, essentially untrained/unskilled workers (primarily teenagers). In addition, Congress was responding to concerns from businesses about the credit to be charged against the minimum wage on behalf of workers who received tips. Finally, Congress recognized the administrative and practical difficulties of maintaining two separate tests for determining whether different types of businesses (retail and non-retail) met their respective "annual dollar sales" volume for purposes of FLSA coverage. All these concerns were addressed in the 1989 amendments, which:

- Raised the minimum wage in increments, from $3.35 per hour to $4.25 per hour (see "Minimum Wages" later in this chapter);
- Introduced a subminimum training wage for teenage workers, aged 16–19 (see "Minimum Wages" later in this chapter);

- Increased the amount of "tip" credit that could be applied toward a tipped employee's minimum wage (see "Minimum Wages" later in this chapter); and
- Set a new, uniform "business-volume" (annual dollar sales) threshold for determining whether a business meets the minimum for FLSA enterprise coverage (see "Dollar-Volume Test" later in this chapter).

In addition to these major concerns, the FLSA Amendments of 1989 created an exemption to the overtime provisions, not to exceed 10 hours per week, for employees receiving "remedial education" under certain circumstances (see "Overtime" later in this chapter).

Finally, the 1989 amendments extended the protections of the FLSA to employees of the House of Representatives and to employees of the Architect of the Capitol.

## INTERSTATE COMMERCE REQUIREMENT

The Act extends coverage over employers based on the nature of the employer's business. The interstate commerce aspect of the employer's business allows the courts to extend the Act's coverage to the "farthest reaches of interstate commerce." (*Overstreet v. North Shore Corp.*)

The courts have established the following principles for determining the appropriateness of extending coverage based on the interstate character of the employer's business:

- If an establishment produces goods for sale in interstate commerce, there is a presumption that all employees who worked in the establishment contributed to the production of the goods. To overcome this presumption, the employer must establish that the functions of certain employees were segregated from the production of the goods for interstate commerce. (*Guess v. Montague*) However, such segregation will not assist employers in avoiding coverage if their employees qualify under the "enterprise" concept.
- Employers are deemed within the Act's coverage as producing goods for commerce where the employer intends, hopes, or has reason to believe that the goods

or any unsegregated part of them will move in interstate commerce. (*United States v. F.W. Darby Lumber Co.; Walling v. Burch*)

- If only a minor part of the employer's business is shipped in interstate commerce or is involved in the production of goods for interstate commerce, the employer may still be covered under the Act where the interstate shipments are "regular and recurrent." (*Mabee v. White Plains Publishing Co.*)

The FLSA prohibits "any person" from introducing into interstate commerce goods produced in violation of the Act's minimum wage and overtime provisions. This prohibition is called the "hot-goods" provision, and it has led to numerous court decisions about what is meant by "person," "introduced," "interstate commerce," "goods," and "produced." The Supreme Court has expanded the meaning of "person" to include allegedly *innocent* secured creditors who have acquired security interests in goods manufactured by debtor-employers in violation of the Act. The Court rejected the argument that the ban on shipping "hot goods" applies only to culpable parties. (*Citicorp Indus. Credit v. Brock*)

## EMPLOYER COVERAGE

The FLSA was intended, as remedial legislation, to cover the broadest possible scope of employment situations. To that end, the Act does not define covered employers, but describes them in terms of the amount of business transacted per year. On the other hand, the Act emphasizes who is an employee, and whether individuals are in fact involved in an employer-employee relationship under the so-called "economic realities" test, which is discussed later in this chapter under Employee Coverage.

### Dollar-Volume Test

The basic determining factor for employer coverage involves the size of the employer's business. Congress found that the larger the business, the greater its harm to the public by its FLSA violations and the easier it would be to identify and regulate because of its size. Congress therefore established a minimum gross receipts amount—the dollar-volume test— that would serve as the cutoff between covered and noncovered employers.

The 1989 amendments to the FLSA simplified the enterprise coverage test by establishing a uniform $500,000 "business-volume" threshold in place of prior thresholds for retail and non-retail businesses. Under the new uniform threshold, effective April 1, 1990, enterprises with annual gross sales exceeding $500,000 are covered by the FLSA if they meet the Act's definition of "enterprise," and if they have at least two employees who engage in commerce or in the production of goods for commerce (see "Interstate Commerce Requirement" for more information).

Small enterprises with less than $500,000 in annual gross sales are exempt from FLSA enterprise coverage. Such firms, however, may still have FLSA obligations with respect to workers covered by the Act on an individual basis.

Excise taxes at the retail level which are separately stated and identified in the customer's bill need not be included in the calculation of gross dollar volume of sales. As a general rule, a tax is "separately stated" where it has been added to the sales slip or invoice or stated orally at the time of sale or visually by means of a poster or other sign reasonably designed to inform the purchaser that the amount of the tax is included in the sales price. (WH Publication 1431, January 1977).

Under the prior coverage rules, certain types of enterprises, i.e., public agencies, hospital and health care facilities, construction and reconstruction businesses, and laundry and dry cleaning establishments were covered by the FLSA, regardless of their annual business volume (assuming they met other applicable requirements for enterprise coverage). However, the amended rules provide an exemption to small laundry or dry cleaning and small construction/reconstruction businesses by making such enterprises subject to the "business volume" test. The theory underlying this provision is that a small business will not meet the $500,000 threshold, and thus will not fall under FLSA coverage. Coverage of public agencies, hospitals and health care facilities is unaffected by the 1989 amendments.

## "ENTERPRISE COVERAGE"

Under the 1961 amendments to the FLSA, Congress specifically acknowledged the necessity of the enterprise concept for FLSA coverage, to reach subsidiary branches of an employer's operations. The Act defines enterprise as:

> The related activities performed (either through unified operation or common control) by any person or persons for a common business purpose, and includes all such activities whether performed in one or more establishments or by one or more corporate or other organizational units including departments of an establishment operated through leasing arrangements, but shall not include the related activities performed for such enterprise by an independent contractor.

In the absence of the enterprise concept, an employer's subsidiary branches might otherwise be exempt from FLSA coverage, based on the dollar-volume standard. The Act extends coverage to employees, not specifically exempted otherwise, who are employed by certain enterprises engaged in interstate commerce or in the production of goods for commerce.

Where an employer operates several small entities, none of which individually may meet the minimum dollar-volume tests discussed above, the employer may still be covered under the Act by virtue of the enterprise concept of coverage.

The enterprise concept is not independent of the other bases of coverage, because it is still necessary to determine whether the enterprise or two or more of its employees are engaged in interstate commerce or the production of goods for interstate commerce.

However, unlike other bases of coverage, the enterprise concept does not base coverage on the activities of the individual employees: all of the employees in a particular enterprise or establishment may be covered, provided the enterprise and two or more of its employees are sufficiently engaged in interstate commerce or the production of goods for interstate commerce.

An employer that operates an investigative agency specializing in background and surveillance checks on individuals claiming workers' compensation benefits for clients in more than one state and that has an annual dollar-volume of over

$250,000 is an enterprise within the meaning of the Act, a federal court in Maryland has ruled. Under the current FLSA definition of the word "commerce," the court reasoned, the employer was clearly engaged in commerce. (*Brock v. Commercial Index Bureau*)

The interstate character of the goods as a product that has been moved in interstate commerce is not destroyed by the fact that the product is used to make a different product, which is then sold to intrastate purchasers. And the mingling of the intrastate goods with this product does not negate the product's origin in interstate commerce. (*Wirtz v. Melos Constr. Corp.*)

Although the courts have held that the coverage of the law must be liberally interpreted, they consistently have placed the burden of providing coverage on the employee in an employee-initiated wage suit, and on the Secretary of Labor in a wage-recovery suit or in a suit to restrain violations of the Act. The Act is set up in a way that employees may only sue on their own behalf, and only for the recovery of wages due, while the Labor Secretary may sue on behalf of a class of employees and may obtain injunctive relief in addition to obtaining wages due the employees.

In determining whether a particular business is covered under the enterprise concept, the courts have examined such factors as:

- Related activities of separate business entities; (*Wirtz v. Savannah Bank & Trust Co. of Savannah*)
- The relationship between a "house" agency and the parent organization; (WH AdmOp, Feb. 7, 1962)
- Related activities of conglomerates; (FLSA, Sec. 13(g))
- Work performed by an "independent contractor"; (*Rutherford Food Corp. v. McComb*)
- Work performed for an independently owned retail or service establishment; (*Wirtz v. Charleston Coca-Cola Bottling Co.*)
- Whether there was a common business purpose, common control, and unified operations. (*Wirtz v. Mack Farland & Sons Roofing Co.; Wirtz v. Hardin & Co.; Donovan v. Janitorial Servs.;* and *Donovan v. Sideris*)

## Church-Operated Schools

The existence of schools operated by religious organizations has posed problems for the FLSA. The courts have had to resolve such issues as the following:

- Whether a church-operated school is an "enterprise" for purposes of FLSA coverage;
- Whether individuals who work in such a school are "employees" under the Act; and
- Whether the First Amendment to the U.S. Constitution, which guarantees free exercise of religion, precludes FLSA coverage of such a school.

A federal appeals court ruled that the school is an "enterprise" under the Act and that the history of the FLSA indicates an affirmative intention to treat church-operated schools as enterprises. Rejecting the claim that the individuals who work in the school fall under the Act's exemption for ministerial employees, the court said that the teachers perform no "sacerdotal" function, do not serve as church governors, and do not belong to any clearly delineated religious orders. Finally, the court held that FLSA coverage did not impermissibly burden the church members' exercise of religion under the Constitution. (*Dole v. Shenandoah Baptist Church*)

## EMPLOYEE COVERAGE

### Employees Engaged in Commerce

In view of the congressional intent to extend the FLSA, as remedial legislation, to the farthest reaches of interstate commerce, Congress and the courts have delineated categories of employees whose employers are involved in interstate commerce. The employees are categorized according to the functions they perform under the "employees engaged in commerce" doctrine:

- Employees in the telecommunications and interstate transportation industries;
- Employees who participate in the distribution of goods that move through channels of commerce; and

- Employees who directly aid or facilitate the operation of instrumentalities of commerce by providing materials or power used by the instrumentalities or by maintaining or reconstructing or repairing them.

Since employees engaged in interstate transportation and telecommunications generally are conceded to be covered by the Act, most litigation under the commerce test of coverage involves the "distribution of goods" and "operation of instrumentalities of commerce" prongs of the test.

Reflecting the congressional intent to extend the FLSA as broadly as possible, Congress wrestled with one category of employees which pitted two important social goals against one another: illegal aliens. Interestingly, both social goals were embodied in federal legislation designed to regulate employment practices, and these twin goals came into conflict in 1988.

In 1986, the Immigration and Reform Control Act (IRCA) became effective. This statute was intended to restrict the flow of illegal immigration into the United States, which Congress perceived as being fueled by employment opportunities. IRCA provisions have three main objectives:

- To prohibit the employment of illegal aliens;
- To require employers to make a good-faith determination whether potential employees are legal aliens; and
- To penalize employers that fail to make this determination or that make less than a good-faith determination. The penalties range from fines to imprisonment.

An illegal alien working for a motel sued his employer for unpaid wages under the FLSA. The employer argued that IRCA indicated the congressional intent to ban employment of illegal aliens, and that this intent would be thwarted by enforcing the FLSA wage provisions against the employer of an illegal alien.

A U.S. Court of Appeals ruled, however, that failure to enforce the FLSA in these circumstances would unjustly enrich the employer and would imply that the IRCA stripped employees of statutory rights under the FLSA. The court reasoned that this result would also encourage other employers to take advantage of illegal aliens, knowing that the IRCA would protect them from having to pay wages. Since Congress nowhere indicated an intent that the IRCA would deprive illegal aliens of FLSA rights, the court concluded that illegal aliens are "employees" under the FLSA, even though the IRCA prohibits the employment of such undocumented aliens. (*Patel v. Quality Inn South*)

Cutting against the congressional intent of broad coverage of the FLSA is the complex statutory scheme that exempts many employees covered under other laws such as railway labor, motor carriers, airlines, small telephone exchanges, and water transportation acts, which preempt FLSA coverage in those areas.

*"Production for Commerce" Test.* Under the "production for commerce" test of coverage, the Act defines "produced" as:

- Employees producing, manufacturing, mining, handling transporting, or in any other manner working on goods shipped in commerce; or
- Employees engaged in any "closely related process or occupation directly essential" to the production of such goods.

Under these criteria, courts have attempted to define the parameters of "actual production operations" (*Western Union Tel. Co. v. Lenroot*), and to define the meaning of "goods" (*Powell v. U.S. Cartridge Co.*). Section 3(i) of the Act excludes goods "after their delivery into the actual physical possession of the ultimate consumer thereof." Consequently, the courts have also had to address what was intended by the phrase "ultimate consumer." (*Marshall v. Brunner*)

### "Fringe" Production Employees

Section 3(j) of the Act provides for coverage of any employee engaged in "any closely related process or occupation directly essential" to production. These fringe production employees were specifically described in the Statement of the House Managers in the 1949 amendments to the Act, which listed some fringe employees who still would be covered under the "closely-related and directly-essential" test. Applying these provisions, the Court of Appeals for the Ninth Circuit ruled that employees of a liquid waste disposal company who regularly remove liquid waste from customers' plants producing goods for interstate commerce, and who perform services for airlines directly related to interstate commerce, are engaged in the production of goods for such commerce under the Act. (*Brennan v. Carrasco*)

Congress intended by these amendments to exclude from FLSA coverage those employees whose work is several degrees or stages removed from the production of goods for interstate commerce. These provisions were interpreted in *Allstate Construction Co. v. Durkin*, where "off-the-road" employees employed by a road contractor in the production of material to repair interstate roads were found to be covered by the Act, even though the material was produced in a state for use on the roads within that state. The U.S. Supreme Court reasoned that these employees were engaged in the production of goods for interstate commerce because "he who serves interstate highways and railroads serves commerce. By the same token, he who produces goods for these indispensable and inseparable parts of commerce produces goods for commerce."

Construction workers on a dam, however, were found not to be involved in an activity that was closely related or directly essential to the production of goods for interstate commerce, according to the Supreme Court, in view of the remoteness of construction from the production of the goods, and the absence of the dedication of completed facilities either exclusively or primarily to such production. The Court also observed that the purpose of the dam—to provide water to a locality—could not be regarded as the production of goods for commerce. (*Mitchell v. H.B. Zachry*) This case illustrates the fact that the employer may meet the dollar-volume test and be engaged in interstate commerce, only to be excluded from coverage because its employees do not produce the type of goods that the Act was intended to cover.

## EMPLOYEE EXEMPTIONS

The Act contains a complex scheme of exemptions for employees and employers in certain specified industries. In addition, the Act also carves out specific exemptions for employees having certain responsibilities, where coverage of the employee is thought to be inconsistent with the Act's purpose. These employees fall under one or several of the exemptions for executive, administrative, or professional employees, depending on job duties. These three classes of exemptions are collectively referred to as the "white collar exemptions." Each exemption carries with it a specific set of criteria, or test, that must be met for the employee to fall within the exemption. (See Appendix B for a summary of white-collar exemptions.)

Some employee exemptions suspend only the overtime requirements, while others suspend only the minimum-wage and equal pay requirements. Still others suspend two or all four standards—minimum wage, overtime, equal pay, or child labor. Exemptions may apply to all the employees in an establishment, or only to certain individuals. As an added complication, the exemptions freqently overlap. (See Appendix C for a summary of FLSA exemptions from minimum wage and overtime requirements.)

All of the exemptions under the Act are subject to a rule of "strict construction," that is, any doubt must be resolved in favor of the employee's coverage. (*Calaf v. Gonzalez*) The burden of proving that a particular exemption applies lies with the employer who asserts it. (*Coast Van Lines, Inc. v. Armstrong*)

### White-Collar Exemptions

The Act expressly exempts "executive, administrative, and professional" employees from its minimum wage and overtime provisions. The Act charges the Secretary of Labor with responsibility to define and limit these exempt categories.

An executive employee is limited to one whose duties "include some form of management authority—to persons who actually direct the work of other persons." To qualify as an "exempt executive" employee under the Department of Labor regulations, the employee must:

- Have as his primary duty the management of (*a*) the enterprise in which he is employed or (*b*) a customarily recognized department or subdivision of the enterprise;

- Regularly supervise the work of two or more full-time employees;
- Have the authority to hire, discharge, and promote, or effectively to recommend such action;
- Regularly exercise discretion in the course of his primary duty;
- Spend at least 80 percent of the workday engaged in the primary duty and receive a stipulated amount of pay per week. This stipulated amount per week is either $155 (under the "long test") or $250 (under the "short test"). The regulations were drafted with an eye to expeditious determinations. To that end, individuals who are proffered as executives will be examined under a more detailed set of factors if they are paid less than $250 per week, and under a more streamlined test if they earn more than $250 per week. (The tests have not been revised for many years and, for all practical purposes, no executive earns less than $250 per week. Therefore, the long test has very little applicability. However, the Labor Department is considering changes in these dollar amounts.)

The courts have held that an employee must meet *all* the applicable tests to qualify for the exemption. (*Wirtz v. C.&P. Shoe Corp.; Wirtz v. Williams*) The employee's job title is not controlling, but the duties involved determine whether the executive exemption should apply. (*Associated Builders v. Brennan*) In addition to receiving the minimum-dollar amount specified in the regulations, the employee must be paid on a "salary basis." The Wage-House Administrator has stated that this means the employee must receive his full salary for any week in which he performs any work, regardless of the number of hours or days worked.

The salary aspect of the executive employee exemption is complicated and may involve such factors as offsets for jury duty or military leave, salary plus bonus calculations, bona fide reductions not intended to circumvent the salary basis requirements, offsets as credit for board and lodging, and other issues. Specific problems should be addressed to the local office of the U.S. Department of Labor, Employment Standards Administration, Wage-Hour Division. (See Appendix D)

Finally, the regulations provide that an employee who is in "sole charge" of a particular operation is to be deemed an "executive" employee. In addition, an employee may fall under an executive, administrative, and professional exemption simultaneously. (*Legg v. Rock Prods. Mfg. Corp.*, WH-463, WH AdminOp, Aug. 21, 1978)

The second white-collar exemption removes the administrative employee from protection of the minimum wage and overtime provisions of the FLSA. The salary tests are similar to those that apply to the executive employee. The administrative employee must:

- Perform office or nonmanual work directly related to management operations;
- Regularly exercise discretion beyond clerical duties;
- Perform specialized or technical work, or perform special assignments with only general supervision; and
- Spend at least 80 percent of work time on exempt work. Retail-service employees must spend at least 60 percent of work time on exempt work.

The phrase "directly related to management policies or general business operations" contained in the regulations may cover the responsibilities of a wide variety of employees who carry out major assignments in conducting the business or whose work affects business operations to a substantial degree. The Wage-Hour Division warns that job titles will not control.

Highly paid *administrative employees* (those earning over $250 per week on a salary basis) are exempt if they meet all the criteria of the short test:

- The employee's position must include work requiring the exercise of independent judgment and discretion; and
- The employee's primary duty is office work or work that is not of a manual nature, and is directly related to management policies or to general business operations of the company or its customers. The Wage-Hour Administrator has issued an Explanatory Statement con-

cerning the meaning of "administrative employee" under the regulations (WHM 92:561-92:572).

The last white-collar exemption is the professional employee category, which covers a wide variety of occupations from law and medicine to writing, acting, and other artistic professions. Elementary and secondary school teachers are covered under this exemption by virtue of the 1966 amendments to the Act. As with other white-collar employees, the professional employee is exempt from both the minimum wage and overtime provisions of the Act.

A former senior research associate in a chemical development department who earned more than $250 per week brought suit against his employer claiming he should have been paid overtime during the two years preceding his dismissal because he did not consider his status as that of a professional employee. A federal district court in Pennsylvania found to the contrary because the associate was engaged in a learned profession and had as his primary duty the "performance of work . . . requiring knowledge of an advanced type in a field of science or learning" under the regulations. In addition, he was part of a research team that investigated and evaluated new syntheses for pharmaceutical products, he had discretion to exercise professional judgment, and he did not contest the employer's evidence which proved that he was fully qualified to perform professional work. (*Molinari v. McNeil Pharmaceutical*)

A newspaper employee who wrote radio and television commentary and criticisms was found to be within the professional-employee exemption, since he primarily performed tasks which relied on his creativity, initiative, imagination, talent, and flair. (*Lewis v. News World Communications*; but see *Sherwood v. Washington Post*)

As with administrative employees, the professional employee exemption is available if the employee is paid on a salary basis and the salary meets the minimum-dollar amount specified in the regulations for 40 hours of work per week. Lawyers and doctors actually practicing in their fields need not meet the minimum-dollar amount.

*"Long Test."* The Wage-Hour Division has devised an elaborate test ("long test") for determining whether low-paid (between $155 and $250 per week) white-collar employees qualify for exempt status. It has also devised a streamlined test ("short test") for higher-paid employees (more than $250 per week). For each category of exempt employee (executive, administrative, professional), there is a separate long test and short test. (Ed. note: These tests share some common criteria, but differ in significant ways. Consult Appendix B in this Primer for more information.)

Because the minimum-dollar amounts under both the long and short tests were devised many years ago, the long test is not in use for any practical purpose. Nevertheless, it has historical significance. Under the long test, a low-paid white-collar employee is required to have as his primary duty work that either:

- Requires advanced knowledge in a field of science or learning, of a type customarily acquired by a prolonged course of specialized study; or
- Is original and creative in character in a recognized field of artistic endeavor, so that the result depends primarily on the employee's invention, imagination, or talent.

Since this description is fraught with subjective, ill-defined phrases, the Wage-Hour Division has attempted to provide guidance by issuing a plethora of Administrative Opinions.

*"Short Test."* For white-collar employees earning more than $250 per week on a salary basis, the short test requires that an exempt employee must:

- Have as his primary duty the performance of work requiring advanced knowledge in a field of science or learning, including work that requires the consistent exercise of discretion and independent judgment; or
- Have as his primary duty the performance of work requiring invention, imagination, or talent in a recognized field of artistic endeavor.

The short test is truly shorter than the cumbersome and ambiguous long test. To facilitate matters, the Wage-Hour Division has issued a chart of professions whose employees fall within the exemption. Such professional employees include registered or certified medical technologists, registered nurses, computer systems analysts, and supervisory programmers.

## Nonemployees

In addition to employees and exempt employees, the Act recognizes "nonemployees" as individuals who do not qualify for employee status. For example, apprentices are regarded by the Wage-Hour Division as nonemployees, because apprentices are not what Congress intended to cover by the word employee. According to the Division, an apprentice is a person at least 16 years old (or older, if required by state or federal law) who is employed to learn a skilled trade pursuant to the terms of a *written* apprenticeship agreement with the employer. (Regulations covering employment of apprentices appear at 29 C.F.R. 521, WHM 92:25.) Trainees for work on railroads are not employees, according to the U.S. Supreme Court, since two important qualifications are lacking: (a) any benefit to the employer and (b) compensation or an intent that the services rendered be paid for. (*Walling v. Portland Terminal Co.*)

A major category of nonemployee is the independent contractor. Certain jobs may be performed with an independence in judgment that is contrary to an employer-employee relationship which is characterized by the employer's direction of the employee on the job. This is one of the wide range of factors the courts examine to determine whether a particular individual is an employee or an independent contractor. The determining factors include:

- The extent to which the services rendered are an integral part of the employer's business;
- The permanency of the relationship;
- The amount of the individual's investment in facilities and equipment;
- The individual's opportunity for profit or loss;
- The degree of independent business organization and operation;
- The nature and degree of control exercised over the individual by the employer; and

- The degree of independent initiative, judgment, or foresight used by the individual providing the service. (*Real v. Driscoll Strawberry Assocs., Inc.*)

This set of criteria for independent contractor status has come to be known as the economic realities test. The courts have applied these factors in a way that no one factor will be regarded as determinative; rather, all must be weighed in order to decide the economic realities of the situation. (*Brock v. Lauritzen Farms*) Central to a court's decision is whether the worker is *economically dependent* upon the business to whom he or she renders services. (*Usery v. Pilgrim Equip. Co., Inc.*) The difficulty with independent contractors is that they receive, and expect to receive some compensation for their efforts. The *dependency* on the employer is the litmus test for determining whether a particular individual is an independent contractor or an employee. The language of the Act defines "employ" as "to suffer or permit to work," and the courts have adopted a common sense understanding of the term, with respect to a claimed independent contractor, in the context of the relationship that existed at the time. (*Walling v. Jacksonville Terminal Co.*)

Migrant farm workers have occasionally been the subject of independent contractor disputes. An additional complexity in such cases is the presence of the farm labor contractor, who stands between the farm worker and the farm owner. The courts have had no difficulty finding an employer-employee relationship involving the farm worker and both the contractor and the farm owner. (*Hodgson v. Griffin & Brand of McAllen, Inc.*)

Trainees are another category of nonemployee. The U.S. Wage-Hour Administrator applies a six-part test to determine whether a particular individual falls into this category. The individual must meet *all six* factors:

- The training, even though it includes actual operation of the employer's facilities, is similar to that which would be provided in a vocational school;
- The training is for the benefit of the trainee;
- The trainee does not displace regular employees, but works under closer supervision;

- The employer providing the training gains no immediate advantage from the trainee's activities—on occasion, the employer's operation may in fact be hindered;
- The trainee is not guaranteed a job at the completion of his training; and
- The employer and the trainee understand that the employer is not obligated to pay wages during the training period.

Typically, a graduate research assistant and a senior in college who are required to do on-the-job training as part of their course work are regarded as "trainees." (WH AdminOp, June 7, 1967 and WH-20, Mar. 31, 1970 (WHM 91:417))

Airline trainees for the position of flight attendant have given rise to much litigation, with the courts holding that these trainees are not employees under the FLSA. (*Donovan v. American Airlines*)

Other categories of individuals who may perform work for an employer but who are exempt from FLSA coverage include volunteers, apprentices, handicapped workers, outside salespersons, mental patients or patient workers at rehabilitation facilities, and certain agricultural and prison laborers.

## HOURS OF WORK

Prior to determining whether an employee is entitled to minimum wages or overtime or both, it frequently becomes necessary to establish that the employee was engaged in compensable activity or that the time reserved for the employer was compensable time.

Where the issue is whether the activity engaged in was compensable, the courts generally examine whether the employer knew that the employee was engaged in such activity, whether the employee was specifically ordered to refrain from such activity, and whether the activity benefitted the employer. (*Mitchell v. Caldwell; Davis v. Food Lion*)

For example, the Secretary of Labor brought suit to recover allegedly unpaid wages on behalf of employees who worked at satellite pumping stations located in isolated areas substantially removed from any community. The U.S. Court of Appeals for the Fifth Circuit found that the employees spent "on-call" time with their families, that they were only rarely required to respond to employer needs, and that they were fully aware of the employer's on-call time policy when they were hired. Applying the well-accepted rule concerning on-call time, the court declared that these employees were "waiting to be engaged," and were not "engaged to wait." (*Brock v. El Paso Natural Gas Co.*)

An agreement between chauffeurs and the limousine service which employed them entitled the chauffeurs to compensation for time spent waiting for an assignment. However, they were not entitled to compensation for time spent waiting *away* from the employer's premises or outside of the terms of the agreement, since this time was spent primarily for the chauffeurs' rather than the employer's benefit. (*Caryk v. Coupe*)

Idle time that a casino required its employees to spend at the casino was compensable, because the principal benefit inured to the casino and the employees were not completely free to use the time for their own purposes. (*Brock v. Claridge Hotel & Casino*)

The most common disputes over whether certain time is compensable involve activity that occurs before ("preliminary") or after ("postliminary") the employee's principal work activity. If such work is part of an employee's principal activity, then it is compensable. If such work is not, then it is usually found to be noncompensable. Disputes involving preliminary and postliminary activities fall under the Portal-to-Portal Act. (For information concerning preliminary and postliminary activity, see the introduction to "Preliminary and Postliminary Activities," Chapter 3.)

## MINIMUM WAGES

The "Fair Labor Standards Amendments of 1989," signed by President George Bush in November 1989, affected the minimum wage in three important respects: it raised the minimum wage in increments from $3.35 to $4.25; it created a "subminimum" training wage for teenagers; and it raised the percentage of the amount of money received by employees in the form of tips which could be credited against minimum wages due those employees. Those changes are:

*Minimum Wage Hike.* The two-step hike in the federal minimum wage is to be phased in through two 45-cent installments to help ameliorate the economic impact on employers. The first increase, from $3.35 per hour to $3.80 per hour, became effective on April 1, 1990. The second increase, to $4.25 per hour, becomes effective on April 1, 1991. The new rates apply to all 50 states and U.S. territories and possessions, except American Samoa, where minimum wages are set by the Secretary of Labor based on recommendations from Special Industry Councils. However, a special phase-in schedule applies to certain industries in Puerto Rico.

*Subminimum Training Wage.* The 1989 amendments provide that teenagers, age 16 to 19 years old, may be employed at a subminimum training wage for a period as long as 180 days, but nor more than 90 days by any one employer.

While the amendments do not impose any specific training requirements for an employee's first 90-day training period, certain training requirements must be met if a second 90-day period occurs: Employers must provide "job-specific skills [training] and personal skills [instruction]."

Job-specific skills under Labor Department regulations involve the "development of skills and knowledge necessary for full and adequate performance. The training shall provide knowledge and skills beyond those customarily learned by observation and incidental work exposure," according to the Department of Labor. Personal skills are defined by the Labor Department regulations as "skills other than specific job-related skills that affect an individual's employability and satisfactory work adjustments to any job." (See Appendix K for the Training Wage Regulations published in the Federal Register by the Department of Labor.)

On April 1, 1990, the minimum wage rose to $3.80 per hour, while the training wage was set at $3.35 per hour. The training wage is linked to scheduled increases of the minimum wage, and may not be less than 85 percent of the federal minimum wage. When the federal minimum wage increases to $4.25 per hour on April 1, 1991, the minimum training wage will rise to $3.61 per hour. However, the training-wage provisions, which are the most complicated aspect of the 1989 amendments, are set to expire on April 1, 1993.

Only persons 16 to 19 years of age are eligible to receive the special training wage. Moreover, employers may not under any circumstances pay training wages to migrant and seasonal farm workers and non-immigrant aliens admitted to perform temporary farm labor.

An additional restriction provides that during any given month, the total hours that an employer pays at subminimum training wages may not exceed a proportion equal to one-fourth of the total hours worked by all employees. An employer is also prohibited from paying training wages to any employee under either of the following conditions:

- The employer has laid off employees from the position—or any substantially equivalent position—that the employer intends to fill with training-wage workers; or
- The employer has terminated the employment of regular employees or otherwise reduced their number with the intention of replacing the affected workers with employees eligible for training wages.

Two final aspects of the training-wage provisions should be noted: there must be some showing of "proof" that an individual is eligible to receive the training wage; and the employer must provide notice to such an individual of the conditions under which the training wage is paid.

Information about an employee's employment history is necessary to determine whether he is eligible for training wages. Providing "proof" of previous employment generally is the worker's responsibility. For these purposes, individuals may provide an employer with an accurate list of previous employers, including dates and durations of employment. Generally, an employer's good-faith reliance on such a list suffices to protect the employer from charges of violating the 180-day maximum time allowed for paying an individual at training-wage rates.

The 1989 amendments require the employer to provide employees who are eligible for the training wage with a special written notice describing the training wage, legal restrictions on employers paying training wages, and the remedies available to employees where such restrictions are violated. Copies of this notice and of the new poster concerning training-wage requirements are available from the U.S. Labor Department's Wage-Hour Division. (See Appendix K for the "Notice to Employees About the Training Wage.")

*Tip Credit Increases.* The 1989 amendments allow employers of tipped employees to count tips as covering a greater portion of the required federal minimum wage. After March 31, 1990, the amendments increase the permitted tip credit from 40 percent to 45 percent, and to 50 percent after March 31, 1991.

Aside from setting limits on the amount of money which can be offset against minimum wages due tipped employees, the FLSA also provides rules for averaging wages over a given period of time to comply with the minimum wage requirements. However, the old rule still applies that the credit may not exceed the value of the tips actually received.

Exceptions to the minimum wage are made for learners, apprentices, messengers, and superannuated workers. However, an employer should obtain a certificate of exemption from the Wage-Hour Division before paying the reduced rate. In addition, certain industries and occupations are exempt from the minimum wage requirement; the Wage-Hour Division should be consulted for such information.

In 1986, the FLSA was amended to simplify the administration of sheltered workshops. Prior to this legislation, handicapped workers were exempt from the minimum wage provisions and sheltered workshop employers were required only to pay their handicapped workers at least 50 percent of the minimum wage. The 1986 amendments eliminated separate certification requirements for various categories of handicapped workers and based all wages on individual productivity.

The Wage-Hour Administrator has established rules for computing and paying the minimum wage, the unit of time over which the minimum wage may be averaged, the types of deductions permitted, the effect of piece rates or bonuses, and other matters. Although the Act requires employers to maintain adequate and accurate records, the employer may decide for itself *how* to maintain its records if it is able to provide the Administrator with basic data on the subjects specified above concerning minimum wages.

The two main sources of difficulty in administering this part of the Act concern the length of time over which wages may be averaged to comply with the minimum wage and which deductions may be legally made from employees' wages.

Employees receive pay in various forms: hourly, fixed weekly, fixed monthly, fluctuating workweek, piece rates, bonuses, and commissions. Since the Act sets $3.80 as the minimum for each hour, an hourly paid employee must receive this rate for all hours worked. An employer may not "juggle" the books to pay the employee less than this rate for some hours and more than this rate for other hours in the workweek, even if the average hourly rate meets the minimum wage rate.

A fixed weekly salary is determined by the number of hours worked during a week divided by the actual compensation received. This amount must equal or exceed the minimum hourly wage rate. For a fixed montly rate, or for any fixed rate that exceeds one week, the employer must translate the salary into a weekly wage rate and satisfy the fixed weekly salary standard set forth above. Under this formula, the fixed monthly salary is multiplied by 12 (months) and divided by 52 (weeks per year) to ascertain the weekly rate; the bimonthly salary is multiplied by 24 (bimonthly periods) and divided by 52 (weeks per year) to determine the weekly rate under the payment schedule.

For employees who are paid on a piece-rate basis, or for those paid under an incentive plan, the salary must meet the average hourly minimum wage rate for all hours worked in the week, although the employee may not earn the mininum wage for every hour worked.

Where there is a mixed rate, such as where an employee receives an hourly rate for some hours worked and a piece rate for other hours in the same week, the hourly rate must be at least the minimum and the piece-rate wages must average at least the minimum for the piece-rate hours.

The minimum wage required by the FLSA must be paid in cash or "facilities furnished" and not in scrip, tokens, or anything else that is not readily convertible into money, at face value. The Wage-Hour Administrator treats any kickbacks that reduce the employee's wages below the hourly minimum as illegal.

Under the Act, employers are entitled to deduct from an employee's wages the "reasonable cost of fair value (not retail value) of meals, lodgings, and other facilities" provided to employees, provided the employer satisfies the conditions listed below. The Wage-Hour Division has defined "other facilities" used in Section 3(m) of the Act as being "like board or lodging," such as:

- Meals furnished at company restaurants or cafeterias;
- Housing furnished for dwelling purposes;
- General merchandise furnished by company stores and commissaries;
- Fuel;
- Electricity and other utilities for the employee's non-commerical use; and
- Transportation for the employee between home and work, where the travel time is noncompensable under the Act, and the transportation is not an incident of and necessary to the employment.

Such facilities may be considered wages paid to the employee only if they are customarily furnished by the employer. Employee discounts at retail establishments may not be considered part of the wage, since these discounts simply accommodate employees by reducing the prices of purchases they make. (WH AdminOp, Oct. 5, 1961)

In order for the employer to deduct the reasonable cost or fair value of meals, lodging, and other facilities from employees' minimum wages, the employer has the burden of establishing that:

- The facilities were furnished for the employees' benefit;
- The employees were told that the value was being deducted from their wages;
- The facilities were of a kind customarily furnished by the employer; and

- The employees accepted the facilities voluntarily.

Reasonable cost to the employer may not include any profit to any other "affiliated persons" such as:

- Spouse, child, parent or other close relative of the employer;
- Partner, officer, or employee in the employer's organization;
- Parent, subsidiary, or other closely connected operation of the organization; and
- An agent of the employer's organization.

An employer may make other deductions from minimum wages, such as taxes, uniform cleaning, credit union loans, payroll savings plans, insurance premiums, and voluntary contributions to church, charitable, or other institutions. Illegal deductions include those for meal periods, breakage of merchandise, cash register shortages, and theft losses. However, where there is a debt that the employee owes the employer, a deduction to remove this indebtedness will be allowed, but only if the deduction does not reduce the employee's wages below the minimum wage rate. (*Brennan v. Veterans Cleaning Serv.*) (State minimum wage requirements appear in Appendix E.)

## OVERTIME

The FLSA requires the payment of overtime at a rate of one-and-one-half times (or time-and-a-half) the employee's regular rate of pay for all hours worked in excess of 40 per week. The Act does not establish a daily maximum hours limit, after which overtime would be required. Overtime need be paid over to the employee only on the regular payday for the workweeks in question. (Appendix F sets for the Wage-Hour Division's explanation of how to calculate overtime via its coefficient table.)

The question occasionally arises whether the employer authorized the employee to work the overtime for which he seeks compensation. The Act authorizes overtime if the employer "suffered or permitted" the employee to work the overtime hours. If the employer knew the employee was working the additional hours or if the overtime appeared on the payroll records, the employer will be presumed to have suffered or permitted the employee to perform the overtime work. If the circumstances indicate that the employer knew or should have known that the employee was working overtime for the employer's benefit, then the employer may be liable for those hours.

A hospital employee who was required to be on call 24 hours a day for 365 days per year, and to report within 20 minutes of being paged, prepared to repair complicated equipment is entitled to a trial on his claim for overtime, according to a U.S. appeals court. The all-consuming nature of the restrictions, which barred him from taking vacations or furthering his education, created a genuine dispute of fact as to whether his on-call time constituted time that he was engaged to wait. (*Bright v. Houston Northwest Medical Center Survivor*; but see *Townsend v. Mercy Hosp. of Pittsburgh*)

Since overtime is calculated based on the employee's regular rate of pay, it often becomes crucial to determine that regular rate. Items usually included in this rate are:

- Wages, salary, commission, or piece rate;
- Incentive bonuses;
- Shift premiums;
- Cost-of-living allowances;
- Premiums for hazardous duty or "dirty" work; and
- Other payments that are regarded by the employee as part of his regular compensation.

Types of compensation usually excluded from overtime, as not being part of the regular rate of pay, include:

- Premium pay under union contracts for work on Saturdays, Sundays, and holidays;
- Pay for time not worked, for example, vacations, sick leave, and holidays;
- Contributions to a pension or insurance plan;
- Outright gifts;
- Bonuses that are completely discretionary with the employer;

- Distributions from a profit-sharing plan that meets the Wage-Hour Administrator's regulations; and
- Contributions to a bona fide thrift or savings plan that meet the Wage-Hour Administrator's regulations.

The FLSA requires that the "regular rate of pay" be more than one-and-one-half times the applicable minimum wage. An employer that paid its banquet waiters at least $14 per hour (consisting of an hourly wage plus a percentage of the service charge applied to banquet bills) was found to have complied with the Act. (*Mechmet v. Four Seasons Hotels*)

On the other hand, a premium payment to employees for evening and night shift work was not, in all cases, one-and-one-half times the employee's regular rate and, as a result, could not be excluded from the regular rate for purposes of calculating required overtime pay. (*Brock v. Wilamowsky*)

As mentioned earlier, the method of payment determines the overtime calculation. Where an employee performs more than one job for the employer, or is paid partially on an hourly rate and partially on a piece rate, or on a commission basis, the overtime rate will vary according to what the employee's regular rate is determined to be. (State maximum hours and overtime requirements appear in Appendix G.)

The FLSA Amendments of 1989 created a new exemption to the overtime provisions, not to exceed 10 hours per week, *in the aggregate*, for employees receiving "remedial education" that is:

- Provided to employees who lack a high school diploma or educational attainment at the eighth-grade level; and
- Designed to provide reading and other basic skills at an eighth-grade level or below; and
- Does not include job-specific training.

## Fluctuating Workweek

An important variation on the standard overtime situation involves the employee whose workweek fluctuates. In order for the employer to comply with the Act's overtime provisions where the employee works irregular hours that fluctuate from week to week, there must exist an agreement—preferably written—that provides at least for the FLSA minimum wage, for overtime at the statutory rate for all hours worked per week, and for a weekly wage guarantee for not more than 60 hours calculated according to the rate specified in the agreement.

These agreements, called Belo agreements, are named after the 1942 U.S. Supreme Court decision in *Walling v. A.H. Belo Corp.* Belo agreements require two essential elements:

- Neither the employer nor the employee can anticipate or control with any certainty the number of hours worked from one week to the next; *and*
- the employee's workweek must fluctuate both *above and below* the FLSA overtime limit of 40 hours per week.

The failure of an employee's workweek to dip below the 40-hour mark will constitute a failure to meet the "irregular hours" requirement of the Belo plan. (*Donovan v. Tierra Vista*)

The Belo agreements allow employers to control labor costs and limit overtime expenses, while guaranteeing the employee a fixed weekly pay regardless of the irregular hours worked. Where the agreement fails to meet the Belo requirements, the employer will be required to pay overtime based on fixed pay for fluctuating hours.

## STATE AND LOCAL GOVERNMENT EMPLOYEES

Congress amended the FLSA to allow a proper "fit" of the Act over previously noncovered employees of state and local governments, following the U.S. Supreme Court's decision in *Garcia v. San Antonio Metropolitan Transit Authority*.

The Fair Labor Standards Act Amendments of 1985, effective April 15, 1986, allow for the payment of compensatory (comp) time off in lieu of cash payments for overtime work, and provide standards for determining payment of comp time upon termination of employment for state and local government employees. The amendments also provide for the treatment of volunteers and sporadic employment and substitute employment in a public agency, compensatory time limits, and protection against discrimination or adverse treatment in retaliation for an assertion that an employee is covered by the FLSA overtime provisions.

The ban against retaliation (the "anti-discrimination" provisions) prohibits an employer from discriminating against an
employee "because" the employee asserted that the FLSA applies to him or her. After the 1985 amendments were passed,
a municipality reduced the base wages of its firefighters when
they asserted coverage under the FLSA. The municipality stated
that it reduced wages because of the fiscal necessity to stay
within the previously approved budget. According to the city,
the word "because" in the Act means that there must be a
showing that the claimed retaliation was the "motivating" or
determining factor of the adverse action (in this case the reduced wages).

The appeals court acknowledged that the city's position
had merit, but ruled that the language of the Act does not
compel this interpretation. Further, it held that the legislative
history of the Act precludes such an interpretation. Absent
compelling arguments to the contrary, the appeals court de-
ferred to the U.S. Department of Labor's position that it is not
necessary to prove the employer intended to retaliate to prove
a violation of the Act, where the employer's action nullifies
the effect of extending the Act to state and local government
employees. (*Blanton v. City of Murfreesboro*)

Although the 1985 amendments became effective more
than one year after *Garcia v. San Antonio*, and were designed
to change the impact of that decision, Congress did not specifically state that the amendments were retroactive. Further,
a question usually arises about a retroactive "taking" such as
the amendments taking of overtime that was approved by the
Supreme Court in *Garcia*. In 1987, a federal appeals court declared that the 1985 amendments retroactively relieved the
state of any liability for unpaid overtime occurring after *Garcia*
but prior to the effective date of the amendments. The court
also rejected an argument that employees had been deprived
of a property interest without due process, concluding that
the amendments further the rational legislative purpose of
protecting the fiscal integrity of states and are thus constitutional. (*Rhinebarger v. Orr*)

However, employees may sue for FLSA overtime for periods prior to *Garcia*, if they can show that their work during

these periods did not fall within the area of "traditional governmental functions," under *National League of Cities v. Usery.* (*Ackinclose v. Palm Beach County*)

The amendments treat differently accrual of comp time by public safety, emergency, and seasonal personnel, and accrual by all other public employees. They also provide special rules for firefighters and police personnel concerning tour-of-duty regulations.

### Comp Time Limits

Comp time may be paid in lieu of overtime, but it must be computed on the basis of time-and-one-half for each overtime hour worked.

Public safety, emergency, and seasonal employees may earn up to 480 hours of comp time before cash payments are required; under the time-and-one-half measure, this means that these employees can only work 320 actual overtime hours before becoming eligible for cash payments. All other state and local workers may accrue up to 240 comp time hours, or 160 overtime hours actually worked. Volunteers to state and local governments who receive no compensation or varying forms of compensation (e.g., expense reimbursements or a "nominal fee") are not considered employees under the Act. The hours in which public employees perform occasional or sporadic part-time work that is different from their regular assignments will not count toward overtime calculations.

Section 7(o) of the FLSA requires a government employer to enter into a comp-time agreement prior to electing comp time for its employees. A federal district court was presented with the "difficult question": when a public agency or political subdivision of a state does not have a collective bargaining agreement, memorandum of understanding, or any other agreement between itself and its employees' designated representative regarding compensation for the employees' overtime work, does Section 7(o) of the Act *compel* the public agency to compensate such employees monetarily, rather than with time off, for the overtime hours worked?

Responding in the affirmative, the court observed that the city determined, "in its sole discretion," which employees would receive comp time and which would receive wages. In addition, the court rejected the city's sole defense that state law bars the type of agreement contemplated under Section 7(o) as being without merit. (*Wilson v. City of Charlotte*)

According to the U.S. Court of Appeals for the Tenth Circuit, if the employees are represented, the following rules apply:

- The employer may not use agreements it obtained from employees to pay comp time instead of wages, even where it has a history of paying comp time;
- The employer may not withhold recognition of the employees' representative, where they have designated this representative in a letter and petition to the employer;
- The employer may not rely on the Tenth Amendment to the U.S. Constitution to refuse to bargain with employees' designated representative, since Section 7(o) of FLSA is constitutional; and
- The employer may only use a comp-time agreement obtained through the representative. (*Firefighters (IAFF) Local 2203 v. West Adams County*)

Where state law prohibits a government employer from entering into agreements with employees' representative, Section 7(o) of the FLSA preempts this prohibition. (*Abbott v. Virginia Beach*)

### Tour of Duty for Fire and Police Personnel

The rules allow state and local employers to establish a longer work period than the normal seven-day week for purposes of computing overtime pay for firefighters and police officers. (The FLSA exempts from overtime pay firefighters or law enforcement personnel employed by public agencies with fewer than five employees; this exemption was unchanged in the 1985 amendments.)

Under the special overtime rules, a public employer may establish a work period or "tour of duty" for its firefighters or police officers of up to 28 consecutive days. Overtime eligibility for firefighters begins once they work more than 212 hours during a 28-day work period (based on a 7.57-hour workday).

Public employers may use a shorter tour of duty for firefighters and police officers, provided that the maximum hours are reduced proportionally. For example, firefighters on a 14-day tour would be eligible for overtime after 106 hours. Under these rules, the shortest permissible work period is seven days, during which a firefighter may work 53 hours and a police officer may work 43 hours (based on a 6.11-hour workday). (Appendix H reproduces the Overtime Compensation Rules for police officers and firefighters of state and local governments.)

A county did not violate the FLSA when its firefighters, who worked a 21-day work period, were paid pursuant to a plan that averaged payments of straight time and overtime with each bi-weekly paycheck, even though they did not earn specific amounts paid bi-weekly, where:

- The plan complied with the collective bargaining contract;
- Averaging of straight time payments is permissible under the Act; and
- The overtime payments, which must be paid on the next regularly scheduled payday, were either paid during the work period and in advance of the time when they were payable, or were paid at the end of the work period. (*Mullins v. Howard County*)

## RECORDKEEPING

The Act requires employers to maintain adequate records of all hours worked, all employees, the wages received, and other terms and conditions of employment. Where records were inadequate or nonexistent, courts have ruled that:

- Employers must "disprove" the evidence of hours worked by the employee; (*Skipper v. Superior Dairies, Inc.*)
- Employers may not claim that there is no evidence of the precise amount of time worked; (*Wirtz v. First State Abstract & Ins. Co.*)
- An employer's failure to rebut the employee's evidence based on employee testimony allows a court to establish the hours actually worked; (*Wirtz v. Durham Sandwich Co.*)

- An employee may establish by "just and reasonable inference" the amount of hours worked in the absence of employer records. (*Anderson v. Mt. Clemens Pottery Co.; Duchon v. Cajon Co.*)

An employer did not violate the overtime provisions when it refused to compensate an employee for five minutes of overtime work, according to a federal appeals court, since the employer had a policy of compensating overtime work only if it constituted at least six minutes per week. The appeals court held that nonpayment for the five-minute segment was a *de minimis* (i.e., trifling) violation. The amount of overtime for which the employee would not be paid accrued over a period of one year, the court noted, but did not constitute a substantial measure of his time and effort. (*Brandon v. United States*)

There is no required format for maintaining records, so long as the information is accurate and complete. Employers are advised to retain these records for six years, which is the general statute of limitations adopted by Congress in Title 28 of the U.S. Code (28 U.S.C. Sec. 241(a)). Although the Portal-to-Portal Pay Act establishes a three-year limitations period for willful violations, an administrative proceeding may reach back six years to the employer's records.

Finally, the Act requires the display in a prominent place of the FLSA poster which states the minimum wage, overtime, and equal pay requirements of the Act, and how an employee may pursue wages due and the exercise of other statutory rights. The Wage-Hour Division provides copies without charge.

## CHILD LABOR

The employment of minors is regulated by the FLSA and by many state laws. Section 12 of the FLSA prohibits the use of "oppressive" child labor and bans the shipment of any such "hot goods" produced by such oppressive child labor. In addition, employers may be personally liable for child-labor violations and may face fines, levied on a daily basis, along with the corporation which may be fined daily for its violations. (*McLaughlin v. McGee Bros. Co.*)

The Act also requires that if minors are employed, they

must be above 18 years old in any "hazardous" occupation, as defined by the U.S. Department of Labor. In other cases, the minors must be above 14 or 16, depending on the type of employment and by whom employed. For example, the child-labor restrictions in the FLSA may apply to employees of small newspapers, railroads, or airlines, even though the employees in such establishments are exempt from the minimum wage and/or overtime requirements.

## ENFORCEMENT

Congress provided that the Act would be enforced only through lawsuits, initiated either by the Secretary of Labor or by private individuals. The Act provides for the following actions:

- Suits by the Secretary of Labor to collect unpaid minimum wages and overtime pay due employees and an equal amount in liquidated damages;
- Suits by the Secretary for injunctions to restrain employers from violating the law. The 1961 amendments to the Act grant jurisdiction to the federal courts to order payment of back wages in such an injunction action, and as part of such an order, a federal court may enjoin the interstate shipment of goods produced by employees not paid in accordance with the Act's wage requirements (hot goods injunction);
- Suits by employees themselves to recover any back wages due them under the Act, an equal additional amount as liquidated damages, and attorneys' fees and court costs;
- Criminal actions by the U.S. Department of Justice against "willful" violators of the Act. Conviction in such an action may lead to a fine or, in the case of a second offense, imprisonment.

The primary responsibility for enforcing and administering the FLSA rests with the Wage and Hour Division of the Labor Department. The Division makes inspections and investigations to determine compliance with the Act, issues rules, regulations, and interpretations, and makes determinations on requests for exemptions.

In addition, the FLSA requires the Secretary of Labor to conduct certain studies and reports and to present the results to Congress. These provisions require the Secretary to:

- Investigate whenever he has reason to believe that, in an industry subject to the Act, foreign competition has resulted or is likely to result in increased unemployment in the United States. Should the Secretary determine that increased unemployment has resulted or is likely to result, he then must make a full report of his findings and determinations to the President and to Congress;
- Conduct studies on the justifications or the lack thereof for each of the exemptions provided by Section 13(a) and (b) of the Act. The studies are to include an examination of the extent to which employees of "conglomerates" are subject to these exemptions and the economic effect of their inclusion in such exemptions;
- Study and report to Congress biennially on ways to prevent curtailment of employment opportunities for disadvantaged minorities, youth, and the elderly;
- Report to Congress annually on the economic impact of the FLSA—the so-called (Section) "4(d)" reports.

Finally, employers may be liable for amounts found due as underpayments, plus an equal amount as liquidated damages, plus attorneys' fees and court costs. Employers who are found to have "willfully" violated the Act (with the knowledge that the Act was "in the picture") (*Coleman v. Jiffy June Farms*) may be fined up to $10,000, imprisoned up to six months, or both.


## STATUTE OF LIMITATIONS

Under the FLSA, an aggrieved employee has two years from the date of the alleged violation to file an action. In civil rights and other litigation, a body of case law has developed as to when the right to file accrues. The courts have had to choose between the time when the employee receives notice of the adverse decision, or when the decision is implemented. Generally, the courts have held that the time when the employee receives notice is the time when his right to file an action accrues. (*Delaware State College v. Ricks*)

In the context of FLSA litigation this conflict of when the right to bring an action accrues has not been an area of contest. However, the prudent employee will file an action as soon as he learns of the alleged violation in order to preserve his rights.

Under the Portal-to-Portal Pay Act, the limitations period for filing an FLSA action is extended to three years if the employee can show that the employer engaged in a "willful" violation of the FLSA. It should be noted that such a finding will be persuasive, if not conclusive, as to any good-faith belief defense to the imposition of liquidated damages liability on the employer. (See Chapter 3 for further information on this subject.)

Finally, there is a general six-year limitations period enacted by Congress in 1966 under Title 28 of the U.S. Code (28 U.S.C. Sec. 241(a)) to an administrative action before a federal agency. In those cases where the Portal Act does not apply, the six-year period controls. (*Glenn Elec. Co. v. Donovan*)

## LIQUIDATED DAMAGES

The Act provides that employers who violate the minimum wage and/or overtime provisions of the FLSA are liable for these wages, plus liquidated damages equal to the unpaid wages. Under the Act, the liquidated damages are mandatory; once the employer is found to have violated the Act's wage provisions, the employee stands to collect twice the amount of the unpaid wages. The employee may also collect costs and reasonable attorneys' fees. The employer's liability can therefore be quite extensive.

An employer was found liable for liquidated damages based on the facts that the employer:

- failed to pay FLSA overtime;
- violated the state minimum wage law;
- failed to maintain adequate records of hours worked;
- showed "manifest" bad faith in failing to maintain records and pay statutorily required amounts. (*Caryk v. Coupe*)

The Portal Act provides that courts may use discretion in awarding liquidated damages, if the employer can show that it had a good-faith belief based on reasonable grounds that its conduct did not violate the Act. Under this good-faith belief defense, the court may reduce or deny entirely an award of liquidated damages that is otherwise mandatory under the FLSA. (For further discussion of this issue, see Chapter 3.)

# 3
# PORTAL-TO-PORTAL PAY ACT

Congress passed the Portal-to-Portal Pay Act (Portal Act; WHM 90:121) in May 1947 as an amendment to several statutes. The Portal Act was created as a result of the U.S. Supreme Court's decision in *Anderson v. Mt. Clemens Pottery Co.* in which the Court examined a situation involving nonpayment for time employees spent walking to and from their workplaces within the employer's compound. Studies indicated that it took approximately 14 minutes for employees to enter the premises, punch in, walk to their respective worksites, put on uniforms, and begin working. The employer credited the employees for time worked in a manner that resulted in their being compensated for 56 minutes less *per day* than the time recorded by the time clocks.

The Supreme Court held that the time necessarily spent by the employees walking to work on the employer's premises, following the punching of the time clocks, was working time within the scope of the FLSA overtime provisions. The time employees spent pursuing "preliminary" activities after arriving at their places of work, such as putting on aprons and overalls, removing shirts, taping or greasing arms, putting on finger cots, preparing equipment for productive work, turning on switches for lights and machinery, opening windows, and assembling and sharpening tools, was also working time within the scope of the Act's overtime provisions.

The Court ruled that time spent by employees must be counted as work time under the FLSA whenever all of the following conditions are present:

- Physical or mental exertion by the employee (whether burdensome or not);

- Exertion controlled or required by the employer; and
- Exertion pursued necessarily and primarily for the benefit of the employer and its business.

These standards were first applied by the Court in cases involving underground travel time of iron and coal miners. (*Tennessee Coal, Iron & R.R. v. Muscoda Local 123; Jewell Ridge Coal Corp. v. Mine Workers Local 6167*) However, *Mt. Clemens Pottery* represented the first application of these criteria in a manufacturing environment. This prework activity, literally from the entry "portal" of the workplace, to the exit "portal" off the employer's premises at the end of the shift, became known as preliminary activity (and the courts now recognize its counterpart—postliminary activity) in issues involving compensable time under the FLSA.

## PRELIMINARY AND POSTLIMINARY ACTIVITIES

The most common disputes over whether certain time is compensable involve activity that occurs before ("preliminary") or after ("postliminary") the employee's principal work activity. If such work is part of an employee's principal activity, then it is compensable. If such work is not, then it is usually found to be noncompensable. Such activities include:

- Walking, riding or traveling to and from the actual place of performance of work;
- Checking in or out and waiting in line to do so;
- Changing clothes;
- Washing up, showering or bathing; and
- Retrieving or returning tools of the trade.

These activities can be regarded as part of the principal activity or can be found to be incidental to that activity, depending on the facts of each case. For example, miners who must travel substantial distances underground before beginning work are more likely to be credited for such travel time than are individuals walking from the parking lot to the factory.

In *Mt. Clemens*, the Court also held that these preliminary activities must be included in overtime computations under these rules, unless such time is so inconsequential as to fall within the rule on trifles. Today this rule is known as the *de minimis* rule.

Once it has been shown that an employer has violated the FLSA, the employer is liable for damages for those violations. The damages can be augmented if the violations are "willful" (see "Willful Violations" later in this chapter), but at a minimum, the employer must compensate the employee for all unpaid minimum and overtime wages due. But what happens if the records are inaccurate or nonexistent? The Supreme Court in *Anderson v. Mt. Clemens* established the principle of a "reasonable inference," that is, whatever may be reasonably inferred from the type of work practices that exist in the relevant industry will be held against the employer.

This "reasonable inference" standard was the basis for a federal appeals court's decision to affirm the imposition of damages liability under the Portal Act on an employer that violated wage and recordkeeping provisions of the FLSA. Although the damages were only an approximation, the appeals court reasoned, the employer failed to negate the reasonable inferences to be drawn from the Secretary of Labor's evidence concerning the extent of uncompensated work performed for the employer. (*McLaughlin v. Ho Fat Seto*)

The effect of the *Mt. Clemens* decision was explosive. In the months following the decision, the courts were flooded with what were called portal-pay suits, involving an estimated five billion dollars in back pay and liquidated damages. The impact was nationwide.

## BASIC PURPOSE

Congress responded to *Mt. Clemens* by passing the Portal-to-Portal Pay Act, which affected not only the FLSA, but also the Walsh-Healey Act and the Davis-Bacon Act. The basic objective of the Portal Act was to relieve employers from the unforeseen liabilities of the *Mt. Clemens* decision. The most significant aspects of the Portal Act's changes are:

- The Act banned future suits by employees to recover back pay for activities that take place before the start or after the completion of an employee's "principal activities," unless these preliminary or postliminary activities must be paid for under a contract, custom, or practice in the plant;

- Actions brought by unions or other representatives of employees on their behalf were prohibited. However, actions by employees on behalf of additional employees similarly situated were still permitted, provided each participant gave his consent in writing; and
- A two-year statute of limitations was established on all claims under the FLSA and the Walsh-Healey and Davis-Bacon acts. The limitations period is calculated back from the date the action is filed in court. This means that only violations occurring within two years (three years if the court finds willful violations) of the date the action is filed will be heard.

An action *accrues*, for purposes of the two-year limitations period, when the employee becomes or should become aware of the violation. Accrual of an action is determined so that a prospective calculation can be made, from the date the employee learns of the violation to two years forward from that time. For example, if a violation occurred in December 1984, then the employee must bring the action by December 1986 or he is "time-barred" by the two-year statute of limitations.

The limitations period theoretically protects the employer from having to defend against "stale" claims where the evidence and/or witnesses are no longer available for the employer's best defense. On the other hand, the accrual rule is intended to encourage aggrieved employees to bring timely claims.

Courts have readily accepted the theory of the "continuing violation" which consists of an employer's repeated violation of the Act for a period of time. Each new violation renews the accrual date, so that the two-year period begins to run from the date of the most recent violation.

## WILLFUL VIOLATIONS

The Portal Act was amended in 1966 to provide that where a cause of action arises out of a willful violation of the FLSA, the action may be commenced within three years after the *accrual* of the cause, when the employee knew or should have known of the violation. This extension of the limitations period from two to three yeaers also extends any back pay due by a significant degree (an additional year of unlawfully withheld wages), and also exposes the employer to substantially greater liquidated damages liability. An employer who has not engaged in any willful violation of the FLSA may face up to two years of back-pay liability. If the employer is found to have committed willful violations, the monetary liability is potentially three times the amount facing the nonwillful violator (three years of back pay plus an equal amount as liquidated damages equals six years of back pay).

Consequently, the determination of what is a willful violation has taken on additional importance to contesting parties, and to the courts which must attempt to formulate clear, predictable, and fair standards for determining when a willful violation has occurred.

The first important pronouncement of what was meant by the term willful in the context of the FLSA arose in the case of *Coleman v. Jiffy June Farms*. In this case, the Court of Appeals for the Fifth Circuit said that an employer willfully violates the FLSA where the employer "knew or suspected that his actions might violate the FLSA. Stated most simply . . . Did the employer know the FLSA was *in the picture?*" (Emphasis supplied.) This came to be known as the "in the picture" standard for determining willfulness.

In 1988, the Supreme Court rejected the "in the picture" standard, reasoning that this approach imposed liability even if the employer was merely negligent. Since employers are required by law to post notices about the applicability of the FLSA, the Court observed, employers knew that the Act was "in the picture" in virtually every case in which FLSA violations were alleged. Under these circumstances, the Court concluded, every violation of the Act would lead to a finding of a willful violation because the Act was "in the picture" in every case. This was not what Congress intended by referring to "willful" violations, the Court declared. (*McLaughlin v. Richland Shoe Co.*)

Having rejected the "in the picture" standard, the Court had to establish what standard would be appropriate for determining whether a violation was "willful." The Court first acknowledged that the Portal Act's imposition of liquidated damages liability was intended to be punitive, in view of the congressional perception that willful violations are more culpable than negligent violations.

Turning to a decision it rendered under the Age Discrimination in Employment Act (*Trans World Airlines v. Thurston*), the Court examined its formulation of what constitutes a "willful" violation under the ADEA: a "willful" violation requires a showing that the employer "knew or showed reckless disregard" for whether its conduct was prohibited by the Act. This standard appeared workable, but the Court had a third standard to examine.

In *Laffey v. Northwest Airlines*, the U.S. Court of Appeals for the District of Columbia ruled that a violation of the FLSA is willful if the employer recognizes it might be covered by the Act and acts without reasonable basis for believing that it was complying with the Act. The Supreme Court reasoned, however, that this standard would permit a finding of willfulness based on mere negligence or on a good-faith but incorrect assumption about a pay plan. On that basis, it rejected this intermediate standard.

The only remaining standard—the *Thurston* "knew or showed reckless disregard" standard developed under the ADEA—was adopted by the Court for use in FLSA cases as well.

The 1966 amendments also removed the two-year time limit from injunction actions brought by the Secretary of Labor, unless the Secretary also seeks an order requiring payment of back wages. And there is no time limit on contempt proceedings for violation of an injunction issued in an earlier proceeding.

Finally, there are two generally applied limitations periods that also affect actions under the FLSA. There is a five-year limitations period on criminal actions brought by the federal government, and this period applies to criminal actions brought by the government under the FLSA.

There is also a general six-year limitations period for administrative proceedings (WHM 98:206) and a general six-year period for lawsuits that were not affected by the Portal Act (*Glenn Elec. Co. v. Donovan*)

## OTHER PROVISIONS

The Portal Act amended the FLSA, and the Walsh-Healey and Davis-Bacon acts in other significant ways. In addition to the limitations-period changes discussed above, which control all three statutes, the Portal Act also amended these laws in the areas of:

- Barring future suits for back pay for preliminary or postliminary activities, unless these activities are otherwise to be compensated at the worksite;
- Barring representative suits, except where the employees sue on behalf of themselves and other employees similarly situated. However, joining in such a suit requires the employee affirmatively to "opt-in" to the lawsuit, in writing;
- Establishing a good-faith defense to any liability under the Act, as to back pay and liquidated damages. The employer must plead and prove that it acted in good-faith reliance on and in conformity with a written administrative regulation, order, ruling, approval, interpretation, practice, or enforcement policy issued under the respective statute. Under an FLSA claim, the employer must point to a ruling of the Wage-Hour Administrator; under Davis-Bacon Act claims, the employer must refer to a ruling or order of the Secretary of Labor; and under Walsh-Healey Act claims the Labor Secretary or any federal official designated by him in administering the Act may be the source of an order or ruling on which the good-faith defense may be based;
- Granting courts hearing FLSA actions discretion to deny or reduce liquidated damages if the employer acted in "good faith" and had "reasonable grounds" for believing that no violation of the Act was being committed; and

- Relieving employers of all retroactive liability that arose as a result of the Wage-Hour Division's definition of the term "area of production" within the meaning of the FLSA's agricultural processing exemptions.

Shortly after the Portal-to-Portal Pay Act was passed, the Wage-Hour Division issued a detailed Interpretative Bulletin (WHM 90:731) setting out its interpretation of the Act. According to the Division, the Act's legislative history indicates that a strict construction of the statutory terms is warranted, and that the Act was not intended to modify the general policy of the FLSA as remedial legislation. The Portal Act in fact was intended to relieve employers in certain situations where liability was both unforeseen and catastrophic. The Bulletin counsels that the FLSA is to be liberally interpreted to foster the congressional policy of establishing fair labor standards, and that the FLSA exemptions are to be narrowly construed for the same reason.

## GOOD-FAITH DEFENSE

Perhaps the most heavily litigated aspect of the Portal Act involves the good-faith defense contained in Sections 9 and 10 of the Act because a finding that the employer acted in good faith when it violated the FLSA precludes any determination that the violation was willful. A willful violation, as we have seen, entitles the prevailing plaintiff to an award of liquidated damages equal to the amount of the unpaid wages, and exposes the employer to an extended limitations period from two to three years. Of course, this exacerbates the employer's monetary liability for back wages from two years to potentially six years.

The good-faith defense provides the employer with a shorter limitations period for back-pay liability, and it grants the courts *discretion* to deny or reduce any liability for liquidated damages. However, the court must find that the employer's violation occurred in good faith, that it had reasonable grounds for believing that no violation was being committed.

The Act defines "good faith" as compliance with a written administrative regulation, order, ruling, approval, or interpretation, or any administrative practice or enforcement policy issued by the specified official administering the FLSA, the Walsh-Healey Act, or the Davis-Bacon Act. Such writing or practice will provide a complete defense to any claim of willful conduct under the language of the Act.

The good-faith defense protects government employers, as well as private sector employers, even though this provision of the Act was not changed when the FLSA was amended to apply to the federal government and the Civil Service Commission was vested with authority to oversee the government's compliance with the FLSA's overtime provisions. A federal district court has reasoned that Congress sought to provide federal employees with as much, but not more, protection than counterparts in the civilian economy enjoyed, and to deny government employers this defense would frustrate the purposes of the Act. (*Palardy v. Horner*)

It appears from a review of the case law decided under the Portal Act that the good-faith defense is most frequently contested when there is no written administrative regulation, order, ruling, or the like, and the employer has proffered some evidence that its actions were reasonably based. Such evidence could take the form of a written opinion from privately retained legal counsel in an unsettled area of law. The employer must show that it *received* such advice, and that it relied in good faith *on that advice*. A post hoc awareness of the existence of such a writing is insufficient to demonstrate that the employer in fact relied on that advice in selecting its course of action.

The Wage-Hour Division's Interpretative Bulletin (WHM 90:731) discusses the good-faith defense in detail, and is the most thorough and reliable discussion of this aspect of the Portal Act available.

In construing this defense, the Division emphasizes that the employer's action must have been (*a*) in comformity with the ruling, administration opinion, order, and the like; (*b*) in reliance on the ruling; and (*c*) in good faith. An action may not be considered to have been "in conformity with" the administrative ruling or interpretation, unless it is in *strict* conformity with that determination, according to the Interpretative Bulletin. An erroneous belief by the employer that it acted in conformity with the ruling would not be sufficient to meet the good-faith defense prerequisites. Actual and substantial conformity is required.

Likewise, it is pointed out in the Bulletin, an employer's action may not be considered to have been "in reliance on" an interpretation or ruling unless the employer had actual knowledge of the ruling or interpretation at the time of the employment decision, and in fact, relied upon *that* ruling.

As to the final requirement, the Division's position is that good faith is not the actual state of mind of the employer, but an objective test as to whether the employer, in acting or omitting to act as it did, and in relying upon the regulation, order, ruling, and the like acted as a "reasonably prudent man would have acted under the same circumstances." Part II of the Bulletin also defines the terms "regulation and order," "interpretation," "ruling," "approval," and "practice or enforcement policy."

Following the 1985 amendments to the FLSA, government employers were faced with a host of questions concerning employees whose status under the Act was unclear. Where these government employers acted in good faith, based on reasonable, objective evidence, they did not incur liquidated damages. For example, a city employer declined to pay overtime to its fire department employees on two grounds:

- The paramedics were classified as fire protection employees, and thus exempt under federal regulations (29 C.F.R. Section 553.215) from a 40-hour workweek; and
- The fire department employees were executive employees exempt from overtime under the "salary basis" test under the regulations (29 C.F.R. Section 541.1(f)).

Declining to impose liquidated damages in both cases, the federal district court ruled in the first dispute that there was no clear legal precedent advising the city that its conduct was manifestly condemned under law, the standards found in the regulations were ambiguous, and application of the regulations to the paramedics was a question for the jury. (*Bond v. City of Jackson*)

In the second case, the court ruled that the city acted in

good faith and reasonably believed that it did not violate the Act. The court noted that the city earnestly sought to determine its obligations, and the city offered proof in court as to the *bona fides* of its efforts and of its belief. Finally, the fact that the court submitted the question whether these employees were managers or supervisors to the jury indicates that the city had a reasonable basis for its belief. (*Wright v. City of Jackson*).

# 4
# EQUAL PAY ACT

On June 10, 1963, President John F. Kennedy signed the Equal Pay Act (WHM 90:131), which was designed to eliminate wage differentials based on sex. The Equal Pay Act (EPA) amended Section 6 of the Fair Labor Standards Act (FLSA) and shares the FLSA's minimum-wage coverage standards, with certain exceptions.

In 1977, Congress passed the Reorganization Act of 1977, authorizing President Jimmy Carter to "reorganize" and streamline certain federal government agencies. Under Reorganization Plan No. 1 of 1978, the Equal Employment Opportunity Commission (EEOC) was given authority, previously vested in the Department of Labor, to enforce the EPA and the Age Discrimination in Employment Act (ADEA). Executive Order 12144 (1979) implemented the transfer of authority. (See Appendix I for a directory of EEOC offices.)

The EEOC adopted regulations established by its predecessor, the Labor Department's Wage-Hour Division, for recordkeeping under the EPA. While the Act was under the authority of the Wage-Hour Division, the Wage-Hour Administrator had issued numerous Administrative Opinions and an Interpretative Bulletin concerning agency policy toward enforcing the EPA.

Upon assuming responsibility for this new task, the EEOC stated that an employer who acted in good-faith reliance on and in conformity with any written interpretation by the Wage-Hour Administrator may establish a good-faith defense to liquidated damages liability under the EPA, in line with Section 10 of the Portal-to-Portal Pay Act (Portal Act), as it modifies the FLSA. The Commission cautioned, however, that an employer could not establish a good-faith defense where it relied on any interpretation contained in the regulations promulgated under the EPA that had been rejected by the courts.

## MAJOR PROVISIONS

The EPA, incorporated into the FLSA, requires that male and female workers receive equal pay for work requiring equal skill, effort, and responsibility, and performed under similar working conditions. The Act's coverage is essentially the same as that of the minimum-wage provisions of the FLSA. An employer covered by the FLSA's minimum-wage provisions is most likely to be covered by the EPA. However, the EPA does not share the FLSA's exemption from coverage for certain categories of employees, such as executive, administrative, and professional employees and outside salesmen. These categories are covered by the EPA. The EPA provides specific exemptions from liability where wage differentials are:

- Based on any factor other than sex;
- Paid pursuant to a bona fide seniority system;
- Paid pursuant to a bona fide merit system; and
- Paid pursuant to a system which measures earnings by quantity or quality of production.

In equalizing past wage disparity based on sex, an employer may not lower the wages of the higher-paid worker to those of the lower-paid worker. As with the FLSA, unpaid wages may expose an employer to liquidated damages for willful violations, and to attorneys' fees and costs.

In applying the test of "equal pay for work requiring equal skill, effort, and responsibility, performed under similar working conditions," the courts have discerned a number of crucial questions that must be answered. The litigants must present the question of which jobs are properly to be compared ("comparators"), when equal salaries may not constitute equal "pay," and whether equal work is being performed under "similar" working conditions, among others. The plethora of variables makes this area of wage-hour law particularly fertile.

For example, a federal appeals court, affirming the district court, has ruled that a female former college professor was not

assigned a heavier instructional workload than male profes-
sors. The female professor alleged that the heavier workload
precluded her from coaching extramural activities, but the appeals court observed that she attempted to compare herself
with five male "comparators" who were primarily assigned
administrative duties. (*Berry v. Board of Supervisors, LSU*)

Wage comparisons are made only between wages paid to
employees of the opposite sex within the same establishment,
rather than between members of the same sex, or between
employees within different establishments. The EPA meaning
of establishment follows the FLSA definition: a "distinct physical place of business" and not "any entire business or enterprise" that might encompass separate places of business. (29
C.F.R. Sec. 1620.9) However, in determining an employer's
obligations under the EPA, employer and establishment are
not synonymous terms. An employer may have more than one
establishment in which it employs workers within the meaning
of the Act. In such cases, the legislative history makes clear
that there shall be no comparison between wages paid to employees in different establishments. (20 C.F.R. Sec. 1620.7)

The courts and the EEOC have attempted to provide definitive answers to the meaning of equal "pay," (i.e., "wages"),
equal "work," equal "skill," equal "effort and responsibility,"
and the effect of additional duties on this evaluation. The
Wage-Hour Administrator had previously called for a "practical" approach to the interpretation and application of the
"similar working conditions" criterion. The regulations currently control this element of the equal pay standard. (29 C.F.R.
Sec. 1620.13, WHM 95:601–95:615; *Maguire v. Trans World
Airlines*)

## ENFORCEMENT

Prior to the 1978 transfer of enforcement authority to the
EEOC, the Commission solely administered equal pay issues
under Title VII of the Civil Rights Act of 1964. Under Title VII,
the Commission is required to attempt informal methods of conciliation before resorting to litigation. Congress failed to specify
in the Reorganization Act of 1977 whether the same philosophy
of conciliation-before-litigation applied to EPA enforcement.

A federal district court decided in 1982 that the Commission was indeed required to engage in good-faith conciliation efforts before it could bring an action under the EPA. (*EEOC v. Home of Economy, Inc.*) Imposing the conciliation requirement fulfills the congressional intent embodied in the Reorganization Act of 1977 that the EEOC's enforcement functions "should not be limited" to the functions related to equal pay administration previously vested in the Secretary of Labor, the Wage-Hour Administrator, and the Civil Service Commission (currently the Office of Personnel Management). The court reasoned that the Commission should act as a conciliator before it acts as a litigator under the EPA, in conformity with its conduct under Title VII.

## Arbitration

Can an employment agreement's arbitration provision bar a former employee's lawsuit alleging that the employer violated the EPA? A female former stock broker filed an EPA action following her layoff and the employer argued that the broker signed an employment agreement containing an arbitration clause. A federal district court stayed the lawsuit, pending arbitration, in view of her failure to show that Congress intended to bar arbitrators from hearing such claims.

The U.S. Court of Appeals for the Second Circuit dismissed the broker's appeal, on the ground that the party who has been compelled to arbitrate can argue that the arbitral forum was the incorrect one when the arbitration award is before a federal court for enforcement. Therefore, according to the appeals court, the decision as to the correct forum can be reviewed and upholding the lower court's stay was proper. (*Steele v. L.F. Rothschild & Co.*)

## COVERAGE

### Employees

As with the FLSA, the EPA covers employees engaged in interstate commerce, employees who participate in the distribution of goods which move through channels of commerce, and employees who directly aid or facilitate the operation of instrumentalities of commerce. This last group includes such instrumentalities as railroads, highways, waterways, and airports.

The Act also applies to employees engaged in the production of goods for interstate commerce, such as:

- Employees producing, manufacturing, mining, handling, transporting, or in any other manner working on goods shipped in commerce; and
- Employees engaged in any "closely related process or occupation directly essential" to the production of such goods.

The "closely related" and "directly essential" language was inserted in the 1949 amendments to the FLSA to narrow the coverage of "fringe" production workers. Certain fringe workers are still covered under the FLSA. (For a more detailed discussion on this subject, see Chapter 2 under Fringe Employees.)

Although the EPA relies on the FLSA case law for coverage principles, there are significant differences. For example, the white-collar exemption under the FLSA for professional employees does not apply under the EPA. One federal court stated that the professional employees of a state university medical school are covered by the EPA, despite the FLSA exemption, because Title IX of the Education Amendments of 1972 makes the FLSA exemption inapplicable to equal pay claims. (*Friedman v. Weiner*)

### Employers

An employer under the EPA is defined as "any person acting directly or indirectly in the interest of an employer in relation to an employee and includes a public agency." The Act specifically excludes "any labor organization (other than when acting as an employer), or any one acting in the capacity of officer or agent of such labor organization."

Subsequent to the passage of the EPA, the U.S. Supreme Court ruled in *National League of Cities v. Usery* that Congress lacked authority under the Commerce Clause to extend coverage of the FLSA to state and local governments. *National League of Cities* was decided in 1976, and following this decision, numerous circuit courts held that this decision did not affect

Congress' extension of the EPA to a "public agency." (*Usery v. Dallas Indep. School Dist.; Usery v. John J. Kane Hosp.*)

In 1985, the U.S. Supreme Court ruled in *Garcia v. San Antonio Metropolitan Transit Authority* that the FLSA in fact did extend to state and local governments without violating the Tenth Amendment to the Constitution's protection of state sovereignty. This decision created a consistent, cohesive federal statutory scheme of wage-hour regulations over all sectors; federal, state, local, and private sector employers.

Under FLSA case law, employers are covered under two concepts; the enterprise coverage theory, and the establishment standard. Although these concepts were alluded to earlier in this chapter, they are discussed in detail below.

### "Enterprise" Coverage

Under the 1961 FLSA amendments, Congress specifically acknowledged the necessity of the enterprise concept for FLSA coverage to reach subsidiary branches of an employer's operations. In the absence of the enterprise concept, these branches might otherwise be exempt from FLSA coverage, either based on the minimum-employee test or the dollar-volume standard. The Act extends coverage to employees, not specifically exempted otherwise, who are employed by certain enterprises engaged in interstate commerce or in the production of goods for commerce. The enterprise must:

- Have two or more employees engaged in interstate commerce or in the production of goods for commerce, including handling, selling, or otherwise working on goods that have moved in or were produced for commerce by any person; and
- Meet the appropriate dollar-volume test specified for the five types of enterprises and establishments falling under the enterprise test for coverage. Currently, the minimum dollar-volume test is $362,500 per annum for retail and service establishments not covered by the FLSA prior to December 31, 1981. There is a general $250,000 dollar-volume test for enterprises engaged in the laundry or drycleaning business, construction or

reconstruction, the operation of hospitals, institutions or schools, or for public agencies. The dollar-volume test has been "grandfathered" with each revision in the minimum amount established, so that companies covered under a lower limit will not be deemed exempt under a higher limit.

## "Establishment" Coverage

Prior to 1974, the FLSA covered certain retail or service stores in a chain based on an establishment test for coverage. The 1974 FLSA amendments phased out the establishment test incrementally, so that today, retail and service establishments are subject only to the general $362,500 dollar-volume test for businesses.

The establishment concept still applies, however, in EPA enforcement. The Act specifically prohibits discrimination on the basis of sex between employees "within any establishment in which such employees are employed." The employee bringing an EPA action has the burden to show that the allegedly unlawful wage disparity exists between employees within the same establishment. A federal district court illustrated the parameters of an establishment when it ruled that predominantly male pursers on an airline's international flights are not employed within the same establishment as the lower-paid and predominantly female cabin attendants on the airline's domestic flights. (*Maguire v. Trans World Airlines*)

## EXCEPTIONS TO COVERAGE

As noted earlier, the EPA specifically excepts four categories of wage differentials, if they are:

- Based on a bona fide seniority system; or
- Based on a bona fide merit system; or
- Based on a system which measures earnings by quantity or quality of production; or
- Based on any factor other than sex.

According to the Wage-Hour Administrator, the first three bases are not limited to formal, written programs. If the criteria of a particular system or plan have been communicated to the employees, the employer may rely on that system or plan. However, a formal, written plan will serve both parties more effectively in an EPA dispute.

The fourth base, sex-based wage differentials, will be in violation of the Act according to the Wage-Hour Administrator. Regardless of the proffered basis for a wage differential, the Wage-Hour Division will examine the elements of any particular system or plan that allegedly discriminates on the basis of sex to determine whether the differential is sex-based or otherwise. As in FLSA enforcement, "titles" or labels will not determine the validity of a particular wage plan or system.

In examining the validity of wage differentials, courts have held:

- A hospital maintained an unlawful wage differential between janitors and maids, since all work was within the general cleaning function and there were only insubstantial or minor differences in the degree of effort, skill, or responsibility of the respective jobs; (*Brennan v. South Davis Community Hosp.*)
- An insurance company did not violate the Act by paying more to a male underwriter than to a female underwriter, since the differential was based on two different salary programs, neither of which had sex discrimination as its purpose or effect; (*EEOC v. Aetna Ins. Co.*) and
- An employer violated the Act when it paid a newly hired male employee $10,000 more than it paid a female worker, despite the employer's belief that it expected to gain greater profits from his work, since the employer failed to show that the male's work was actually more profitable. (*EEOC v. Hay Assocs.*)

Employers have come under scrutiny in the context of Equal Pay Act allegations for their job classification systems, "red circling" rates, merit-pay plans, and other wage and benefit programs.

The "factor other than sex" prong of the four statutory exceptions in the Act has provided a wide range of examples where employers have demonstrated that some sex-neutral element of the job warranted a wage differential. (The EPA creates this exception with the language "any other factor other than sex," the first "other" in the exception apparently resulting from a clerical error by the drafters.) Such sex-neutral elements as experience (*Trent v. Adria Laboratories, Inc.*), training programs (*Hodgson v. First Victoria Nat'l Bank*), and economic benefit to the employer (*Hodgson v. Anclote Manor Found.*) have been found to justify an employer's wage differential for certain work. On the other hand, the "market force" theory— that employers must pay more to acquire male workers in certain industries, and may pay less to female workers because this is what the "market will bear"—has been soundly rejected. (*Hodgson v. Brookhaven Gen. Hosp.; Brennan v. Victoria Bank & Trust Co.*)

The "factor other than sex" exception continues to be a fertile area for development of EPA law. For example, this exception has been applied in the following cases:

- A state statute requiring veterans service officers to be wartime veterans can be a legitimate factor other than sex that could justify the payment of a higher salary by the state Department of Veterans Affairs to employees in the all-male job of veterans service officer than to employees in the all-female job of veterans service officer associate. The court found eminently reasonable the state's belief that wartime veterans will have a "special camaraderie" with veterans needing the Department's help, enabling them to open up to a veterans service officer, when they otherwise might not do so. (*Fallon v. Illinois*)

- An employer that was opening a restaurant and hiring employees on an accelerated basis articulated a legitimate nondiscriminatory reason for paying female employees less than male employees doing substantially the same work, where it offered evidence that the decision on starting salaries was based on the strength of the employment application, the showing at the personal interview, past experience, and whether the current employee had personal knowledge of the applicant's abilities. (*Ebert v. Lamar Truck Plaza*)

- An employer failed to prove that its payment of a higher salary to a male employee than to a female employee was based on a factor other than sex, given the pure subjectivity of the process by which the employer set their salaries, the lack of testimony from the supervisor explaining his evaluations of their work, and the fact that the woman's sales goals were set as high or higher than the male's goals. (*Keziah v. W.M. Brown & Son*)

With regard to fringe benefits, the Wage-Hour Administrator has stated that unequal insurance benefits provided for male and female employees is lawful, if the premiums paid or costs incurred by the employer are equal. Similarly, unequal premiums paid or costs incurred by the employer are lawful, if the benefits provided are equal. (WH AdminOp, Oct. 14, 1965)

Similarly, a university's tuition remission program for faculty members who have children in college must treat male and female faculty members equally. The Wage-Hour Division has approved such a plan for married couples who are both on the university's faculty, where each received a one-half tuition payment for each child. The Division reasoned that the failure to pay this category of faculty members full tuition for each child does not appear to have an adverse impact on either sex. (WH AdminOp, Feb. 6, 1978, WHM 95:631)

The Act bars unions from causing or attempting to cause an employer to discriminate against an employee in a manner that would violate the equal pay standard. The union can be held liable in damages for such conduct. (*Hodgson v. Sagner, Inc.; Hodgson v. Clothing & Textile Workers, Baltimore Regional Joint Bd.*)

However, an employer that was found to have violated the Act may not obtain contributions from the union to alleviate some of its back-pay liability, where the union that negotiated the discriminatory contract clauses was not sued by the aggrieved employees who sued the employer. (*Northwest Airlines v. Transport Workers*)

## PENALTIES

As an amendment to the FLSA, the Equal Pay Act carries the same penalties for violations as FLSA violations: a two-year limitations period for nonwillful violations; a three-year limitations period plus liquidated damages for willful violations; and prejudgment interest and costs, where appropriate. (*Hill v. J.C. Penney Co.*)

## REMEDIES

As stated earlier, an employer may not cure its equal pay violation by reducing the wage rate of the higher-paid employee to the rate of the lower-paid employee. The employer is required to raise the lower rate to equal the higher rate.

An employer may not cure a violation where males and females work in different classifications by merely permitting lower-paid female workers to transfer into the higher-paid male classifications as vacancies occur. (*Corning Glass Works v. Brennan; Schultz v. American Can Co.*)

Finally, an employer hoping to avoid a longer limitations period and liquidated damages liability may not rely on the advice of its attorney nor on the apparent complexity of the law to defend against a claim of "willfully" violating the Act. (*Hill v. J.C. Penney Co.*)

# 5
# WALSH-HEALEY PUBLIC CONTRACTS ACT

The Walsh-Healey Public Contracts Act (WHA; WHM 90:201) predates the Fair Labor Standards Act of 1938 by two years. As originally designed, the WHA established employment standards for contractors furnishing or manufacturing materials, articles, or equipment for the U.S. government. In tandem with the National Recovery Act, the WHA was intended to move the country out of the depths of the Great Depression by directly aiding the common man by regulating the wage rates that had to be observed when doing business with the federal government.

Although the National Recovery Act was eventually ruled unconstitutional, the WHA is alive and well, and was most recently amended by Congress via the Department of Defense Authorization Act of 1986, which repealed the WHA's eight-hour day limit after which overtime rates had been mandatory.

Overtime under the WHA must be paid at a rate of one-and-one-half times the employee's "basic" rate of pay, instead of the "regular rate" as under the FLSA. The Department of Labor, however, has taken the position that the terms "regular rate" and "basic rate" are synonymous.

In applying this rule, the Department has consistently followed court decisions construing overtime obligations under the FLSA in deciding questions relating to overtime pay under the WHA. (See Chapter 94, WHM.) Thus, the basic rate of pay on which overtime pay is calculated is ordinarily determined by dividing the employee's total weekly pay, excluding any "overtime premiums, " by the total number of hours worked by the employee during that week. Under the WHA, overtime is calculated on a weekly rather than a daily basis.

In addition to regulating hours of work and wages for work performed under government contract, the Act addresses child labor, convict labor, and hazardous working conditions.

## REQUIREMENTS

Under the WHA, all contractors who agree to undertake performance contracts for the federal government for the manufacturing or furnishing of materials, supplies, articles, and equipment in any amount exceeding $10,000 must stipulate that:

- All employees on the project. with certain exceptions, will be paid not less than the prevailing minimum rate determined by the Secretary of Labor for similar work in the locality;
- No employee will be permitted to work in excess of 40 hours in any week without the payment of overtime at a rate of time-and-one-half the employee's regular rate of pay for all hours in excess of 40 per week;
- No male worker under 16 years of age or female worker under 18 years of age will be employed on the contract;
- No convict laborer will be employed on the contract; and
- No part of the contract will be performed under working conditions that are unsanitary, hazardous, or dangerous to the health and safety of the employees.

The Secretary of Labor is authorized to permit an increase in the maximum hours of labor specified in the contracts executed under the Act, provided he establishes a rate of pay for overtime compensation that is not less than one-and-one-half times the basic hourly rate of pay received by any affected employee. The Secretary is also authorized to establish prevailing wage rates on an industrywide basis.

As administered by the Department of Labor's Wage-Hour Division, the WHA also applies to employees of manufacturers and "regular dealers" supplying the federal government with material, supplies, articles, or equipment on a contract whose value exceeds $10,000. Since the Act covers manufacturing and other public contract statutes cover "servicing" and "construction" and "alteration" and "repair, " the courts have had to distinguish between these performances.

A typical dispute may involve large-scale repair of an engine; the issue becomes: "When does extensive 'repair' constitute wholesale 'manufacture'?" The Davis-Bacon Act (DBA), with the Contract Work Hours and Safety Standards Act, applies to mechanics and laborers engaged in the construction, alteration, or repair of public buildings or public works under contract with the federal government. Similarly, the McNamara-O'Hara Service Contract Act (Service Contract Act) governs service contracts performed for the federal government, and requires employers to pay employees the wages and fringe benefits prevailing in the locality, but in no event will the employees receive less than the minimum wage set under the Fair Labor Standards Act.

With this complex statutory scheme in mind, it becomes clear that some acts may be "cheaper" than others for the contractor performing under a government contract. This situation creates the incentive to operate, and ultimately to litigate, the extent of coverage of one federal contract act over another.

Where the government contract exceeds the $10,000 minimum amount, the WHA requires all primary and most secondary contractors (subcontractors or "subs") to comply with the standards unless their contracts are specifically exempt from the Act. The WHA, and certain regulations, have exempted such contracts as "open-market" agreements: contracts for the sale of perishables and other specified agricultural products, contracts for transport by common carrier, contracts for public utilities, and service contracts and rental agreements. (Contract exemptions will be discussed later in this chapter.)

All employees who actually work on the materials supplied under the government contract are covered by the WHA, including those engaged in manufacturing, fabricating, assembling, handling, supervising, or shipping. Employees who perform any preparatory work or other work necessary for the performance of the contract are also covered. If the contractor fails to segregate the work performed on the government contract from noncontract work, the WHA deems all employees as employed on the government contract and covered under the Act. As with the FLSA, all executive, administrative, and professional employees are exempt. Additionally, the WHA exempts all office and custodial workers from coverage. (Employee exemptions will be discussed in detail later in this chapter.)

## COVERED CONTRACTS

Section 1 of the Act governs coverage over contracts and uses such phrases as "manufacturing," "furnishing," "fabrication," and "production." Such terms are inherently inartful, and changing needs and technology may make yesterdays' "manufacturing" become tomorrow's "repair."

In a series of Wage-Hour Administrative Opinions, the Wage-Hour Division has interpreted these phrases in a way that the Act was found to cover contracts:

- For the "construction" of sled-targets and position buoys. The Administrator rejected a plea that the items were exempt because they were not "manufactured," since they were in fact "produced," "fabricated" and "furnished" to the government; (*In re Anderson & Cristofani*)
- For the reconditioning of tools. Where the work requires a complete or substantial rebuilding, it is regarded as "manufacturing"; (WH AdminOp, Oct. 22, 1941)
- For the erecting or installing of articles or equipment after delivery, such as the installation of generators requiring a prepared foundation; (WH AdminOp, 1941) and
- For the maintenance, servicing, and repair of government vehicles, since such a contract assumes that the contractor will provide a substantial amount of parts and supplies. (WH AdminOp, Oct. 7, 1964)

The Act also applies to the "construction, alteration, furnishing, or equipping of any naval vessel."

The Act specifies a dollar-amount of $10,000, and administrative practice has established several rules for applying this standard to individual contracts. For example, the stated price of the contract controls, even if prompt payment may reduce the amount due on the contract to less than the statutory minimum. Similarly, a postexecution reduction in contract price, even where both parties mutually agree on the reduction, will not remove the contract from the Act's coverage. (*United States v. Ozmer*)

If the contract price exceeds the statutory minimum, individual component parts of the contract and separate manufacturers are all covered, even if each component would sell for less than $10,000. Not surprisingly, where several contracts, each less than the statutory minimum, are awarded simultaneously by the government's acceptance of a single bid, then each contract is covered as if it met the statutory minimum. (WH AdminOp, May 3, 1957)

Contracts for indefinite amounts are covered, if they *may exceed* the $10,000 figure. When a contract's price is undetermined because of exigent circumstances, most commonly the "needs of the government," these open-ended contracts also fall under the Act. (*In re Norris, Inc.; In re Pelham's*) Additionally, purchase-notice agreements, also known as "supply" contracts, are covered.

## COVERED CONTRACTORS

The Act covers a manufacturer whose contract with the government exceeds $10,000. The Wage-Hour Administrator has interpreted this phrase to encompass a person, corporation, partnership, or other, that owns, operates, or maintains a factory or establishment that produces on its premises the materials, supplies, articles, or equipment which is the basis for the contract. A prime contractor may be held liable for the violations of his subcontractor. (*United States v. Davison Fuel & Dock Co.*)

The Act also applies to a "regular dealer" in commodities, and the dealer's participation in a contract may expose a manufacturer who is not directly on the contract to liability under the contract. (*In re Negri*)

However, a regular dealer who contracts to furnish goods to the government may not be held liable for the failure of his manufacturing supplier to comply with the Act's wage and over-time provisions. (*United States v. New England Coal & Coke Co.*)

On the other hand, a substitute manufacturer, or successor contractor, who subcontracts part of the work he is obligated to perform may not be found liable for the violations of the "sub-substitute" manufacturer. (*In re Lyon & Borah, Inc.*)

## PERSONAL LIABILITY

Section 2 of the Act provides that liability shall extend to the "party responsible." This provision has been used to impose personal liability on employer/contractor officials who would otherwise escape liability. The test for determining when personal liability should attach is whether the official *controlled* and *managed* the company during the relevant time in which the contract was performed. Under this test, employer officials were found liable, even though they did not sign the government contract, where they owned a majority of the stock and exercised exclusive control and supervision over the affairs of the contractor. (*In re A-AN-E Mfg. Corp.*)

On the other hand, a personnel director was found not to be personally liable, since he was not an officer of the contractor, had no property interest in it, and did not determine labor policy or control or manage the contractor's affairs.

However, financial interest of corporate officers, standing alone, is insufficient to bring these individuals within the meaning of "party responsible," such that personal liability would attach. (*United States v. Hudgins-Dize Co.*)

## EXEMPTIONS

After it has been ascertained that an employer meets the Act's criteria for coverage (e.g., type of contract, dollar amount), the employer may attempt to fall within any of a number of exemptions contained both in the Act and in the regulations promulgated under the Act. There are three avenues for avoiding the Act's provisions: (*a*) subcontractor or successor employer exemptions; (*b*) employee exemptions, and (*c*) contract exemptions.

The Act specifically exempts open-market contracts (contracts which authorize the work to be done at rates currently available on the open market); contracts for the purchase of perishables, including dairy, livestock, and nursery products; agricultural or farm products processed for first sale by the original producers; contracts by the Secretary of Agriculture for the purchase of agricultural products; contracts for transportation by common carriers under published tariffs; and contracts with common carriers subject to the Federal Communications Act of 1934.

Under the regulations, the list of exempt contracts includes contracts for the construction of public works; rental of real or personal property; public utilities; delivery of newspapers, magazines, or periodicals by the publisher to sales agents or publisher representatives; and exclusive services.

The Secretary of Labor is authorized to exempt any contract that may impair the federal government's ability to conduct business, following a determination to that effect by the head of the federal agency involved in the contract. This authorization was used during World War II, but has fallen into disuse in recent years. (For further information, consult Walsh-Healey Rulings and Interpretations No. 3, issued in 1955 and last amended in 1963, WHM 99:151.)

Most of the confusion/litigation in this exemption scheme has involved the exemptions for specified employee classifications and for specified contracts. These will be examined in detail.

### Subcontractor/Successor Exemption

Generally, the Act does not apply to work performed by a manufacturer other than the original contractor, unless that work would *normally* have been performed by the contractor itself. Thus, subcontractors who actually fill part or all of the government contract are not covered by the Act if it is the "regular practice" in the industry for the prime contractor to purchase such goods rather than to manufacture them.

Where, however, a contractor subcontracts part of the work to another manufacturer, the producer of the commodities not manufactured by the original contractor is a "substitute manufacturer" who is considered fully covered by the Act. A prime contractor is liable for damages arising from violations committed by its substitute manufacturer.

## Employee Exemptions

The Act covers *all* employees under a government contract, except office, supervisory, custodial, and maintenance workers who do any work in preparation for or that is necessary for performance of the contract. The Wage-Hour Division maintains an extensive list of workers who are not "directly working in production" but who are nevertheless covered by the Act. The line of demarcation appears to be whether the employee is doing *any work connected with* the manufacture, fabrication, assembling, handling, supervision, or shipment of materials, supplies, or equipment required under a government contract under the Act. If there is no work done in connection with such a contract, the employee most likely will not be covered by the Act. Employees performing commercial work on a contract who are separated from employees performing work on a government contract, for example, will be treated as exempt, provided the contractor's records keep such employees separate from the employees on the government contract.

The list of employees who are exempt by virtue of their not being directly involved in production under a government contract covered by the Act includes employees who only perform office work and whose work is not connected with the production of goods under the contract; custodial employees whose work is directed to the maintenance of the plant or facility and who are not involved in any work necessary for the fulfillment of the government contract; executive, administrative, and professional employees, as defined by the Wage-Hour Administrator under FLSA enforcement (exempt only from Walsh-Healey overtime provisions); foremen and instructors who do not operate machinery, perform manual work, or handle materials involved in a government contract; chief inspectors who are compensated on a salary basis and have a high degree of responsibility and authority; experimental workers who are not connected with the fulfillment of a government contract; requisition clerks who do nothing but prepare material orders and route orders through the plant; marine workers, if they are "seamen" under the FLSA; and convict laborers. However, paroled, pardoned, or discharged criminals, or prisoners participating in a work-release program are not deemed convict laborers for the purposes of this exemption.

**Contract Exemptions**

Several types of government contracts are exempt from the wage, hour, and child-labor provisions of the Act:

- Contracts for the construction of public works, which are covered by the Davis-Bacon and Contract Work Hours acts and the Anti-Kickback Law (Copeland Act);
- Contracts for agricultural or farm products processed for first sale by the original producer;
- Contracts made by the Secretary of Agriculture for the purchase of commodities or the products thereof;
- Contracts for the purchase of such materials, supplies, articles, or equipment "as may usually be bought in the open market" (the so-called open-market exemption). This exemption is construed by the Public Contracts Administrator as applying only to such purchases as the government *usually makes* in the open market, including purchases without ads for bids and purchases which the procurement agency is authorized to buy in the open market;
- Contracts for the "carriage of freight or personnel by vessel, airplane, bus, truck, express, or railway line where published tariff rates are in effect";
- Contracts exclusively for *personal* services;
- Contracts for the rental of real or personal property;
- Contracts for perishables, including dairy, livestock, and nursery products;
- Contracts for public utility services;
- Contracts for the furnishing of service by radio, telephone, telegraph, or cable companies subject to the Federal Communications Act of 1934; and

- Contracts to sales agents or publisher representatives for the delivery of newspapers, magazines, or periodicals by the publisher itself.

The Act also contains an exemption for "stockpiling" of goods, where the contractor "customarily" maintains a stockpile of material that cannot be identified as to the time work was done on any item in the pile.

## RECORDKEEPING

The Act requires the contractor to maintain complete payroll records for each employee working on the government contract. These records must comply with FLSA requirements, and for purposes of Walsh-Healey compliance, must also contain injury-frequency rates, a record of the sex of each employee, and the number which identifies the contract on which each employee works.

## ENFORCEMENT

The Secretary of Labor is authorized to investigate and decide cases involving alleged violations of the Act. This authority has been delegated to the Wage-Hour Administrator for daily enforcement purposes. Employers are liable for any underpayment of base wages or overtime and a penalty of $10 for each day an underage minor is employed.

The Defense Contract Administration Services is responsible for conducting compliance reviews, pre-award reviews and complaint investigations for covered federal contractors performing defense work. (See Appendix J for list of regional offices.)

Serious and willful violations of the Act may subject a contractor to the blacklist penalty which bars the receipt of a government contract by that contractor for a period of three years.

Back-pay claims under the WHA, like those under the FLSA, are governed by the Portal-to-Portal Pay Act, including limitations periods and liquidated damages liability. (See Chapter 3 for more on this issue.)

The WHA may apply to both the "manufacture" of equipment and the "installation" of equipment on the job site. Where more than an incidental amount of installation work is required, however, the Davis-Bacon Act (DBA) may enter the picture. Whether the WHA or DBA should govern such installation work will be determined by the Solicitor of Labor, who has issued "interpretative guidelines" in the past.

Similarly, if a contractor manufacturers goods under a government contract and the goods are shipped across state lines, the contractor will be subject both to the WHA and the FLSA. (WH AdminOp, Oct. 11, 1941) The Supreme Court rejected a contractor's claim that the two laws could not apply concurrently, finding that the two laws are not mutually exclusive. (*Powell v. U.S. Cartridge Co.*)

## SAFETY AND HEALTH STANDARDS

The WHA was the first of the federal laws regulating wages and hours to contain a provision requiring compliance with safety and health standards for the protection of workers. The Act provides that contracts entered into by any agency of the federal government calling for the manufacture or furnishing of materials, supplies, or equipment in any amount exceeding $10,000 must contain a stipulation that no part of such contract will be performed in any plant, factory, building, or surroundings or under working conditions that are unsanitary, hazardous, or dangerous to the health and safety of the employees engaged on contract work.

Failure to maintain proper safety and health standards in the performance of a contract subject to the Act constitutes a breach of that contract. This may provide the basis for the cancellation of the contract and make the party or parties responsible subject to the Act's blacklist penalty. Blacklisted persons are ineligible to receive federal contracts for a period of three years from the date the Secretary of Labor determines that the violation occurred.

To assist contractors in complying with these safety and health requirements, the Secretary of Labor has established specific safety and health standards in the regulations. These regulations set the *minimum* standards that will be applied in the enforcement of the law to determine whether particular contracts are being performed in compliance with the WHA's safety and health standards.

The regulations apply to all types of industrial plants and deal with such subjects as building and machine guarding, fire prevention and protection, sanitation, first aid facilities, ventilation, personal protective equipment, and the like.

# 6
# McNamara-O'Hara
# Service Contract Act

The McNamara-O'Hara Service Contract Act of 1965 (Service Contract Act or SCA; WHM 90:225) covers contracts with the federal government for the provision of services to the government. This differs from the Walsh-Healey Act, which covers contracts for the furnishing or manufacturing of goods, materials, and equipment to the federal government; and from the Davis-Bacon Act, which covers contracts for the provision of construction or supplies for construction of public buildings or public works.

Service employees generally include persons engaged in a recognized trade or craft or in a manual labor occupation. Such employees working under an SCA-covered contract must be paid the wages and fringe benefits prevailing in the locality, as determined by the Secretary of Labor. The Act allows the contractor to provide the service employee with any equivalent combination of fringe benefits or to make differential payments in cash.

The Act authorizes the Secretary of Labor to withhold accrued payments due on any contract to the extent necessary to pay covered workers the difference between wages and benefits required by the contract and those actually paid. Other sanctions against a noncomplying contractor include contract termination and debarment.

The Secretary of Labor is authorized to maintain a lawsuit against the contractor for any underpayments to SCA-covered employees. The Secretary is also authorized to determine if "unusual circumstances" exist to warrant a lesser penalty than the three-year blacklist penalty under the debarment provision of the Act. The courts have ruled that only the Secretary is authorized to bring an action under the Act, while individual employees are restricted to administrative proceedings.

## COVERAGE

The SCA covers all contracts with the federal government exceeding $2,500 in amount, whose primary purpose is the providing of *services* to the government. SCA regulations (29 C.F.R. Part 4.6) require the Secretary of Labor to include in SCA contracts language incorporating the Act's labor standards provisions for all government contracts in excess of the statutory minimum. Failure to include verbatim language from the Act formed the basis for a contractor's claim that it was thus not subject to the Act's minimum-wage and fringe-benefit provisions. The claim was unsuccessful. (*National Electro-Coatings v. Brock*)

### Covered Contracts

The Act applies to contracts the "principal purpose" of which is the furnishing of services to the United State through the use of service employees. Unless specified otherwise, any contract with the government that is not for construction or supplies is a contract for services, according to the Wage-Hour Administrator. In a series of Administrative Opinions, the Division has determined that the SCA covers contracts for:

- Equipment or vehicle rental including the equipment or vehicle operator;
- Surveying;
- Mapping;
- Spraying operations;
- Cafeteria and dormitory services;
- Car-washing, wheel-packing, chassis lubrication, vehicle maintenance, and storage;
- Office-equipment repair;
- Landscaping and grounds maintenance;
- Laundry services for the Armed Services;

- Subsurface exploration, involving drilling for soil samples and rock cores;
- Mail transportation;
- Shipping and storing of household goods;
- Printing and duplicating services, but only if the principal object of the contract is for services and the furnishing of printed or duplicated matter is secondary to the contract's main purpose;
- Computer maintenance and watch repair;
- Fire protection services;
- Engineering, design, programming, and testing;
- Furnishing hotel accommodations to military personnel;
- Inspection and maintenance services;
- Veterans' convalescent care in nursing homes; and
- Garbage removal.

This is only a partial list of covered contracts under the current $2,500 threshold. Suffice to say that, with a low threshold, few contracts for services for the government will ever be lower than the $2,500 minimum.

Section 7 of the Act concerns exemptions from SCA coverage. Where the Act is silent, and in line with the Administrator's pronouncements, certain operations may be regarded as covered in the absence of specific exclusions. These operations include:

- Galvanizing of steel products;
- Design functions;
- Motion-picture production; and
- Preparing title certificates for real property transactions.

Section 7 of the Act provides a list of exemptions from SCA coverage. This list includes:

- Contracts for constructing or repairing public works or public buildings;
- Contracts covered by the Walsh-Healey Act;
- Contracts for the carriage of freight or personnel where published tariffs are in effect;
- Contracts for the furnishing of services by radio, telephone, telegraph, or cable companies;
- Contracts for public utility services;

- Contracts for employment where an individual or individuals are to provide direct services to a federal agency; and
- Contracts with the U.S. Postal Service for the operation of a postal contract station.

The Wage-Hour Division, in determining which contracts are covered under the Act, has also established which contracts are not covered. The Division's list of exempt contracts includes contracts for:

- Medical services at a hospital under a Medicare program;
- Renting parking spaces;
- Creating topographic maps;
- Renting motor vehicles;
- Managing, operating, and maintaining research centers and a job corps center for women;
- Relocating persons under an agreement with a local redevelopment agency under the Federal Urban Renewal Program, even though the federal government pays all the expenses of moving an occupant displaced by urban renewal; and
- Tree-trimming, tree removing, and landscaping functions that are part of an urban renewal project.

In many of these instances, the Division has treated a contract as exempt if the contract is not "entered into by the United States" as a contracting party. (WH AdminOp, Apr. 20, 1966, WHM 99:2114)

**Covered Employees**

Under the Act, service contractors are required to pay the wages and fringe benefits prevailing in the locality to all "service employees" engaged in contract performance, including guards, watchmen, and any person in a recognized craft or trade, in a skilled mechanical craft, or in unskilled, semiskilled, or skilled manual labor occupations. The Act extends to foremen and supervisors whose jobs primarily require trade, craft, or laboring experience.

In addition to those employees who actually perform the service required under the contract, the Act covers workers whose duties are "necessary" to contract performance. Such employees include office workers who do clerical work in connection with the contract, for example. (WH AdminOp, May 16, 1966, WHM 99:2114) Additionally, an individual who meets the definition of a service employee under the Act is also covered, regardless of the relationship existing between the individual and the contracting entity.

In 1976, Congress amended the Act by including in Section 8(b) a complete definition of "service employee":

> The term "service employee" means any person engaged in the performance of a contract entered into by the United States and not exempted under section 7, whether negotiated or advertised, the principal purpose of which is to furnish services in the United States (other than any person employed in a bona fide executive, administrative or professional capacity, as those terms are defined in part 541 of title 29, Code of Federal Regulations, as of July 30, 1976 and any subsequent revision of those regulations); and shall include all such persons regardless of any contractual relationship that may be alleged to exist between a contractor or subcontractor and such persons.

The language was intended to be all-inclusive. It obviates a series of Administrative Opinions issued by the Division that interpreted a publication by the Civil Service Commission (now the Office of Personnel Management, OPM) entitled "Handbook of Blue-Collar Occupational Families and Series." Under the present scheme, the OPM administers the Act. Whether a particular individual falls under the Act turns on whether he/she may be classified as a bona fide executive, administrative, or professional employee within the meaning of the FLSA.

## PREVAILING WAGE STANDARD

The Act provides three bases for determining what rates will be paid to service employees:

- The wage rates for similar employment prevailing in the locality, as determined by the Secretary of Labor; or
- The rates established in a collective bargaining contract covering service employees including future wage increases; or
- The minimum wage rate under the FLSA, where no prevailing wage rate determination has been made.

The Act does not contain an overtime standard, but it states that all SCA contracts are covered by the Contract Work Hours and Safety Standards Act, which provides that in computing overtime compensation, the regular or basic rate of pay will be the same as that under the FLSA. The Secretary is required to establish prevailing wage rates for all contracts where five or more service employees are employed.

A primary element of an SCA prevailing wage case concerns the parameters of the locality which governs the wage rate determination. One federal court has held that "locality" should be given its ordinary and common meaning and that this phrase has a meaning under the SCA that is different from its meaning under the Walsh-Healey Act. Rejecting the Labor Secretary's claim that a nationwide locality was appropriate, the court advised that in 98 percent of cases, the Standard Metropolitan Statistical Area standard used by the EEOC was an adequate basis for establishing the locality. (*Southern Packaging & Storage Co. v. United States*)

Another court held that the prevailing rates should have been those for comparable employment in the area where the services were to be performed, rather than the location of the government installation which sought the contract. (*Descomp, Inc. v. Sampson*)

Finally, an administrative law judge determined that the locality was the county, not the federal enclave involved, where the appropriate criteria were:

- Comparability of similar employment in the surrounding area;
- The area in which the work force possessing similar skills resides; and
- An identifiable and related geographical area that may serve as a basis for making the required comparison. (*In re Applicability of Bargained Wages*)

## SUCCESSORS

Section 4(c) of the Act binds successor contractors to the collective bargaining contract of the predecessor contractor, according to the Secretary of Labor. (*In re Eastern Serv. Mgmt.*

*Co.*) However, successorship and seniority rights under the contract are not fringe benefits within the meaning of Section 4(c), and therefore a successor contractor did not violate the Act when he failed to hire some of the predecessor's employees and hired others at lower pay. (*Clark v. Unified Servs.*)

Nevertheless, a financing institution that purchased a contractor's accounts receivable cannot recover contract proceeds that had been withheld due to SCA violations, since the contractor had no right to the funds. (*United Cal. Discount Corp.*)

In addition, the Secretary of Labor does not have authority under the SCA to set aside the plain terms of a successor collective bargaining contract's wage and benefit provisions that are less than the Act's prevailing wage rates in the locality for similar work, even though the contract rates exceed the rates in the predecessor's contract. The Act requires only that the rates of the successor equal the rates of the predecessor and permits the Secretary to suspend the predecessor's rates only when wages are already higher than local rates for similar services. (*Holt Co. v. Electrical Workers (IBEW) Local 1340*)

## VARIANCE PROCEEDINGS

Section 4(c) also relieves a contractor from the obligation to comply with the contractually established wages and fringe benefits of the predecessor's contract, if the Labor Secretary finds that such wages and fringes are "substantially at variance with those which prevail for services of a character similar in the locality." (*In re Applicability of Bargained Wages*) The variance determination can therefore legally interfere with the collective bargaining process.

Where a contracting officer modified the prevailing wage rate on a construction project, a question was raised whether the federal government was bound by the modification based on the officer's erroneous interpretation of the regulation governing effective modifications. The court found that the contractor's request for an adjustment in the contract price was justified and that the government was bound to it since the officer's modification was not "palpably illegal" and there is nothing in writing saying that an officer is not authorized to make mistakes of law. (*Broad Ave. Laundry v. United States*)

## WAGE PAYMENTS AND DEDUCTIONS

Noncompliance with the Act's wage provisions, either by nonpayment or underpayment, was found in the following rulings:

- Employees may not bargain away the payment of wages secured to them by the Act, and therefore, their signatures on erroneous time cards do not affect their entitlement;
- The contractor cannot attempt to comply with the Act by reallocating portions of payments made for other hours which are in excess of the specified minimum wage; and
- Payments to employees of amounts in excess of the minimum wages required in one workweek may not be credited toward amounts required to be paid in another workweek, since workweeks stand independent of one another. (*In re Roman*)

An employer was found to have violated the prevailing minimum wage requirements, as a result of certain deductions that lowered the employee's wages below the statutory minimum, in the following decisions;

- Where the employer deducted the cost of uniform laundering for food service employees; (*In re Quality Maintenance Co.*) and
- Where the employer required a prospective employee to pay for the cost of a uniform required to be worn on the job. (WH AdminOp, July 7, 1974, WH-274, WHM 95:138)

Finally, the Act requires the contractor to maintain adequate records of hours worked and wages paid to service employees. This requirement has led to a series of rulings on whether the employer has complied with the Act:

- Where an employee performs work on a covered contract and on nongovernment work in the same workweek, the records must effectively segregate the types of work performed. If the records are inadequate, the employee must be paid according to the Act's requirements for all hours in any workweek if he works for any part of a day in that workweek on a covered contract; (WH AdminOP, Mar. 14, 1966, WHM 99:2435)

- Where a maintenance worker spent part of his time on government work and part of his time on nongovernment work, the employer was not allowed to apply a pro rata system of wage payment, as an alternative to adequate recordkeeping, since this did not constitute compliance with the Act; (WH AdminOP, July 19, 1968) and

- Failure to maintain adequate records of segregated work only requires the government to show the amount and extent of work as a matter of "just and reasonable inference," even though the result is only approximate. (*In re Roman*)

## FRINGE BENEFITS

The Act requires the contractor to furnish such fringe benefits as the Secretary determines to be prevailing for such employees in the locality. A contractor may satisfy its obligation to furnish specific fringe benefits by providing any equivalent combination of benefits or by making equivalent or differential payments in cash.

Since a contractor may discharge its fringe benefit obligation by paying the employee an equivalent amount in cash, the question has frequently arisen whether the cash value of the payment was in part equal to the fringe that would otherwise have been provided. For example, to find the hourly cash equivalent of a "one-week paid vacation," the employee's rate of pay is multiplied by the number of hours of vacation, using a standard 8-hour day and 40-hour week, unless otherwise specified. The total annual amount is divided by 2080, the number of regular working hours in a 52-week period, to arrive at the cash equivalent. (WH AdminOp, Aug. 15, 1966)

Where the determination lists the holidays for which payment is required under the Act, the contractor must furnish the holiday off with pay. The contractor may substitute another day off with pay if the substitution is done according to a plan that has been communicated to the affected employees. The contractor may pay the employee cash equivalents for specific holidays. (WH AdminOp, Jan. 28, 1970, WHM 99:2351)

A contractor may meet the health and welfare benefits requirement by maintaining a self-insured plan, where the contractor has not refused to pay a claim or to provide an employee with a benefit required by the contract, and there has been no evidence of bad faith by the contractor. (*White Glove-Building Maintenance v. Hodgson*) The contractor's notice of its self-insured plan to all new employees satisfies the requirement that the substitution be made according to a plan that has been communicated to the affected employees.

Severance pay is a fringe benefit and must be included in the wage determination and the new government contract, unless after an administrative hearing, it is found to be inconsistent with the prevailing wages in the locality. (*Trinity Servs. v. Usery*)

## FRINGE OFFSETS AND PAYMENTS

Under the Act a contractor may not:

- Obtain contributions toward fringe benefits from its employees to satisfy the fringe benefit standards set by the Secretary; (WH AdminOp, Apr. 7, 1966)
- Offset social security payments by decreasing its contribution to employee retirement funds; (WH AdminOp, Apr. 14, 1966) and
- Offset fringe benefit payments made for hours spent on nongovernment work against an employer's fringe obligation for work done on a government contract. (WH AdminOp, June 7, 1967)

Service employees of a contractor are entitled to receive fringe benefit payments for hours they do not work but for which they are paid even though such hours are holidays or vacation time. The Labor Department has ruled that the contractor does not have the prerogative to apply the wage determination in a manner that it considered reasonable. (*In re Emerald Maintenance, Inc.*)

Finally, as with the segregation of government- and non-government work, the Act requires adequate recordkeeping of fringe benefit payments that are made as cash equivalents in lieu of fringes. (*In re Aarid Van Lines*)

## ENFORCEMENT

The Act may not be enforced through a private action, since the enforcement responsibilities are assigned exclusively to the Labor Secretary. (*Teamsters Local 427 v. Philco-Ford Corp.; Foster v. Parker Transfer Co.*) Although the Act limits the right to bring an action to the Secretary, it provides a range of mechanisms for obtaining compliance and/or imposing liabilities and penalties. The Act authorizes:

- The withholding of amounts due under a contract sufficient to pay employees the difference between the wages and the benefits required under the contract and those actually received;
- Court action against the contractor, subcontractor, or surety bond to recover any remaining amount of underpayments;
- Termination of the contract with the contractor liable for any resulting cost to the federal government;
- Imposition of a debarment list (blacklist), banning a contractor from receiving a government contract for a period of three years, unless the Labor Secretary finds "unusual circumstances."

Where the Labor Secretary withholds sums due the contractor based on a finding of noncompliance with the wage and fringe benefit provisions of the Act, the amounts withheld are deposited in a special fund, and paid to the employees directly upon determinations of how much each is to receive.

The Secretary is authorized to maintain an action for deficiencies where amounts withheld are insufficient to cover underpayments due employees. Any money not disbursed to employees is turned over to the U.S. Treasury. However, a contractor's bankruptcy proceeding does not affect a default proceeding under the SCA concerning the contractor's failure to respond to charges that it violated the Act's wage provisions. (*In re Beal*)

If the contractor violates any provision of the contract, the contracting agency may cancel the contract upon written notice to the contractor. The government may charge the original contractor with any added costs incurred in obtaining contract completion through a substitute contractor.

## LIMITATIONS PERIOD

An important distinction between the SCA and other federal public contract acts is that the SCA contains its own statute of limitations rather than borrowing the two-year period from the FLSA.

The Portal-to-Portal Pay Act does not include the SCA within its coverage, and the Fourth Circuit reasoned that this omission by Congress was not inadvertent. Although this omission creates an inconsistency in enforcement of public contracts acts, the court ruled, the SCA limitations period is the six-year general statute of limitations under 28 U.S.C. Sec. 2415. (*United States v. Deluxe Cleaners & Laundry*)

Although the SCA does not follow FLSA limitations periods (through the Portal Act), it does adopt FLSA case law in appropriate circumstances. Approving the imposition of prejudgment interest on a noncomplying contractor, a federal district court held that silence on this issue within the SCA was not enough to defeat FLSA case law authorizing the grant of prejudgment interest in similar cases. (*United States v. Powers Bldg. Maintenance Co.*)

The SCA contains recordkeeping requirements similar to those in the Walsh-Healey Act, particularly with reference to the segregation of government and nongovernment work. These records must be made available for inspection by authorized representatives of the Wage-Hour and Public Contracts divisions.

## BLACKLIST PENALTY

The Act requires that a noncomplying contractor be placed on the debarment list for a period of three years. The 1972 amendments to the SCA limited the Secretary's authority to deviate from this penalty, such that variance may only be granted upon a finding by the Secretary of "unusual circumstances." (*In re Dokken*)

The Act does not define "unusual circumstances, " but certain elements should be present to justify such a finding. These include:

- Where the violation is clear and the contractor's conduct is culpable, willful, or aggravated, relief is not appropriate;
- Where there is a legitimate dispute as to a contract term leading to the violation, a contractor should not be penalized for electing to litigate an issue in doubt;
- Where the contractor's conduct is not culpable, consideration should be given to the nature and gravity of the violation, its impact on the unpaid employees, and any good-faith conduct by the contractor to correct the violation and comply with the Act. (*In re Emerald Maintenance, Inc.*)

"Unusual circumstances" have been found in the following situations:

- Undercapitalization and poor bookkeeping; (*In re Glover*)
- No prior history of violations, a bona fide dispute, the contractor's position was not frivolous, and the amount in dispute was small; (*In re Taskpower Int'l.*)
- Confusion concerning the number of years of experience necessary to qualify for accumulating vacation benefits and the contractor's reliance on statements of the contracting officer; (*In re Myers & Myers, Inc.*) and
- Action by the contracting agency that resulted in substantial monetary loss to the contractor. (*In re Quality Maintenance Co.*)

Contractors have been debarred based on a failure to demonstrate "unusual circumstances" in the following cases:

- Financial difficulties; (*In re Van Elk*)
- Ignorance of legal requirements and a nonchalant approach to ending violations; (*In re McLaughlin Storage*)
- Wage determination was at substantial variance with the prevailing rate in the locality but the contractor made

no effort to have the determination corrected or modified; (*In re Electric City Linoleum*) and

- Simple negligent conduct. (*In re Dynamic Enters.*)

A federal district court refused to preliminarily enjoin enforcement of the debarment penalty against a contractor that
violated the wage and fringe-benefit provisions of the SCA,
pending review of the Labor Department's final administrative
action, even assuming the violations were *de minimis.* The court
noted that the contractor failed to prove the existence of unusual circumstances, inasmuch as:

- The violations were deliberate and of an aggravated
  nature;
- The contractor did not show that it would suffer irrep-
  arable harm from the debarment penalty; and
- The harm to other interested parties and the public interest weigh against an injunction. (*Kirchdorfer v. McLaughlin*)

## ATTORNEYS' FEES

The SCA is silent on the matter of attorneys' fees awards.
However, Congress has provided for an award of reasonable
attorneys' fees "to the prevailing party in any civil action brought
by or against the United States . . . in any court having jurisdiction of such action." (Equal Access to Justice Act, 28 U.S.C.
Sec. 2412(b))

The U.S. Court of Appeals for the Federal Circuit had an
opportunity to address the application of the Equal Access to
Justice Act (EAJA) in the context of a contractor that successfully protested an action of a federal contracting agency.

A public contractor was denied an upward price adjustment in the contract by a contracting officer. The Armed Services Board of Contract Appeals upheld the denial, even though
it conceded that the officer's decision was based on her erroneous interpretation of an SCA regulation.

The contractor successfully appealed the Board's ruling to
the U.S. Court of Claims, which granted the price adjustment
but said nothing about the cost of the litigation. (*Broad Ave.
Laundry v. United States*) The contractor then filed its request

for fees under EAJA with the U.S. Court of Appeals for the Federal Circuit.

The EAJA provides that an agency or a court, in any "adversary adjudication" or "civil action . . . brought by or against the United States, shall award to a prevailing party other than the United States fees and other expenses, unless the position of the agency or the United States 'was substantially justified or that special circumstances make an award unjust.' "

The contractor was clearly a prevailing party as a result of the Claims Court's decision in favor of the price adjustment. The issue to be resolved by the appeals court was the meaning of the "position of the government" language in EAJA. The court rejected the claim that the Act was intended to cover the government's position at the administrative proceeding before the Board. It held, instead, that the "position of the government" meant the government's stance in litigation. The position of the government was therefore "substantially justified" in litigation, the court concluded, and no attorneys' fees were awarded.

A contractor that was relieved from the debarment penalty for its violations of the SCA and the CWHSSA was not entitled to attorneys' fees under EAJA, where:

- The regulations implementing EAJA exclude SCA and CWHSSA;
- The right to such fees arises under EAJA and not the labor standards acts; and
- EAJA authorizes fees only in "adversary adjudication," defined as proceedings required by law, and the SCA authorizes but does not require the proceeding in the instant case. (*In re Verticare*)

# 7
# DAVIS-BACON ACT

The Davis-Bacon Act of 1931 (DBA; WHM 90:251) along with the Anti-Kickback Law (Copeland Act) and Contract Work Hours and Safety Standards Act, establishes employment standards for laborers and mechanics on public construction projects let under federal contracts for amounts in excess of $2,000. Since the $2,000 floor was established in 1935, Congress has considered, but not approved, many attempts to raise that floor.

The DBA requires covered contracts to specify prevailing minimum wage rates for various classes of mechanics and laborers employed on the project. Covered contracts include highway building, dredging, demolition, cleaning, and painting and decorating of public buildings. Covered employees include all mechanics and laborers employed directly on the site of the project, including subcontractor employees. Employees of "materialmen" (companies that supply material for the work away from the construction site and that maintain establishments where their goods are sold to the general public) are exempt if they do not spend more than 20 percent of their worktime at the construction site.

## COVERAGE

In an early dispute concerning coverage of the Act, a conflict arose between the Comptroller General and the Attorney General over the status of workers performing dredging operations. The Secretary of Labor had originally found that these workers were akin to mechanics and construction laborers, and therefore subject to the Act. The Attorney General held, to the contrary, that these workers are more like "seamen" and should be covered by the Maritime Workers Act rather than the DBA. The Comptroller General settled the dispute by siding with the Labor Secretary on the ground that the administration and enforcement responsibilities were delegated to the Labor Department and the Labor Secretary's position must control. (Comp Gen Dec. B-105067, Nov. 6, 1951)

This dispute illustrates the difficulty in establishing the parameters of the Act's coverage. The Act extends coverage based on the type of work called for in the contract, the type of contract involved, and the type of contractor involved.

The Act covers any lease-purchase agreement with the government for buildings or conversions, extensions, additions, or remodeling of existing structures. (Labor Solic Op, Dec. 1954) However, the Act does not apply to construction, alteration, or repair of buildings for occupancy by the federal government under any term-lease or lease-option agreement, since these types of contracts evidence a lack of a *firm commitment* by the government to acquire more than a lease-hold interest in the property. (Comp Gen Dec. B-122382, July 18, 1962)

Demolition work as part of a contract for initial construction or demolition performed as part of "initial construction" (i.e., closely related or immediately incidental thereto) is covered by the labor standards provisions of the Act. (Asst. Labor Solic Op, June 20, 1961)

The Act has been interpreted to cover other contracts, including:

- The plugging of oil and gas wells and the removal of above-ground equipment in connection with the construction of a reservoir; (Solic Op, June 13, 1961)
- The spreading of oil on road surfaces during the construction of a highway, at the construction site; (Solic Ops, Oct. 8, 1962 and Nov. 6, 1962)
- The renting of equipment to a covered contractor, where the rental agreement calls for the employees of the rental company to operate the equipment on the construction project at the worksite; (*In re Griffith Co.*)

- The cleaning operations on public buildings or works performed by the process of steam or sandblast cleaning; (Solic Op, July 17, 1961)
- Contracts performed under the Area Redevelopment Act of 1961 must comply with the DBA's prevailing minimum wages (and overtime provisions of the Contract Work Hours and Safety Standards Act); and
- Contracts performed under the Federal-Aid Highway Act of 1956 (Sec. 115 of the Act).

In each of these agreements, it was determined that the work in question essentially constituted an "integral part" of the prime contractor's performance of its government contract. (*Sansone Co. v. California Dep't of Transp.*) Although not determinative, the "integral part" element is important in establishing the scope of the Act's coverage. The Act does not cover contracts for:

- The preparation of materials for a construction project away from the construction site and delivery in final form at the worksite, if the workers do not spend more than 20 percent of their time at the worksite; (Solic Op, Oct. 1942)
- The delivery of crushed stone from a quarry to a construction site, where the workers unload the stone merely by lifting the "tailgate" on the truck and perform no other work at the site; (Asst. Solic Op, Oct. 11, 1961)
- The delivery of standard materials (e.g., concrete aggregate, hot mix, and sand) to a construction site, performed independently of the contract; (*Zachry Co. v. United States*)
- The prefabrication of component roof panels for the contract, where the prefabrication work normally cannot be done at the construction site; (Solic Op, Aug. 2, 1961)
- The supplies, including installing or maintaining work that is only incidental to the furnishing of such supplies. However, the Act covers contracts for installation involving substantial construction, for transportation of

supplies to or from the building site by the contractor or subcontractor, such as window frames or millwork;

- Servicing or maintenance work in a building that is completed or substantially completed; the Act covers servicing or maintenance performed as part of the construction or repair of the public buildings or works;
- The complete dismantling or demolition of a construction site, where no construction is done by the dismantling or demolition company;
- Exploratory drilling;
- Construction work closely related to research and development, where the research work cannot be done separately, or where the construction work is the subject of the research;
- The construction or repair of vessels, aircraft, or other kinds of personal property; and
- Work outside the continental United States or a place not known or reasonably determinable at the time the contract is executed.

In addition, the Act does not cover preliminary survey work such as the preparation of metes and bounds prior to construction, especially if performed pursuant to a separate contract. Survey work done immediately prior to or during construction, performed as an aid to the crafts that are engaged in the actual construction project, is considered covered. (Solic Op, June 1960; Sec. Lab., Aug. 2, 1962)

Other work not regarded as Davis-Bacon work includes work performed off the construction site, whether done by contractors, subcontractors, or materialmen (Comp Gen Dec. B-148076, July 26, 1963) and certain types of installation work performed during the actual construction, that is only incidental to the actual construction. (Solic Op, Mar. 3, 1964)

The distinction between which contracts are covered and which are not is often characterized in terms of the work called for. Where the work brings the workers into close integration with ("integral part" of) the prime contractor's performance, the workers are classified as employees of a subcontractor covered under the Act. Where the workers do not perform work that is integral to the prime contractor's performance, they are classified as materialmen and not covered under the contract. But whether the examination focuses on the language in the contract or on the workers' classification, the determination turns on the actual nature of the work performed in relation to the prime contractor's performance.

Employees engaged in assembling major components of houses to be erected on nearby sites, for example, were deemed to be subcontractor employees, covered by the Act, even though they were employed in a mobile factory that could be located at a different site. The mobile factory operations are distinguishable from those of a factory producing prefabricated homes or components for a variety of customers, which may be regarded as a variant of the traditional materialman serving the construction industry. The employees performed work that was integrally related to the final assembly or conventional construction activities on the worksite, and thus constitute a part of the overall assembly or construction. (Solic Op, Aug. 27, 1969)

A variety of factors enters into the determination of whether a particular contract is covered by the Act, but the most decisive would appear to be the degree of integration or integral relations between the sub and prime contractors' performance.

In view of the variety of factors that can enter into the determination of whether a particular contract may be covered by the Act, it is advisable to contact the U.S. Labor Department, Davis-Bacon Office for clarification. (See Appendix J, Contract Standards Operations Division)

## CONFLICT WITH OTHER LAWS

When a contract calls for installation work, there may be some doubt as to whether the amount of installation work is substantial enough to justify coverage by the DBA, or whether the installation is merely incidental to the construction project, thus warranting Walsh-Healey Act coverage. A contract calling for the installation of Minuteman missile equipment at a construction site was determined to be only "incidental" to the construction project, since it involved a minimal amount of time. Therefore, the Act did not apply. (Solic Op, Apr. 16, 1962)

But where the construction costs were the major part of an installation contract, or where the installation was complex and substantial, the installation contract was deemed to be within the Act's coverage. (Solic Ops, Nov. 6, 1961 and Nov. 30, 1961)

An employer who was the subject of an FLSA action by employees loading and unloading government goods at an Army reservation was unsuccessful in establishing that the Davis-Bacon Act covered, and thus shielded it, from FLSA liability. The court declared that only laborers engaged in the construction or repair of public works, and not employees of a private firm working on a government reservation, were covered by the DBA. It added that the DBA and FLSA statutes are not necessarily incompatible. (*Ortiz v. San Juan Dock Co.*; *Walling v. Patton-Tulley Transp. Co.*)

## PREVAILING WAGES

Unlike the Walsh-Healey Act, the Davis-Bacon Act authorizes the Labor Secretary to establish prevailing wage rates on a contract-by-contract basis. The Secretary is required to conduct a survey of the wage rates prevailing in the "locality" and to set DBA rates for the contract according to those rates. Area and regional differentials are thus recognized in the setting of rates under the DBA.

The Secretary is also required to establish a scale of rates for the various classifications of workers on a particular project, rather than establishing one minimum prevailing wage rate for the project or industry. The classifications range from "helpers" to apprentices to laborers to journeymen, and each rate takes into consideration the locality. Thus the setting of such rates is a very complex and time-consuming process that has led to much litigation.

The constitutionality of the statutory mechanism for setting the prevailing wage rates for separate job classifications under the Act was contested and upheld in 1938. (*Gilioz v. Webb*) Similarly, the U.S. Supreme Court has declared that the Secretary's determination is not subject to judicial review. (*United States v. Binghamton Constr. Co.*) However, changes in the regulations implementing the process of setting the wage rates may be challenged, where the charging party demonstrates a substantial likelihood that it will prevail on the merits based on such things as improper promulgation of the regulations under the Administrative Procedure Act. (*Building & Constr. Trades v. Donovan*)

Because the Secretary's wage determinations are nonreviewable by a court, Congress established the Wage Appeals Board in 1964 to review:

- Wage determinations;
- Debarment cases;
- Controversies concerning payment of wages or proper classifications involving large sums of money or large groups of employees, or novel situations; and
- Adjustment of liquidated damages assessed under the Contract Work Hours and Safety Standards Act (WHM 90:271). Determinations of the Wage Appeals Board are reviewable on the grounds of lack of due process (*Framlau Corp. v. Dembling*) and fraud or gross error (*Southwest Eng'g Corp. v. United States*).

Wage determination disputes usually arise at the time the rates are set, but do not get adjudicated until well after contract completion. Therefore, most disputes involve a contractor's attempt to gain reimbursement for what it regards as improperly high rates. In denying reimbursement, the U.S. Supreme Court has ruled that the rates established by the Secretary and included in the contract are not a representation or a warranty that such rates are prevailing in the local community. (*United States v. Binghamton Constr. Co.*)

In 1989, the Wage Appeals Board (WAB) ruled that the Davis-Bacon Act applied retroactively to privately funded construction of an outpatient clinic, built for exclusive lease by the Veterans Administration. The Labor Department's Wage-Hour Administrator had previously concluded that the VA solicitation resulted in a "contract to construct" within the meaning of the Act. The Administrator further determined that the clinic was a "public" building within the meaning of the Act, even though the federal government would not acquire title to the facility. (*In re Lease of Space for Outpatient Clinic, Crown Point, Ind.*)

The *Crown Point* decision affirmed a 1985 decision by the WAB, wherein the Board held that the Act should apply if more than an incidental amount of construction-type activity is involved in the execution of a government contract. (*Military Housing, Ft. Drum*)

Contractors have pursued reimbursement under three theories: (*a*) equitable adjustment, (*b*) mutual mistake of fact, and (*c*) redetermination of rates. The first two theories stem from basic contract law, and the third theory is the result of administrative practice by the Wage-Hour Division.

Under the equitable adjustment theory, a contractor was entitled to obtain $18,000 that a contracting officer had withheld following a downward redetermination of rates by the Labor Secretary. The rates had originally been set higher than what prevailed in the locality, and the contractor had originally submitted its bid based on the actual rates prevailing in the locality. The Court of Claims ruled that there was no equitable basis for the contracting agency to obtain the completed contract at a price less than that which it agreed to pay. The contractor was thus found equitably entitled to the reimbursement it sought. (*Burnett Constr. Co. v. United States*)

Under the mutual mistake of fact theory, the contractor obtained reimbursement based on the Labor Department's delay in adjusting the prevailing rates until after the contract was executed. The contractor incurred increased labor costs at the government's direction, and the court ruled that the parties had contracted under a mutual mistake of fact as to the maximum and minimum rates prevailing in the locality. The contract may be reformed to reflect the true intent of the parties. (*Poirier & McLane Corp. v. United States*)

Under the redetermination of rates concept, a contractor was denied an adjustment, even though he incurred higher labor costs due to higher rates set after the contract was executed. The contract contained a clause for payment of wages to be determined by the Secretary *after* the contract was executed, and the Court of Claims stated that this clause was not against public policy, since it had been included for the benefit of the workers, rather than for the benefit of the contractor. (*Bushman Constr. Co. v. United States*)

However, a union unsuccessfully sought to compel a state transportation department to incorporate the appropriate prevailing wages in bid solicitations for a construction project pursuant to the Act. The Transportation Department had included in the original solicitation the wage rates erroneously published in the Federal Register, and two federal agencies had notified the department of this fact 11 days before the scheduled date of opening of the bids. The court noted that the union had obtained all the substantive relief it sought prior to the instant action, and the union was merely seeking to preserve its status as a "prevailing party" for purposes of an award of attorneys' fees. (*Operating Eng'rs Local 3 v. Bohn*)

States' prevailing wage laws are virtually always involved in state-funded construction projects. These state laws are often called "little Davis-Bacon Acts," since the purpose and language of the state laws generally follow closely their federal counterpart. However, the federal government has also taken note of the existence of these little Davis-Bacon Acts, and of the potential confusion created by a project covering more than one state boundary, especially where federal funds may be involved. To that end, the federal government has issued a rule to resolve such confusion. Federal prevailing wage rates determined under the federal Davis-Bacon Act preempt state prevailing wage rates for a given construction trade on public or Indian housing projects when the state prevailing wage is higher, according to a final regulation issued by the U.S. Department of Housing and Urban Development in 1988 (53 F.R. 30206; see WHM 99:1261).

A final aspect of prevailing wage rate determinations involves Comptroller General rulings, such as:

- Obsolete rates may be adjusted by a change order; (Comp Gen Dec. B-106987, May 8, 1953)
- Issuance of a letter of inadvertence, acknowledging a mistake in the rate included in the contract, does not automatically authorize a change in the contract price; (Comp Gen Dec. B-129205, Nov. 15, 1957)
- Changed wage rates originally included in a contract to require payment of building instead of heavy-highway schedules represents a change in judgment, rather than a correction of inadvertent errors; (Comp Gen Dec. B-150293, Feb. 13, 1963)
- The Labor Secretary cannot restrict the use of spray painting work under a prevailing wage rate determination; (Comp Gen Dec. B-132044, June 10, 1957) and
- A Project Stabilization Agreement negotiated by construction industry employers and unions could be included in contracts for certain missile programs, in the interest of national defense, under the National Defense Contracts Act of 1958. The agreement covered all construction, fabrication, and related work covered by the Act at two military facilities, and called for the payment of fringe benefits and overtime pay. (Comp Gen Dec. B-148930, July 2, 1962)

A federal agency's failure to require that the Davis-Bacon Act's prevailing wage provisions be included in the contract can be remedied, even after performance of the construction work has been started under the contract. The Wage Appeals Board affirmed the Wage-Hour Administrator's order that the prevailing wage provisions be *retroactively* included in the agency's agreement with a private developer to construct a building for lease by the agency. A prior case with similar circumstances had resulted in a WAB ruling against such retroactive inclusion, where the contracting agency had concluded that the Act did not apply. This ruling prompted the Department of Labor to promulgate a regulation authorizing the Wage-Hour Administrator to issue a wage determination after the contract was awarded or after the beginning of construction, if the agency has failed to incorporate a wage determination in a contract required to contain prevailing wage provisions under the Act. (*In re Veterans Admin.*)

## FRINGE BENEFITS

Contributions to fringe benefit funds may not be counted toward satisfying the minimum prevailing wage rates in the contract under the Act, unless the wage rate determination specifically indicates that the fringes are included in the rates. The Act was amended in 1965 to allow contractors to combine wage payments and fringe contributions, if they added up to the total in the wage-fringe determination. However, this does not permit the contract to apply this "mix" formula to wage-only determinations. The Labor Solicitor issued a memorandum in 1965 to clarify the crediting of fringe benefit contributions in meeting Act wage determinations. (Solic Memo, Oct. 15, 1965)

The Wage Appeals Board (WAB) has addressed the situation where a contractor made contributions to an apprenticeship benefit fund and attempted to claim fringe-benefit credits under the Act. The contractor contributed a $500 tuition payment to an apprenticeship training plan on behalf of its sole apprentice and voluntarily contributed 25 cents per hour to an apprenticeship training fund for bricklayers, carpenters, and laborers on behalf of its employees who worked on five federally financed construction projects. The WAB ruled that:

- The contractor may not claim credits for these contributions under the "funded-plans" provisions of the DBA, since the Act provides that only *irrevocable* contributions made "pursuant to a fund, plan, or program" may be credited and these voluntary contributions are not irrevocable and were not made "pursuant" to a fund, plan or program; and
- The contractor may claim credits under the Act's "unfunded-plans" provisions, but only as to actual costs necessary to provide training for apprentices registered in the plan. (*In re Miree Constr. Corp.*)

## ENFORCEMENT

In view of the Act's purpose of protecting the wage standards of workers performing under government contracts, the Act and the regulations provide for a variety of methods for ensuring that workers receive the prevailing wages set in the contract.

For example, noncompliance by the contractor entitles the contracting agency to cancel the contract and to seek money from the contractor for the extra costs incurred in finding a substitute performer on the contract. Similarly, the Comptroller General may pay the workers directly and seek reimbursement from the contractor for any deficiencies. The government may also set off payments due the contractor under one contract for deficiencies under another contract where the contractor has failed to pay the prevailing wages. Finally, the workers themselves may bring an action to recover unpaid wages under Section 3(b) of the Act. If the contract does not contain prevailing wages, however, there is no private right of action under the Act.

Arbitration has recently been applied to resolve disputes arising under the DBA. For example, a state supreme court has ruled that:

- A collective bargaining contract containing an arbitration clause did not contemplate arbitration of disputes over a federal agency's determinations concerning what work the federal contractor was required to subcontract under the Act, where the agency has sole and absolute authority to make such determinations; and
- The union is entitled to an order requiring arbitration as to the federal contractor's duty under the collective bargaining agreement to use its "best efforts" to influence the federal agency's determinations concerning what work the contractor was required to subcontract under the Act, where the contractor officially participates in the agency's decision-making process, and the agency's determinations under the Act affect both the contractor and the union. (*Oil Workers Local 2-652 v. EG & G Idaho, Inc.*)

As with the FLSA and the Walsh-Healey Act, Davis-Bacon Act lawsuits are governed by the Portal-to-Portal Pay Act, including limitations period determinations and imposition of liquidated damages liability. (See Chapter 3 for further information.)

## Employee Actions

The Act does not specifically confer on individual employees the right to bring an action for unpaid wages under a contract. On remand from the U.S. Supreme Court, however, the Court of Appeals for the Seventh Circuit made the definitive ruling on employee actions under the Act. It held:

- Laborers and mechanics are the "especial" beneficiaries of the Act, since the legislative history of the Act reveals that its fundamental purpose was to benefit laborers and mechanics by assuring they receive prevailing wages;
- The Act's grant of a right of action applies only to an action on a surety bond issued under the Miller Act, which requires the posting of a surety bond on most government contracts covered by the DBA;
- Employees have an implied right of action which effectuates congressional intent in passing the statute;
- The right to recover unpaid portions of the prevailing wage is based on congressional policy, despite the fact that an action for breach of an employment contract is traditionally a state-court action. (*McDaniel v. University of Chicago*)

An important aspect of this particular case, which led to the recognition of a private right of action, albeit "inferred," was that the statutory remedies available under the Act were ineffective in remedying the employees' injury from underpayments:

- No funds had been withheld from the contractor, so no monies could be forwarded to the employees or set off against another contract;
- No bond had been required against which the government could move on behalf of the employees;
- The government chose not to invoke the sanctions of

contract termination or blacklisting. Had any of these circumstances not existed, the government would have had a means of using the statutory remedies to make "whole" the victims (employees) of the employer's noncompliance.

The existence of prevailing wages in the contract provides a basis for creating the inference of the private right of action. The absence of such wage rates destroys this inference, and allowing employees to sue under such circumstances would undercut the administrative mechanism created to assure consistency in the administration and enforcement of the Act. (*Universities Research Ass'n v. Coutu*)

Once it was established that a private right of action existed (albeit "inferred") under the DBA, it was not long before penumbral actions were recognized. For example, a union sought information concerning the names, addresses, and Social Security numbers of non-union employees of a federal contractor, ostensibly to monitor the contractor's compliance with the Act, as well as the federal government's enforcement of the Act. The federal government resisted, and the union sued under the Freedom of Information Act (FOIA). The U.S. Court of Appeals for the Third Circuit ruled that the public interest in disclosure of the names and addresses of these non-union workers was not barred, but that the workers' privacy interests barred disclosure of their Social Security numbers. (*Electrical Workers (IBEW) Local 5 v. United States Dept. of Housing & Urban Development*)

### Actions Against U.S. Government

Several unions successfully sued to compel the government to enforce the Act, claiming that Labor Department officials had failed to examine payroll records and conduct investigations to assure compliance with the Act; to send notices and hold hearings on charges of willful violations; to debar contractors who willfully violated the Act; and to withhold underpayments due employees from willful violators. The Tenth Circuit ruled that such actions are nondiscretionary duties under the Act and the regulations, and that mandamus and injunctive relief are available where dereliction of duty is alleged. (*Painters Local 419 v. Brown*)

Where the Comptroller General withholds funds from a contractor on the ground of noncompliance with the prevailing wage provisions, employees seeking to obtain money from the government must show that they had made a demand for payment from the Comptroller General, that there had been a determination of their right to payment by the official, and that the official had refused payment, as a condition precedent to maintaining an action in court against the government. (*Veader v. Bay State Dredging & Contracting Co.*)

The Act requires a federal contractor to maintain payroll records with sufficient particularity so that the contractor, if necessary, may demonstrate that there has been compliance with the Act's wage provisions. The contractor may dispute computations of the Labor Department, but it must have its own records to support its contentions. (*In re Woodside Village*)

A contractor that had submitted false records under the Act was debarred for three years from government contracting. The contractor's claim that its officers went beyond the scope of their duties and that the debarment penalty was thus inappropriate was unavailing. (Comp Gen Dec. B-145606, Aug. 1, 1961)

Receipt from the Labor Secretary of a notice of intent to initiate administrative enforcement procedures does not support a contractor's request to enjoin the Secretary, where the regulations provide levels of administrative proceedings that apparently are adequate to protect the contractor's rights, and in any event, there is no present harm to the contractor and no certainty that there will be future harm. (*Home Improvement Corp. v. Brennan*)

## DEBARMENT

The DBA authorizes debarment from future government contracts for up to three years, for violations of the wage provisions of the Act in the course of performing under a covered contract. The Act specifically states that "the Comptroller General of the United States is further authorized and is directed to distribute a list . . . of persons and firms whom he has found to have *disregarded their obligations* to employees and subcontractors." (Emphasis added.) (40 U.S.C. Section 276-2(a)) This basis for debarment has come to be known as the "disregard-of-obligations" standard.

In 1987, the Labor Department declared that the "disregard-of-obligations" standard for imposing the debarment penalty on a contractor for violating the wage provisions of the DBA requires some review of the contractor's intent, since there is no indication that the legislature intended debarment to be a strict liability offense. In that case, the Labor Department declined to debar a contractor that violated DBA wage provisions in six of seven government contracts that it had been awarded. The Department found that the contractor's violations were not willful or intentional, since lack of knowledge and inadvertent mistake do not amount to disregard of obligations. (*In re Jen-Beck Assocs., Inc.*)

In a case involving a federal contractor's earlier debarment by the U.S. Department of Housing and Urban Development (HUD) for mail fraud in connection with submitting false payroll records under the DBA, the U.S. Court of Appeals for the Third Circuit ruled that:

- The contractor may raise the HUD debarment as a preclusion defense in the Labor Department's debarment proceeding based on alleged DBA violations; and
- The Labor Department's administrative law judge *must* consider the preclusion defense, since the HUD debarment was both adjudicatory and final, and the HUD administrative law judge filed a detailed opinion. (*Facchiano v. Brock*)

# 8

# CONTRACT WORK HOURS AND SAFETY STANDARDS ACT

The Contract Work Hours and Safety Standards Act of 1962 (CWHSSA; WHM 90:271) was enacted to supersede the collection of statues that became law from 1892 to 1917, collectively entitled the Eight Hour Laws. Also called the Work-Hours Act, CWHSSA is intended to regulate the payment of overtime for all mechanics and laborers employed on any public works project under a government contract or a government-financed contract.

The CWHSSA, like the Eight Hour Laws, originally required payment of time-and-one-half for all hours worked in excess of eight in one day to laborers and mechanics on public works. CWHSSA extended this overtime requirement to a workweek maximum of 40 hours in any one week. Congress eliminated the eight-hour day limit, however, in an attempt to allow a more flexible work schedule for covered employees, by enacting the Department of Defense Authorization Act of 1986 (P.L. 99-145).

Although the eight-hour day maximum is no longer in effect, contractors are still required to comply with the Act's 40-hour per week overtime limit. Overtime is computed on the employee's "basic rate of pay," which is the equivalent of the FLSA's "regular rate" of pay. Consequently, weekly salaries and fluctuating workweek (Belo) plans may be applied in computing CWHSSA overtime pay. (See Chapter 2, FLSA, under Overtime for more information on Belo plans.)

The Act also provides that no covered employee shall be employed under working conditions that are "unsanitary, hazardous, or dangerous" to health and safety. Debarment, or the blacklist penalty, is available for willful or grossly negligent violations of the Act.

## COVERAGE

### Covered Contracts

The Act covers any contract that may require or involve laborers or mechanics on a public works project under a contract with the federal government or under a contract financed by the federal government. CWHSSA regulations (29 C.F.R. Part 4.6) require the Secretary of Labor to incorporate the Act's wage and fringe-benefit provisions in all covered contracts. Failure to include verbatim language from the Act formed the basis for a contractor's claim that it was thus not subject to the Act's minimum-wage and fringe-benefit provisions. The claim was unsuccessful. (*National Electro-Coatings, Inc. v. Brock*)

Section 103 specifies which contracts will be covered and provides a limitation on this coverage:

- A contract to which the United States or any agency or instrumentality thereof, any territory, or the District of Columbia, is a party;
- A contract that is made for or on behalf of the United States, any agency or instrumentality thereof, any territory, or the District of Columbia; and
- A contract for work financed in whole or in part by loans or grants from, or loans insured or guaranteed by, the United States or any agency or instrumentality thereof under any statute of the United States providing standards for such work. *Provided*, that the Act shall not apply to work where assistance from the United States or any agency or instrumentality is only in the nature of a "loan guarantee, or insurance."

The Act's legislative history indicates that this proviso was intended to exclude programs that involve only federal guarantees of private loans, such as home construction financed by the Federal Housing Authority or the Veterans Administration.

Under this proviso, municipal employees working on construction and beautification projects were found to be exempt from the Act. (WH AdminOp, Sept. 9, 1969)

### Exempt Contracts

The Act specifically exempts contracts for transportation by land, air, or water (*Martinez v. Phillips Petroleum Co.*); contracts for the transmission of intelligence; and contracts for the purchase of supplies or materials or articles ordinarily available in the open market ("Open market contracts"). The Act also states that it shall not apply to any contract covered by the Walsh-Healey Act.

### Employee Coverage

The Act specifically covers all mechanics and laborers, including watchmen and guards, employed by any contractor or subcontractor in the performance of any part of the work contemplated by a covered contract. Workers performing services in connection with dredging or rock excavation in any river or harbor of the United States or any territory or of the District of Columbia are also covered. The Act exempts any employee working as a "seaman," however.

## HEALTH AND SAFETY STANDARDS

The Act authorizes the Secretary of Labor to set reasonable limits and to make such rules and regulations allowing reasonable variations, tolerances, and exemptions to and from any or all provisions of the Act as he may find necessary and proper in the public interest to prevent injustice or undue hardship or to avoid serious impairment of the conduct of government business.

The Assistant Secretary of Labor for Occupational Safety and Health is responsible for promulgating and administering the regulations governing health and safety standards under CWHSSA.

The Act also authorizes the Secretary to promulgate regulations providing for health and safety standards that must be observed in the performance of any contract or subcontract let under the Act. To this end, the Secretary may make inspections, hold hearings, issue orders, and make decisions that are deemed necessary to gain compliance.

The Secretary may apply to the federal courts to enforce compliance with safety and health standards. Where the contract has been canceled or the contractor has been debarred due to noncompliance, the contractor may seek review in the appropriate circuit court.


## ENFORCEMENT

Under CWHSSA, the contractor who violates the Act may be liable directly to its employees for unpaid overtime and to the federal government for liquidated damages. The Act also provides criminal sanctions for willful violations, including a fine of $1,000 or six months imprisonment, or both.

The major source of disagreement under the Act's predecessor, the Eight Hour Laws, involved whether employees working for a covered contractor or subcontractor had a private right to bring an action for recovery of unpaid wages. The courts rejected any notion of a private right to sue (*Filardo v. Foley Bros. Inc.; McDaniel v. Brown & Root, Inc.*)—some decisions rejected a theory based on an implied right to bring an action, and others rejected a theory based on third-party beneficiary of the contract.

However, CWHSSA specifically grants employees the right to bring an action for wages. The two major sources of litigation under the Act have involved disputes over the debarment or blacklist penalty and over the imposition of liquidated damages.

Under CWHSSA, a contractor's overtime violations may not be excused for alleged miscomputations or alleged inadvertence. And the U.S. Claims Court has upheld the Labor Department's determination that requiring employees to work an extra 15 to 20 minutes as part of their continuing work regimen is not *de minimis*, for purposes of the Act's overtime provisions. (*Cobra Constr. Co. v. United States*)

In another case, the U.S. Claims Court found that it lacked jurisdiction and dismissed a subcontractor's claim to recover payments withheld by the Labor Department for CWHSSA violations. The U.S. Court of Appeals for the Federal Circuit declared that the Claims Court erred, where the subcontractor claimed that there was a *contract* barring the Labor Department from withholding funds until the dispute was resolved. Such a contract, according to the appeals court, would create jurisdiction in the Claims Court under the Tucker Act. (*Cooper General Contractor v. United States*)

## LIQUIDATED DAMAGES

The Act provides that a noncomplying contractor will be assessed a penalty for liquidated damages in the amount of $10 per day for each calendar day on which a covered employee is permitted or required to work without receiving overtime pay for overtime work. The liquidated damages are withheld by and for the use of the federal government. The government withholds overtime pay on behalf of the employees, and the Comptroller General is authorized to pay these overtime wages directly to the employees.

If the amounts withheld under the contract are insufficient to reimburse the workers for their unpaid overtime, they are authorized to maintain private actions or interventions against the contractor and its sureties. The Act invalidates any agreement by the employees to accept less than the required wages or any voluntary refunds by them, as employer defenses to allegations of overtime violations.

A contractor who has had amounts withheld as liquidated damages may appeal this action to the head of the contracting agency, who has authority to issue a final order on the propriety of the withholding. The Secretary of Labor may accept or reject the contracting agency official's recommendation. The contractor has 60 days from the date of the Secretary's disposition of the case to appeal to the U.S. Court of Claims for review.

Most government contracts contain a standard Disputes Clause which establishes the time period within which a party to the contract must assert that a dispute has arisen. Most Dispute Clauses contain only a 30-day time period, even though the CWHSSA allows for 60 days to appeal. The 60-day period for appeal to the U.S. Court of Claims, however, is substantially shorter than the six-year limitations period characteristically allowed for ordinary contract disputes. The various boards of contract appeals have generally taken jurisdiction over such claims. (*In re Anaco Reproductions*)

A 1982 decision by the U.S. Court of Claims illustrates both the enforcement mechanisms for review of contracting agency determinations, and the application of the liquidated damages penalty. A contractor performing work under contracts covered by both the Service Contract Act and CWHSSA was assessed liquidated damages for underpayments under the latter statute. Following an investigation of the employer's recordkeeping and payroll practices, the Department of Labor recommended to the Secretary of the Army—the head of the contracting agency in this dispute—that the contractor be assessed liquidated damages. The Army Secretary imposed a penalty of $12,520 for the contractor's failure to exercise due care. The Court of Claims held that this finding by the Secretary was supported by substantial evidence. The court rejected the contractor's claim that its violations were "inadvertent notwithstanding exercise of due care." It concluded that the amount of damages was not so harsh as to constitute an "abuse of discretion" on the part of the Army Secretary. (*Inland Serv. Corp. v. United States*)

The Work-Hours Act, unlike the FLSA and the Walsh-Healey and Davis-Bacon acts, is *not* covered by the Portal-to-Portal Pay Act's "good-faith defense." Under CWHSSA's predecessor, the Eight Hour Laws, a contractor's reliance on rulings of the War Department was not a defense in an action by an employee to recover overtime pay allegedly due under the Law. (*Finnan v. Elmhurst Contracting Co.*)

## DEBARMENT PENALTY

The CWHSSA does not specifically provide for the debarment (blacklist) penalty, but it does authorize the Labor Secretary to promulgate regulations to impose appropriate sanctions and measures to enforce the Act. Under the regulations (29 C.F.R. Sec. 5), the Secretary has prescribed this penalty for willful or aggravated violations of the Act. The Secretary's authority to impose debarment by promulgating a regulation, the propriety of inferring such a penalty where CWHSSA is silent and other statues specify it, and the appropriateness of imposing it in a particular case, were all upheld by the U.S. District Court for the District of Columbia in 1961. (*Copper Plumbing & Heating Co. v. Campbell*)

Acknowledging that CWHSSA does not specifically mention debarment as a sanction, the U.S. Court of Appeals for the Second Circuit nevertheless ruled that such action is necessary for enforcement of statutory labor standards. The Wage Appeals Board and a federal district court had both found the contractor to have willfully violated CWHSSA on two federally funded construction projects. Resisting the debarment penalty imposed by each, the contractor argued that debarment constituted a penalty and that penalties may not be imposed without specific instruction from Congress. However, the appeals court reasoned that a sanction which serves to compel compliance with statutory goals should not be deemed a penalty, citing the U.S. Supreme Court in *Steuart & Bros. v. Bowles.* (*Janik Paving & Constr. v. Brock*)

Relief from the debarment penalty requires a showing of "unusual circumstances." (See also "Blacklist Penalty" in Chapter 6.) The Labor Department takes the position that financial problems do not constitute unusual circumstances for purposes of relieving a contractor of the debarment penalty. (*Labor Dept. v. Stafford's Might Maid*)

### Attorneys' Fees

The CWHSSA is silent on the matter of attorneys' fees awards. However, Congress has provided for an award of reasonable attorneys' fees "to the prevailing party in any civil action brought by or against the United States . . . in any court having jurisdiction of such action." (Equal Access to Justice Act, 28 U.S.C. Sec. 2412(b))

A contractor that was relieved from the debarment penalty for its violations of the SCA and the CWHSSA was not entitled to attorneys' fees under EAJA, where:

- The regulations implementing EAJA exclude SCA and CWHSSA;
- The right to such fees arises under EAJA and not the labor standards acts; and
- EAJA authorizes fees only in "adversary adjudication," defined as proceedings required by law, and the SCA authorizes but does not require the proceeding in the instant case. (*In re Verticare*)

## OTHER LAWS

CWHSSA specifically exempts contracts covered by the Walsh-Healey Act. Since Walsh-Healey does not cover contracts below $10,000 in amount, CWHSSA will likely cover these contracts without running afoul of Walsh-Healey coverage.

Walsh-Healey applies to an employee in any workweek in which the employee devotes *any time* to work covered by the Act. However, CWHSSA applies only where the employee works on a government contract for more than 40 hours in the workweek. (WH AdminOp, Oct. 7, 1964)

# 9
# OTHER FEDERAL LAWS

In addition to the major statutes that govern wages, hours, recordkeeping, and safety-health standards that have been discussed in previous chapters, there is a plethora of minor statutes that affect these areas in one way or another. These statutes may only govern an area incidentally, rather than as a major intent of Congress, but employers must comply with them nevertheless.

## ANTI-KICKBACK LAW (COPELAND ACT)

The Anti-Kickback Law (Copeland Act) of 1954 (WHM 90:281) is designed to protect employees' wages from illegal "kickback" arrangements in government-financed public construction. It covers contracts governed by Davis-Bacon and Work Hours acts. The Copeland Act prohibits anyone from compelling employees to return wages "by force, intimidation, or threat of procuring dismissal from employment, or by any other manner whatsoever." The Act prescribes a penalty of a $5,000 fine, up to five years' imprisonment, or both.

## TITLE III, CONSUMER CREDIT PROTECTION ACT

Title III of the Consumer Credit Protection Act of 1968 (CCPA; WHM 90:141) covers all employees, regardless of the size of the employer's business. Congress enacted this law under its authority to regulate commerce. The law is intended to create a uniform treatment under the bankruptcy law. Therefore, only a minimal involvement in interstate commerce is necessary for an employer to fall under the Act's coverage. The

Act regulates and makes consistent employer practices regarding garnishments of employee wages. It defines "earnings," "disposable earnings," and "garnishment," and it establishes restrictions on the amount of wages that can be garnisheed.

The maximum amount that may be garnisheed is determined under a formula. Under this calculation, the amount of wages that is subject to garnishment may not exceed (*a*) 25 percent of the employee's disposable earnings for any workweek, or (*b*) the amount by which his disposable earnings are greater than 30 times the federal minimum hourly wage, whichever is less. However, these limits on amounts that may be garnisheed do not apply where:

- The wage deduction is based on a court order for support or on an order of a court of bankruptcy; and
- Wage deductions for any debt due on any state or federal tax.

The CCPA prohibits an employer from discharging an employee for having a "single" garnishment levied against his or her pay. Violation of this ban carries penalties of a $1,000 fine, one year imprisonment, or both. The Secretary of Labor is authorized to enforce the CCPA, and the courts have interpreted this statutory mandate to preclude discharged employees from filing private lawsuits. (*Le Vick v. Skaggs Co.*)

Similarly, there is no implied private cause of action for damages for violations of the CCPA, and therefore, there can be no action under the Civil Rights Act of 1871 for those violations. (*Burris v. Mahaney*)

Because of the large number of state laws that regulate in this area, Congress added a section in the Act stating that the states are not precluded from applying their own garnishment laws, where the state laws prescribe higher or stricter standards restricting garnishment than the CCPA. The Act does not protect an employee who is discharged for having more than a single garnishment.

Long before Congress enacted federal legislation dealing with garnishment, the U.S. Supreme Court held unlawful state laws permitting a creditor to garnish an employee's wages without first giving him a hearing in court. Emphasizing that the state statute did not require the creditor to show that garnishment was necessary to collect the debt, the court ruled that a garnishment without notice or hearing amounts to a seizure of property without the procedural due process required under the Fourteenth Amendment to the U.S. Constitution. (*Sniadach v. Family Finance Corp.*)

Finally, any state may apply to the Secretary of Labor to have garnishments issued under state law exempted from CCPA restrictions, where the state law provides for restrictions that are substantially similar to the Act.

## CHILD SUPPORT ENFORCEMENT ACT

The Child Support Enforcement Act of 1984 (WHM 90:143) revises the Social Security Act and requires all states to have child support withholding laws in effect by January 1, 1986. Employers are required to withhold from an employee's wages any amounts determined to be due under support orders issued by a court or administrative body.

The Act prohibits employers from disciplining, discharging, or refusing to hire an individual because of a withholding order for support. Employees are entitled to advance notice and a hearing before any order becomes effective.

## OCCUPATIONAL SAFETY AND HEALTH ACT

The Occupational Safety and Health Act of 1970 (OSHA; LRX 6201) covers all employers engaged in a business affecting commerce, but does not include the federal government or any state or political subdivision of a state. OSHA defines an employee as any individual employed in a business of the employer affecting commerce.

Although the Secretary of Labor has primary responsibility for enforcing OSHA, the Secretary of Health and Human Services and the Occupational Safety and Health Review Commission also have important duties under the Act. In addition, the states are free to conduct their own safety and health programs in areas where there are no federal standards.

The Act imposes on an employer the general duty to furnish each of its employees employment and a place of employment which are free from recognized hazards that are causing or are likely to cause death or serious physical harm to employees.

To constitute a violation of the employer's general duty, the hazard involved must be preventable by the employer and must therefore be foreseeable. The employer can satisfy this general duty by:

- Promulgating adequate safety rules;
- Enforcing such rules with reasonable sanctions adequate to deter violations;
- Providing adequate training and instruction to all employees involved in hazardous work;
- Providing adequate supervision to employees according to their experience and exposure to dangerous conditions; and
- Providing protective equipment and requiring use of such equipment, where necessary.

In establishing safety and health standards, Congress created the National Institute of Occupational Safety and Health (NIOSH). NIOSH is authorized to conduct research, develop innovative methods and techniques for identifying toxic substances, and set criteria for safe use.

The Act also authorizes "notice and comment" rulemaking, under the auspices of the Labor Secretary. Any person adversely affected by the standard may obtain review by the appropriate U.S. Court of Appeals.

The Labor Secretary is authorized to grant temporary variances, and variations, tolerances, and exemptions from any or all provisions of the Act due to national defense considerations. The Secretary is required to conduct investigations and to issue citations where appropriate.

For all violations, the Secretary must set a period of "abatement," by which time the employer must correct the infraction. However, the employer has several options:

- Challenging the determination and seeking to have the abatement order revoked or modified;

- Seeking to obtain a variance;
- Applying for a temporary variance, to gain time to comply with the abatement order; and
- Petitioning the Labor Secretary for revocation or modification of the order, on the ground that a good-faith attempt to comply has been unsuccessful because of factors beyond the employer's control.

Employers who violate the Act face a range of civil and/or criminal penalties that include fines of up to $10,000 and six months in jail for a first offense of willfully violating the Act, and a fine of up to $20,000 and one year imprisonment for each subsequent offense.

The Act encourages individual employees to contact the Occupational Health and Safety Administration when a violation is suspected. Employees are protected from retaliation for exercising their rights under the Act, such as filing complaints or testifying against their employer in a proceeding under the Act.

## MISCELLANEOUS STATUTES

A variety of laws contain "employee protection" provisions that relate to wages-hours and/or safety-health issues in the workplace, even though the underlying purpose of the law may be to regulate in some other area. These federal statutes include the Energy Reorganization Act, the Surface Transportation Assistance Act of 1982, and the Rehabilitation Act of 1973.

Still other laws that touch on these areas of concern are the Employee Retirement Income Security Act of 1974, the Migrant and Seasonal Agricultural Worker Protection Act, the National Foundation on the Arts and Humanities Act, the Motor Carrier Act, the Mineral Land Act, the Area Redevelopment Act of 1961, the Merchant Marine Act, the Miller Act, and the Age Discrimination in Employment Act of 1967.

For example, the Tucker Act governs certain disputes which arise in federally funded construction projects. This statute has been involved in a dispute that would otherwise be enforced strictly under the Contract Work Hours and Safety Standards Act (CWHSSA; see Chapter 8 for more details). In that dispute, a subcontractor was found to have violated the CWHSSA's overtime provisions and the Labor Department withheld payments to the subcontractor. The subcontractor sued to recover the withheld payments and the dispute reached the U.S. Claims Court, which found that it lacked jurisdiction and dismissed the claim.

The U.S. Court of Appeals for the Federal Circuit declared that the Claims Court erred, where the subcontractor claimed that there was a *contract* barring the Labor Department from withholding funds until the dispute was resolved. Such a contract, according to the appeals court, would create jurisdiction in the Claims Court under the Tucker Act. (*Cooper General Contractor v. United States*)

Similarly, the Miller Act permits a person who has performed work on a government contract covered by the Miller Act to recover under the performance bond executed by the general contractor, if he or she has not been paid in full. Union trust funds sued a contractor under this provision of the Act for contributions for work performed by covered employees under collective bargaining agreements with the general contractor. However, because the trust funds had failed to comply with the Act's notice provisions, they were unsuccessful. (*Laborers' Pension Trust Fund v. Safeco Ins. Co. of Am.*)

In addition to these laws, many states have their own statutory scheme to regulate wages, hours of work, and other aspects of the employee's compensation scheme, such as the accrual and payment of sick or vacation leave, payment upon termination of employment, and other items. (State minimum wage requirements appear in Appendix E; state maximum hours and overtime requirements appear in Appendix G.)

Many states also have laws which establish prevailing wage rates for state-funded construction projects. These state laws are often called "little Davis-Bacon Acts," since the purpose and language of the state laws generally follow closely their federal counterpart. However, the federal government has also taken note of the existence of these little Davis-Bacon Acts, and the potential confusion created by a project covering more than one state boundary, especially where federal funds may be involved. To that end, the federal government has issued a rule to resolve such confusion. Federal prevailing wage rates determined under the federal Davis-Bacon Act preempt state prevailing wage rates for a given construction trade on public or Indian housing projects when the state prevailing wage is higher, according to a final regulation issued by the U.S. Department of Housing and Urban Development in 1988 (53 F.R. 30206; see WHM 99:1261).

Last, but not least, employers may be obligated to pay certain wages and fringe benefits and scheduled increases under collective bargaining agreements or individual employment contracts.

# APPENDIX A

## DIRECTORY OF U.S. DEPARTMENT OF LABOR ADMINISTRATIVE AND REGIONAL OFFICES

## U.S. DEPARTMENT OF LABOR
### Administrative Offices

*Address: U.S. Department of Labor Building, 200 Constitution Avenue,*
*N.W. Washington, D.C. 20210*
*Telephone: (202) 523-8271*

**OFFICE OF THE SECRETARY**
Secretary: Elizabeth H. Dole

**DEPUTY UNDER SECRETARY FOR INTERNATIONAL LABOR AFFAIRS**
Deputy Under Secretary: Shellyn McCaffrey
Associate Deputy Under Secretary, Trade: (*Vacant*)

**DEPUTY UNDER SECRETARY FOR LABOR-MANAGEMENT COOPERATIVE PROGRAMS**
Deputy Under Secretary: John R. Stepp

**INSPECTOR GENERAL**
Inspector General: James Brian Hyland
Deputy Inspector General: Raymond Maria

**OFFICE OF THE DEPUTY SECRETARY**
Deputy Secretary: Roderick A. DeArment
Associate Deputy Secretary: Michael K. Wyatt

**ADMINISTRATIVE LAW JUDGES**
Chief Judge: Nahum Litt
Deputy Chief Judge: John M. Vittone
Associate Chief Judge: G. Marvin Bober
Administrative Law Judges: David A. Clarke, Stuart A. Levin, Frank J. Marcellino

**BENEFITS REVIEW BOARD**
Chief Administrative Appeals Judge: Robert Ramsey
Administrative Appeals Judges: James F. Brown, Roy P. Smith, Nancy S. Dolder, Regina C. McGranery

**EMPLOYEES' COMPENSATION APPEALS BOARD**
Chairman: Michael Walsh
Members: David Gerson, George Rivers

**WAGE APPEALS BOARD**
Chairman: Jackson M. Andrews
Members: Thomas X. Dunn, Stuart Rothman

**ASSISTANT SECRETARY FOR CONGRESSIONAL AFFAIRS**
Assistant Secretary: Kathleen Harrington
Deputy Assistant Secretary: (*Vacant*)

**ASSISTANT SECRETARY FOR ADMINISTRATION & MANAGEMENT**
Assistant Secretary: Thomas C. Komarek
Deputy Assistant Secretary: Betty Bolden
Comptroller: William R. Reise

**ASSISTANT SECRETARY FOR PENSION & WELFARE BENEFITS**
Assistant Secretary: David M. Walker
Deputy Assistant Secretary, Policy: Ann L. Combs

**ASSISTANT SECRETARY FOR POLICY**
Assistant Secretary: Jennifer Dorn
Deputy Assistant Secretary, Program Economics & Research & Technical Support: (*Vacant*)
Deputy Assistant Secretary, Regulatory Economics & Economic Policy Analysis: Roland G. Droitsch

## ASSISTANT SECRETARY FOR MINE SAFETY & HEALTH

Assistant Secretary: David C. O'Neal, designee
Deputy Assistant Secretary: Robert Peluso
Associate Assistant Secretary: Patricia W. Silvey, acting

## ASSISTANT SECRETARY FOR EMPLOYMENT STANDARDS

Assistant Secretary: William C. Brooks
Deputy Assistant Secretaries: John Fraser, William E. Andersen

## ASSISTANT SECRETARY FOR LABOR-MANAGEMENT STANDARDS

Assistant Secretary: William C. White, acting
Deputy Assistant Secretary: Mario A. Lauro Jr., acting

## ASSISTANT SECRETARY FOR PUBLIC & INTERGOVERNMENTAL AFFAIRS

Assistant Secretary: (*Vacant*)
Deputy Assistant Secretary: Johanna Schneider
Associate Deputy Under Secretary, Intergovernmental Affairs: (*Vacant*)

## ASSISTANT SECRETARY FOR VETERANS' EMPLOYMENT & TRAINING

Assistant Secretary: Donald E. Shasteen
Deputy Assistant Secretary: (*Vacant*)

## ASSISTANT SECRETARY FOR OCCUPATIONAL SAFETY & HEALTH

Assistant Secretary: Alan McMillan, acting

## ASSISTANT SECRETARY FOR EMPLOYMENT & TRAINING

Assistant Secretary: Robert T. Jones
Deputy Assistant Secretary: (*Vacant*)

## WOMEN'S BUREAU
Director: Jill Emery

## BUREAU OF LABOR STATISTICS
Commissioner: Janet L. Norwood

### Office of Administration & Internal Operations
Deputy Commissioner: William G. Barron Jr.

### Office of Technology & Survey Processing
Assistant Commissioner: Carl J. Lowe

### Office of Compensation & Working Conditions
Associate Commissioner: George L. Stelluto
Deputy Associate Commissioner: Kathleen M. MacDonald

### Office of Economic Growth & Employment Projections
Associate Commissioner: Ronald E. Kutscher

### Office of Employment & Unemployment Statistics
Associate Commissioner: Thomas J. Plewes

### Office of Field Operations
Associate Commissioner: Laura B. King

### Office of Prices & Living Conditions
Associate Commissioner: Kenneth V. Dalton

### Office of Productivity & Technology
Associate Commissioner: Jerome A. Mark

### Office of Publications
Associate Commissioner: Henry Lowenstern

### Office of Research & Evaluation
Associate Commissioner: Wesley L. Schaible

## OFFICE OF THE SOLICITOR
Solicitor: Robert P. Davis
Deputy Solicitor, National Operations: Jerry G. Thorn

Deputy Solicitor, Planning & Coordination: Judith E. Kramer, acting
Deputy Solicitor, Regional Operations: Ronald G. Whiting

**Office of Management**
Director: Lydia Gardner Leeds

**Black Lung Benefits Division**
Associate Solicitor: Donald S. Shire
Deputy Associate Solicitor: (*Vacant*)

**Civil Rights Division**
Associate Solicitor: James D. Henry
Deputy Associate Solicitor: Joseph M. Woodward

**Employee Benefits Division**
Associate Solicitor: Cornelius S. Donoghue Jr, acting
Deputy Associate Solicitor: (*Vacant*)

**Employment & Training Legal Services Division**
Associate Solicitor: Charles D. Raymond
Deputy Associate Solicitor: Jonathan H. Waxman

**Fair Labor Standards Division**
Associate Solicitor: Monica Gallagher
Deputy Associate Solicitor: Gail V. Coleman

**Labor-Management Laws Division**
Associate Solicitor: John F. Depenbrock
Deputy Associate Solicitor: Barton S. Widom

**Legislation & Legal Counsel Division**
Associate Solicitor: Seth D. Zinman
Deputy Associate Solicitor: Swift Tarbel III

**Mine Safety & Health Division**
Associate Solicitor: Edward P. Clair
Deputy Associate Solicitor: Louis G. Ferrand Jr.

**Occupational Safety & Health Division**
Associate Solicitor: Cynthia L. Attwood
Deputy Associate Solicitor: Donald Shalhoub

**Plan Benefits Security Division**
Associate Solicitor: Marc Machiz, acting
Deputy Associate Solicitor: Gregor B. McCurdy

**Special Appellate & Supreme Court Litigation Division**
Associate Solicitor: Allen H. Feldman
Deputy Associate Solicitor: Charles ˙ adden

**Special Litigation Division**
Associate Solicitor: David H. Feldman
Deputy Associate Solicitor: Daly Temchine

## OFFICE OF THE SOLICITOR
### Regional Offices

**REGION I — BOSTON**
JFK Federal Buidling, Boston, MA 02203. Regional Solicitor: Albert H. Ross, (617) 565-2500.

**REGION II — NEW YORK**
201 Varick St., New York, NY 10014. Regional Solicitor: Patricia M. Rodenhausen, (212) 337-2078.

**REGION III — PHILADELPHIA**
3535 Market St., Room 14100, Philadelphia, PA 19104. Regional Solicitor: Marshall H. Harris, (215) 596-5157. Deputy Regional Solicitor: Kenneth L. Stein, (215) 596-5171.

**REGION IV — ATLANTA**
1371 Peachtree, St., NE, Atlanta, GA 30367. Regional Solicitor: Bobbye Spears, (404) 347-4811.

**REGION V — CHICAGO**
230 South Dearborn St., Chicago, IL 60604. Regional Solicitor: John Secaras, (312) 353-7256.

### REGION VI — DALLAS

525 Griffin St., 107 Federal Bldg, Dallas, TX 75202. Regional Solicitor: James E. White, (214) 767-4902. Deputy Regional Solicitor: William E. Everheart, (214) 767-4902.

### REGION VII — KANSAS CITY

911 Walnut St., Kansas City, MO 64106. Regional Solicitor: T.A. Housh Jr., (816) 374-6441. Deputy Regional Solicitor: Jaylynn Fortney, (816) 374-6441.

### REGION VIII — DENVER

1961 Stout St., Federal Bldg., Denver, CO 80294. Regional Solicitor: Henry Mahlman, (303) 844-5521.

### REGION IX — SAN FRANCISCO

71 Stevenson St., San Francisco, CA 94105. Regional Solicitor: Daniel W. Teehan, (415) 995-5461. Deputy Regional Solicitor: Carol Fickenscher, (415) 995-5461.

### REGION X — SEATTLE

9909 1st Ave., Seattle, WA 98174. Regional Solicitor: Robert A. Friel, (206) 442-0940.

# APPENDIX B

# Chart of FLSA White-Collar Exemption Tests

## CHART OF WHITE-COLLAR EXEMPTION TESTS

**EXECUTIVES**

**Tests: All six must be met.**

A. Primary duty is the management of (1) the enterprise in which he is employed, or (2) a customarily recognized department or subdivision thereof.

B. Customarily and regularly directs the work of **two or more** other employees.

C. Has authority to hire or fire other employees or to make recommendations as to hiring, firing and the advancement, promotion, or change of status of employees.

D. Customarily and regularly exercises discretionary powers.

E. Receives payment on a salary basis at a rate of not less than: (1) $155 a week in the 50 states; $130 a week if employed by other than the Federal Government in Puerto Rico, the Virgin Islands, and American Samoa.

F. Does not devote more than 20 percent of the hours worked in the workweek to activities which are not **directly and closely related to** the performance of exempt work; with the exception of

(1) executive employees in retail or service establishments who may devote up to 40 percent of the hours worked in the workweek to activities not directly or closely related to executive activities,

(2) an employee who owns at least 20-percent interest in the enterprise in which he is employed, and

(3) an employee who is in sole charge of an independent establishment or a physically separated branch establishment.

**Streamlined Tests for High-Paid Executives**

Executive employee paid at least $250 ($200 if employed by other than the Federal Government in Puerto Rico, the Virgin Islands, and American Samoa) weekly may qualify for exemption if he meets these tests:

(1) primary duty consists of the management of the enterprise in which he is employed or of a customarily recognized department or subdivision thereof; and

(2) such duty includes the customary and regular direction of the work of two or more other employees in the establishment or department.

**ADMINISTRATIVE EMPLOYEES**

**Tests: A, B, D, and E must all be met along with one of the three tests in C.**

A. **Primary duty is the performance of office or nonmanual work directly related to management policies or general business operations** of his employer or his employer's customers, or the performance of functions in the administration of a school system or educational establishment or institution, or of a department or subdivision thereof, in work directly related to academic instruction or training; and

B. **Customarily and regularly exercises discretion and independent judgment; and**

## CHART OF WHITE-COLLAR EXEMPTION TESTS—Cont'd.

C. (1) Regularly and directly assists a proprietor, or an employee employed in a bona fide executive or administrative capacity, or (2) performs under only general supervision work along specialized or technical lines requiring special training, experience, or knowledge, or (3) executes under only general supervision special assignments and tasks; and

D. Does not devote more than 20 percent of his hours worked in the workweek to activities which are not directly and closely related to the performance of the work described in subsections (A) through (C) above; with the exception of administrative employees in retail or service establishments who may devote up to 40 percent of the hours worked in the workweek to activities not directly and closely related to administrative activities; and

E. Receives payment on a salary or fee basis at a rate of not less than: (1) $155 a week in the 50 states: (2) $125 if employed by other than the Federal Government in Puerto Rico, the Virgin Islands, and American Samoa, or in the case of academic administrative personnel, is compensated for his services at either of the rates above or on a salary basis in an amount which is at least equal to the entrance salary for teachers in the school system or educational establishment or institution by which he is employed. (3) Administrative employees employed on a fee basis for less than a normal 40 hour week must be compensated at an hourly rate of not less than $3.875 ($3.125 if employed by other than the Federal Government in Puerto Rico, the Virgin Islands and American Samoa). These figures represent the hourly rate at which such employees would ordinarily be compensated to reach the minimum salary rates, based on a 40 hour week, to qualify for exemption.

### Streamlined Tests for High-Paid Administrative Employees

Administrative employees paid at least $250 ($200 if employed by other than the Federal Government in Puerto Rico, the Virgin Islands, and American Samoa) weekly may qualify for exemption if they meet these tests:

(1) primary duty is the performance of office or nonmanual work directly related to management policies or general business operations of his employer or his employer's customers; and

(2) such duty includes work requiring the exercise of discretion and independent judgment.

### PROFESSIONAL EMPLOYEES

Tests: One of the alternate requirements under A and all of the requirements B, C, D, E must be met.

A. Employee must have as his primary duty either (1) work requiring knowledge of advanced type in a field of science or learning, or (2) original and creative work in an artistic field, or (3) teaching, tutoring, instructing, or lecturing in the activity of imparting knowledge as a teacher certified or recognized as such in the school system or educational establishment or institution by which he is employed.

B. Work requires the consistent exercise of discretion and judgment.

C. Work must be (1) predominantly intellectual and varied in character as opposed to routine mental, manual, mechanical, or physical

## CHART OF WHITE-COLLAR EXEMPTION TESTS—Cont'd.

work; and (2) of such a character that the output produced or the result accomplished cannot be standardized in relation to a given period of time.

D. Time spent in activities not "an essential part of and necessarily incident" to professional duties may not exceed 20 percent of employee's own weekly hours worked.

E. Receives payment on a salary or fee basis at a rate of not less than (1) $170 a week in the 50 states; $150 if employed by other than the Federal Government in Puerto Rico, the Virgin Islands, and American Samoa. The salary requirements in this paragraph E need not be met in the case of an employee (a) who holds a valid license or certificate permitting the practice of law or medicine or any of their branches and is actually engaged in the practice thereof, or (b) who holds the requisite academic degree for the general practice of medicine and is engaged in an internship or resident program pursuant to the practice of medicine or any of its branches, or (c) who is employed and engaged as a teacher. (2) Professional employees employed on a fee basis for less than a normal 40 hour week must be compensated at an hourly rate of not less than $4.25 ($3.74 if employed by other than the Federal Government in Puerto Rico, the Virgin Islands and American Samoa). These figures represent the hourly rate at which such employees would ordinarily be compensated to reach the minimum salary rate, based on a 40 hour week, to qualify for exemption.

### Streamlined Tests for High-Paid Professional Employees

Professional employees paid at least $250 ($200 if employed by other than the Federal Government in Puerto Rico, the Virgin Islands, and American Samoa) weekly may qualify for exemption if they meet **either** of these tests:

(1) primary duty consists of the performance of work either requiring knowledge of an advanced type in a field of science or learning, or teaching, including work that requires the consistent exercise of discretion and judgment; **or** (2) primary duty consists of the performance of work in a recognized field of artistic endeavor, including work that requires invention, imagination, or talent.

### OUTSIDE SALESMEN

**Tests: Two must be met.**

A. Employed for the purpose of and is customarily and regularly engaged away from his employer's place of business in (1) making sales or (2) obtaining orders or contracts for services or for the use of facilities for which a consideration will be paid by the client or customer.

B. Hours of work of a nature other than described in the first test must not exceed 20 percent of the hours worked in the workweek by nonexempt employees of the employer. Work performed incidental to and in conjunction with the employee's own outside sales, including incidental deliveries and collections, shall not be regarded as nonexempt work.

# APPENDIX C

## CHART OF FLSA EXEMPTIONS FROM MINIMUM WAGE AND OVERTIME

# NONAGRICULTURAL INDUSTRIES AND OCCUPATIONS: EXEMPTION CHART

*(Agricultural exemption chart appears at WHM 91:547.)*

| INDUSTRY OR OCCUPATION | OVERTIME EXEMPTION | MINIMUM-WAGE EXEMPTION |
|---|---|---|
| **Airlines** | Exemption except for employees engaged in activities not necessary to or related to air transportation. | None. |
| **Amusement & recreational establishments** | Exemption if (a) establishment doesn't operate more than 7 months during calendar year, or (b) its average receipts during any 6 months of prior calendar year don't exceed one third of its average receipts for the other 6 months of the year. 1977 amendments added organized camps or religious or nonprofit educational conference centers as exempt establishments, but specifically deny exemption to concessioners in national parks, refuges, and forests, with exception of facilities operating in these areas that are directly relating to skiing. | Exemption under same terms as overtime exemption. |
| **Apprentices** i.e., one who is at least age 16 and is hired to learn a skilled trade in conformity with established apprenticeship standards). | None. | Subminimum rates may be paid under special certificate. |
| **Auto, farm implement, boat, aircraft dealers** | Exemption for salesmen, partsmen, and mechanics primarily selling or servicing autos, trucks, or farm implements, if employed by nonmanufacturer primarily selling to ultimate consumer. Exemption for salesmen primarily selling trailers, aircraft, or boats if employed by nonmanufacturer primarily selling to ultimate consumer. | None. |
| **Domestic Service Workers in Private Household** | Exemption if not covered by the Social Security Act nor employed for more than 40 hours per week for one employer. Babysitters employed on a casual basis and persons employed to provide companion services are exempt. Live-in domestics are exempt from overtime. | Exemption if not covered by the Social Security Act nor employed for more than eight hours per week in the aggregate. Babysitters employed on a casual basis and persons employed to provide companion services are exempt. |
| **Drivers and drivers' helpers** | Exempt if making local deliveries and compensated on trip rate basis. | None. |

### Checklist II—Other Industries and Occupations—Contd.

| INDUSTRY OR OCCUPATION | OVERTIME EXEMPTION | MINIMUM-WAGE EXEMPTION |
|---|---|---|
| Foreign employment | Exemption for services performed within a foreign country. | Exemption under same terms as overtime exemption. |
| Forestry or logging | Exemption if employer has 8 employees or less. | None. |
| Gasoline stations | Exemption for stations with annual sales of less than $250,000. | Exemption under same terms as overtime exemption. |
| Handicapped workers (i.e., one whose earning capacity has been impaired by age or physical or mental deficiency or injury). | None. | Subminimum rates may be paid under special certificate. |
| Holly-wreath manufacture | Exemption for homeworkers engaged in making of wreaths composed principally of natural evergreens. | Exemption under same terms as overtime exemption |
| Hospital and nursing homes | Hospital may use work period of 14 days, rather than 7 days, in computing overtime if employees agree in advance and 1½ times regular rate is paid for hours over 8 per day, and 80 in 14-day period. Otherwise, overtime rate applies after 40 hours per week. | None |
| Hotels, motels, & restaurants (Other than those qualifying for retail-service exemptions) | Exemption for hotel, motel, and restaurant employees (other than hotel maids and custodial employees (provided they are paid 1½ times regular rate for hours over 44 hours per week effective January 1, 1976. Exemption is repealed effective January 1, 1979. | None |

### Checklist II—Other Industries and Occupations—Contd.

| INDUSTRY OR OCCUPATION | OVERTIME EXEMPTION | MINIMUM-WAGE EXEMPTION |
|---|---|---|
| Learners (i.e., a beginner at a skilled occupation). | None. | Subminimum rates may be paid under special certificates. |
| Messengers | None. | Special certificates for employment at subminimum rates are authorized, but none has been issued. |
| Motion picture theaters | Exemption. | None. |
| Motor carriers | Exemption for employees whose hours of service are subject to regulation by Dept. of Transportation. | None. |
| Newsboys delivering newspapers to the consumer | Exemption. | Exemption. |
| Newspapers | Exemption for employees of paper with 4,000 or less circulation, major part of which is in county in which paper is published or in contiguous counties (paper may be printed elsewhere). | Exemption under same terms as overtime exemption. |
| Outside Salesman | Exempt. | Exempt. |
| Petroleum distributors | Exemption for any employee of independently owned & controlled local enterprise engaged in wholesale or bulk distribution of petroleum products, *provided* he is paid 1½ times the *statutory* minimum rate for work between 40 and 56 hours per week and 1½ times his *regular* rate all work in excess of 12 per day and 56 per week. | None. |
| Professional, executive, and administrative personnel | Exempt if they meet regulatory tests. | Exemption under same terms as overtime exemption. |
| Radio & TV broadcasters | Exemptions for announcers, news editors, and chief engineers of radio or TV station whose major studio is located in (1) city of 100,000 or less that is not part of a metropolitan area of more than 100,000, or (2) city of 25,000 or less, even in such metropolitan area if it is located at least 40 airline miles from principal city in area. | None. |

## Checklist II—Other Industries and Occupations—Contd.

| INDUSTRY OR OCCUPATION | OVERTIME EXEMPTION | MINIMUM-WAGE EXEMPTION |
|---|---|---|
| **Railroad, steamship companies** | Exemption for employees of employer subject to Part I of Interstate Commerce Act, i.e., common carriers engaged in (a) transporting passengers or property wholly by rail, or partly by rail and partly by water when both are used under common control, management, or arrangement for continuous carriage or shipment; or (b) transportation of oil or other commodities, except water and natural or artificial gas, by pipeline or partly by pipeline and partly by railroad or water. | None. |
| **Retail-service establishments** (other than laundry-dry-cleaning establishment, hospital, nursing home, school for handicapped or gifted children, preschool elementary or secondary school, or college | Exemption if (a) more than 50% of establishment's annual sales is intrastate, and (b) at least 75 percent of its annual dollar sales is not for resale and is recognized as retail in the industry. Under the 1977 amendments to the FLSA, the test for coverage of employees of enterprises comprised of one or more retail or service establishments is raised to $362,500 in three steps as follows: <br>● July 1, 1978 ..................... $275,000 <br>● July 1, 1980 ..................... 325,000 <br>● Dec. 31, 1981 ..................... 362,500 | Exemption under same terms as overtime exemption. |
| **Retail commission salesmen** | Exemption provided employee's regular rate (including salary and commissions) is more than 1½ times the statutory minimum, and more than half his compensation comes from commissions. | None. |
| **Retail-manufacturing units** (e.g., bakeries, ice-cream parlors, candy shops) | Exemptions for establishments if (a) it meets tests for retail-service establishments, (b) it is recognized in industry as retail establishment, (c) more than 85 percent of its dollar volume of annual sales is made intrastate; (d) the goods are made or processed and sold in the same establishment. | None |
| **Seamen** | Exemption for all seamen, whether on U.S. or foreign vessels. | Exemption only for seamen on foreign vessels. |
| **Students in agriculture** | None. | Sec. of Labor may permit employment of students part-time (20 hours a week or less) and full-time during vacations at 85 percent of statutory minimum. |
| **Students in higher educational institutions** | None. | Same as above. |

## Checklist II—Other Industries and Occupations—Contd.

| INDUSTRY OR OCCUPATION | OVERTIME EXEMPTION | MINIMUM-WAGE EXEMPTION |
|---|---|---|
| Students in retailing | None | Sec. of Labor may permit employment of students part-time (20 hours a week or less) and full-time during vacations at 85 percent of statutory minimum. |
| Substitute parents for institutionalized children | Exempt if employee and spouse are substitute parents for children residing in private non-profit educational institutions, receive jointly cash wages of $10,000 annually and reside in the same facilities as the children receiving free room and board. | None. |
| Taxicab drivers | Exemption for drivers employed by taxicab company. | None |
| Telephone exchanges | Exemption for employees of independently owned telephone company that has fewer than 750 stations. | Exemption under same terms as overtime exemption. |

# APPENDIX D

## DIRECTORY OF U.S. DEPARTMENT OF LABOR EMPLOYMENT STANDARDS ADMINISTRATION, ADMINISTRATIVE AND REGIONAL OFFICES

## Employment Standards Administration
## Administrative Offices

*Address: U.S. Department of Labor Bldg., 200 Constitution Avenue, N.W., Washington, D.C. 20210. Telephone: (202) 523-6191.*

**Office of Deputy Under Secretary**

Susan R. Meisinger, Deputy Under Secretary
Debbie Bolden, Special Assistant
Ralph Muehlig, Special Assistant
Lawrence W. Rogers, Jr., *Acting* Associate Deputy Under Secretary

**Office of Information**

Linda Tavlin, Director

**Equal Employment Opportunity Coordinator**

Constance M. Davis, Coordinator

**Office of Workers' Compensation Programs**

Lawrence W. Rogers, Jr., Director
Richard A. Staufenberger, Deputy Director

**Office of Management, Administration, and Planning**

Carol Gandin, *Director*
John Fraser, Deputy Director

**Office of State Liaison and Legislative Analysis**

June Mitchell Robinson, Director

**Office of Federal Contract Compliance Programs**

Joseph N. Cooper, Director
Charles E. Pugh, Deputy Director

**Operations Division**

James Warren, Chief Veteran & Handicapped Worker Program
Richard Caliri, Deputy Director, Program Operations
Neil A. Montone, Division of Longshore & Harbor Workers' Compensation
John D. McLellan, Division of Federal Employees' Compensation

**Wage and Hour Division**

Paula V. Smith, Administrator
Herbert J. Cohen, Deputy Administrator
Donald M. Essig, Assistant to the Administrator
James Jones, Chief Management Support Staff

**Office of Program Operations**

Nancy Flynn, *Acting* Assistant Administrator
Nancy M. Flynn, Deputy Assistant Administrator

**Fair Labor Standards Act Operations Division**

Raymond Cordelli, Director
Stephanie R. Glyder, Chief Enforcement Branch
Arthur H. Korn, Chief Special Employment Branch

**Farm & Child Labor Programs Division**

Gordon L. Claucherty, Director
Charles I. Carter, Chief Child Labor Programs Branch
Solomon Sugarman, Chief Farm Labor Progams Branch

**Wage Determinations Division**

Alan L. Moss, Director
Raymond L. Kamrath, Chief Construction

**Office of Policy Planning and Review**

Charles Pugh, Assistant Administrator
Policy & Analysis Division
   William G. Blackburn, Director
Planning & Review Division
   Manuel J. Villarreal, Director

**Contract Standards Operations Division**

Sylvester L. Green, Director

Rae Glass, Chief Construction Contract Operations Branch
William W. Gross, Chief
Service Contract Operations Branch

## ESA Regional Offices

| REGIONAL OFFICES SERVING VARIOUS STATES | | | | | |
|---|---|---|---|---|---|
| Region No. | State | Region No. | State | Region No. | State |
| 4 | Alabama | 3 | Maryland | 1 | Rhode Island |
| 10 | Alaska | 1 | Massachusetts | 4 | South Carolina |
| 9 | Arizona | 5 | Michigan | 8 | South Dakota |
| 6 | Arkansas | 5 | Minnesota | 4 | Tennessee |
| 9 | California | 4 | Mississippi | 6 | Texas |
| 8 | Colorado | 7 | Missouri | 8 | Utah |
| 1 | Connecticut | 8 | Montana | 1 | Vermont |
| 3 | Delaware | 7 | Nebraska | 3 | Virginia |
| 3 | District of Columbia | 9 | Nevada | 10 | Washington |
| 4 | Florida | 1 | New Hampshire | 3 | West Virginia |
| 4 | Georgia | 2 | New Jersey | 5 | Wisconsin |
| 9 | Hawaii | 6 | New Mexico | 8 | Wyoming |
| 10 | Idaho | 2 | New York | | |
| 5 | Illinois | 4 | North Carolina | | *Territories and* |
| 5 | Indiana | 8 | North Dakota | | *Possessions* |
| 7 | Iowa | 5 | Ohio | 1 | Canal Zone |
| 7 | Kansas | 6 | Oklahoma | 10 | Guam |
| 4 | Kentucky | 10 | Oregon | 2 | Puerto Rico |
| 6 | Louisiana | 3 | Pennsylvania | 2 | Virgin Islands |
| 1 | Maine | | | | |

### Region I

Regional Administrator: Walter P. Parker

Address: JFK Federal Building, Room 1612C, Boston MA 02203

Tel.: (617) 223-4305 *Wage and Hour Division*

Assistant Regional Administrator: William L. Smith

Address: Same

Tel.: (617) 223-0995 *Wage-Hour Area Offices* Boston

Address: Park Square Bldg., Room 462, 31 St. James Ave., Boston MA 02116

Tel.: (617) 223-6751 Hartford

Address: Federal Bldg., Rm. 305, 135 High Street, Hartford CT 06103

Tel.: (203) 244-2660 Portland

Address: Area Director, 66 Pearl St., Portland ME 04101

Tel: (207) 780-3344 Providence

Address: Area Director, John E. Fogarty, Fed. Bldg., 24 Weybosset St., Rm. 103, Providence RI 02903

Tel.: (401) 528-4378

### Region II

Regional Administrator: Frank B. Mercurio

Address: 1515 Broadway, Rm. 3300, New York NY 10036

Tel.: (212) 944-3351

*Wage and Hour Division*

Assistant Regional Administrator: Raymond G. Condelli

Address: Same

Tel.: (212) 944-3348

*Wage-Hour Area Offices*

Albany

Address: Area Director, Leo W. O'Brien Federal Bldg., Rm. 822, Albany, NY 12207

Tel.: (518) 472-3596

Bronx

Address: Area Director, 400 East Fordham Rd., Rm. 302, Bronx NY 10458

Tel.: (212) 298-9472

## Brooklyn

Address: Area Director, 271 Cadman Plaza East, Rm. 631, Brooklyn, NY 11201
Tel.: (212) 330-7662

## Buffalo

Address: Area Director, Harry J. Gray, Federal Bldg., Rm. 617, 111 West Huron St., Buffalo NY 14202
Tel.: (716) 846-4891

## Hempstead L.I.

Address: Area Director, 159 North Franklin St., Hempstead, L.I. NY 11550
Tel.: (516) 481-0582

## New York City

Address: Area Director, 26 Federal Plaza, Rm. 2946, New York NY 10007
Tel.: (212) 264-8185

## Newark

Address: Area Director, 970 Broad St., Rm. 836, Newark NJ 07102
Tel.: (201) 645-2279

## Trenton

Address: Area Director, 402 East State St., Rm. 411, Trenton NJ 08603
Tel.: (609) 989-2247

## Caribbean Office

Address: Area Director, F. Degetau Fed. Office Bldg., Rm. 403, Carlos Chardon St., Hato Rey PR 00918
Tel.: (809) 753-4442

### *Wage-Hour Area Offices*

## Hato Rey

Address: Area Director, F. Degetau Federal Office Bldg., Rm. 152, Carlos Chardon St., Hato Rey PR 00918
Tel.: (809) 765-0404, Ext. 263

## Region III

Regional Administrator: James W. Kight
Address: Gateway Bldg. Rm. 15230, 3535 Market Street, Philadelphia, PA 19104
Tel.: (215) 596-1185

### *Wage and Hour Division*

Assistant Regional Administrator: John A. Craven, Jr.
Address: Same
Tel.: (215) 596-1194

### *Wage-Hour Area Offices*

## Baltimore

Address: Area Director, Federal Office Bldg., Rm. 913, 31 Hopkins Plaza, Charles Ctr., Baltimore MD 21201
Tel.: (301) 962-2265

## Charleston

Address: Area Director, 22 Capitol St., Suite 100, Charleston WV 25301
Tel.: (304) 343-6181, Ext. 448

## Harrisburg

Address: Area Director, Federal Bldg., Rm. 774, 228 Walnut St., Harrisburg PA 17108
Tel.: (717) 782-4539

## Hyattsville

Address: Area Director, Al Morrone Presidential Bldg., 6525 Belcrest Rd., Suite 904, Hyattsville MD 20782
Tel.: (301) 436-6767

## Philadelphia

Address: Area Director, 600 Arch St., Rm. 4244, Philadelphia PA 19106
Tel.: (215) 597-4950

## Pittsburgh

Address: Area Director, Federal Bldg., Rm. 1429, 1000 Liberty Avenue, Pittsburgh PA 15222
Tel.: (412) 644-2996

## Richmond

Address: Area Director, Federal Bldg., Rm. 7000, 400 North Eighth St., Richmond VA 23240
Tel.: (804) 771-2995

## Region IV

Regional Administrator: James E. Patching, Jr.
Address: 1371 Peachtree Street, NE, Atlanta GA 30367
Tel.: (404) 881-2818

*Wage and Hour Division*

Assistant Regional Administrator: Richard Robinette
Address: Same
Tel.: (404) 881-4801

*Birmingham, AL*

Assistant Regional Administrator: Sterling B. Williams
Address: 1931 Ninth Avenue South, Birmingham AL 35256
Tel.: (205) 254-1301

*Wage-Hour Area Offices*

Atlanta

Address: Area Director, Citizens' Trust Bldg., Rm. 1100, 75 Piedmont Ave., N.E., Atlanta GA 30303
Tel.: (404) 221-6401

Birmingham

Address: Area Director, 1931 Ninth Ave., south Birmingham AL 35256
Tel.: (205) 254-1305

Charlotte

Address: Area Director, BSR Bldg., Rm. 401, 316 East Morehead St., Charlotte NC 28202
Tel.: (704) 371-6120

Columbia SC

Address: Area Director, Federal Bldg., Rm. 1072, 1835 Assembly St., Columbia SC 29201
Tel.: (803) 765-5981

Fort Lauderdale

Address: Area Director, Federal Bldg., Rm. 307, 299 East Broward Blvd., Fort Lauderdale FL 33301
Tel.: (305) 527-7762

Jackson

Address: Area Director, Billy R. Jones Federal Bldg., Suite 1414, 100 West Capitol St., Jackson MS 39201
Tel.: (601) 960-4347

Jacksonville

Address: Area Director, 3947 Blvd. Ctr. Drive, Suite 121, Jacksonville FL 32207
Tel.: (904) 791-2489

Knoxville

Address: Area Director, 608 South Gay St., Rm. 202, Knoxville TN 37902
Tel.: (615) 637-9300, Ext. 4246

Lexington

Address: Area Director, Concord Square, Suite C, 1460. Newtown Rd., Lexington N.Y. 40505
Tel.: (606) 252-2312 Ext. 2575

Louisville

Address: Area Director, Federal Bldg., Rm. 187-E, 600 Federal Place, Louisville KY 40402
Tel.: (502) 582-5226

Memphis

Address: Area Director, Federal Office Bldg., Rm. 486, 167 North Main Street, Memphis TN 38103
Tel.: (901) 534-3418

Miami

Address: Area Director, Rm. 202, 1150 Southwest First St., Miami FL 33130
Tel.: (305) 350-5767

Mobile

Address: Area Director, 951 Government St. Bldg., Rm. 417, Mobile AL 36604
Tel.: (205) 690-2311

Montgomery

Address: Area Director, 474 South Court St., Montgomery AL 36104
Tel.: (205) 832-7450

Nashville

Address: Area Director, West End Bldg., Rm. 610, 1720 West End Ave., Nashville TN 37203
Tel.. (615) 749-5452

Orlando

Address: Area Director, Orlando Professional Ctr., Rm. 309, 22 West Lake Beauty Drive, Orlando FL 32806
Tel.: (305) 841-1026

Raleigh

Address: Area Director, Federal Bldg., Rm. 408, 310 New Bern Ave., Raleigh NC 27486

Tel.: (919) 755-4190

### Savannah

Address: Area Director, Rm. 104 415 West Broughton St., Savannah GA 31401
Tel.: (912) 232-4321, Ext. 222

### Tampa

Address: Area Director, Suite 402, Interstate Bldg., 1211 N. Westshore Blvd., Tampa FL 33607-4604
Tel.: (813) 228-2154

### Region V

Regional Administrator: William Van Zanen
Address: 230 South Dearborn Street, Chicago IL 60604
Tel.: (312) 353-7280

*Wage and Hour Division*

Assistant Regional Administrator: Richard A. McMahon, Jr.
Deputy Assistant Regional Administrator: Barry J. Haber
Address: Same
Tel.: (312) 353-8845, 7250

*Wage-Hour Area Offices*

### Chicago

Address: Area Director, Federal Building, Rm 412, 2305 Dearborn Street, Chicago, IL 60604
Tel.: (312) 353-8145

### Cincinnati

Address: Area Director, Federal Office Bldg., Rm. 3525, 550 Main St., Cincinnati OH 45202
Tel.: (513) 684-2902

### Cleveland

Address: Area Director, Federal Office Bldg., Rm. 817, 1240 East 9th St., Cleveland OH 44199
Tel.: (216) 522-3892, 3893

### Columbus

Address: Area Director, 646 Federal Office Bldg., 200 N. High St., Columbus OH 43215
Tel.: (614) 469-5677

### Grand Rapids

Address: Area Director, 82 Ionia St., N.W., Grand Rapids MI 49503
Tel.: (616) 456-2337

### Indianapolis

Address: Area Director, Minton-CapeHart Building, Rm. 106, 575 N. Pennsylvania Street, Indianapolis IN 46204
Tel.: (317) 269-6801

### Madison

Address: Area Director, Federal Center Bldg., Rm. 309, 212 E. Washington Ave., Madison WI 53703
Tel.: (608) 264-5221

### Milwaukee

Address: Area Director, Henry Reuss Federal Plaza, 310 W. Wisconsin Avenue, Rm. 1280, Milwaukee WI 53203
Tel.: (414) 291-3585

### Minneapolis

Address: Area Director, Bridge Place, Rm. 102, 220 South Second Street, Minneapolis MN 55401
Tel.: (612) 349-3701, 3702

### South Bend

Address: Area Director, JMS Building, Rm. 523, 108 N. Main Street, South Bend IN 46601
Tel.: (219) 236-8331

### Springfield

Address: Area Director, 524 South 2nd St., Rm. 630, Springfield IL 62701
Tel.: (217) 492-4060

### Region VI

Regional Administrator: Bill A. Belt
Address: 555 Griffin Square Building, Dallas TX 75202
Tel.: (214) 767-6894

*Wage and Hour Division*

Assistant Regional Administrator: Alfred A. Ramsey
Address: Same
Tel.: (214) 767-6891

*Wage-Hour Area Offices*

Albuquerque

Address: Area Director, 505 Marquette Ave. N.W., Suite 1130, Albuquerque NM 87102
Tel.: (505) 766-2477

Baton Rouge

Address: Area Director, Hoover Bldg., Rm. 216-B, 8312 Florida Blvd., Baton Rouge LA 70806
Tel.: (504) 924-5160

Corpus Christi

Address: Area Director, Six Hundred Bldg., Rm. 714, 600 Leopard St., Corpus Christi TX 78473
Tel.: (512) 888-3156

Dallas

Address: Area Director, 1607 Main St., Suite 200, Dallas TX 75201
Tel.: (214) 767-6294

Fort Worth

Address: Area Director, 819 Taylor St., Rm. 7A12, Forth Worth TX 76102
Tel.: (817) 334-2678

Houston

Address: Area Director, 2320 La-Branch, Rm. 2101, Houston TX 77004
Tel.: (713) 226-4304

Little Rock

Address: Area Director, Federal Office Bldg., Rm. 3519, 700 West Capitol St., Little Rock AR 72201
Tel.: (501) 378-5292

New Orleans

Address: Area Director, Federal Bldg., Rm. 703, 600 South St., New Orleans LA 70130
Tel.: (504) 589-6171

San Antonio

Address: Area Director, U.S. Federal Bldg., Rm. A-621, 727 East Durango, San Antonio TX 78206
Tel.: (512) 229-6125

Tulsa

Address: Area Director, Center Mall Professional Bldg., 717 South Houston, Suite 306, Tulsa OK 74127
Tel.: (918) 581-7695

**Region VII**

Regional Administrator: Everett P. Jennings
Address: Federal Office Bldg., Rm. 2000, 911 Walnut Street, Kansas City MO 64106
Tel.: (816) 374-5381

*Wage and Hour Division*

Assistant Regional Administrator: Manuel J. Villarreal, Jr.
Address: Same
Tel.: (816) 374-5386

*Wage-Hour Area Office*

Des Moines

Address: Area Director, Federal Bldg., Rm. 643, 210 Walnut St., Des Moines IA 50309
Tel.: (515) 284-4625

Kansas City MO

Address: Area Director, Federal Office Bldg., Rm. 2900, 911 Walnut St., Kansas City MO 64106
Tel.: (816) 374-5721

Omaha

Address: Area Director, Federal Bldg., Rm. 436 110 North 14th St., Omaha NE 68102
Tel.: (402) 221-4682

St. Louis

Address: Area Director, 210 North Tucker Blvd., Rm. 563, St. Louis, MO 63101
Tel.: (314) 425-4706

**Region VIII**

Regional Administrator: Doyle I. Loveridge
Address: Federal Office Building, Rm. 1442, 1961 Stout Street, Denver CO 80294
Tel.: (303) 837-5903

*Wage and Hour Division*

Assistant Regional administrator:
Loren E. Gilbert
Address: Same
Tel.: Same

*Wage-Hour Area Offices*

Denver

Address: Area Director, U.S. Custom
House, Rm. 228, 721-19th St., Denver
CO 80202
Tel.: (303) 837-4405

Salt Lake City

Address: Area Director, Federal Bldg.,
Rm. 4311, 125 South State St., Salt
Lake City UT 84138
Tel.: (801) 524-5706

**Region IX**

Regional Administrator: William C.
Buhl
Address: 450 Golden Gate Avenue, Rm.
10353, San Francisco CA 94102
Tel.: (415) 556-1318

*Wage and Hour Division*

Assistant Regional Administrator: Her-
bert Goldstein
Address: Same
Tel.: (415) 556-3592

*Wage-Hour Area Offices*

Glendale

Address: Area Director, 115 North Central Ave., Glendale CA 91203
Tel: (213) 240-5274

Los Angeles

Address: Area Director, Federal Bldg.,
Rm. 3251, 300 North Los Angeles St.,
Los Angeles CA 90012
Tel.: (213) 688-4957-4958

Phoenix

Address: Area Director, 2120 North Central Ave., Suite G-130, Phoenix AZ
85004

Tel.: (602) 261-4224, 4223

Sacramento

Address: Area Director 2800 Cottage
Way, Rm. 1603-E, Sacramento CA
95825
Tel.: (916) 484-4447

San Francisco

Address: Area Director, Rm. 341, 211
Main St., San Francisco CA 94105
Tel.: (405) 556-6815, 6816

Santa Ana

Address: Area Director, 1600 North
Broadway, Suite 440, Santa Ana CA
92706
Tel.: (714) 836-2156

**Region X**

Regional Administrator: Joe Garcia
Address: 909 First Avenue, Rm. 4141,
Seattle WA 98174
Tel.: (206) 442-1536

*Wage and Hour Division*

Assistant Regional Administrator: Wil-
bur J. Olson
Address: Same
Tel.: (206) 442-2805

*Wage-Hour Area Offices*

Portland

Address: Area Director, 540 New Feder-
al Bldg., 1220 Southwest 3rd Ave.,
Portland OR 97204
Tel.: (503) 221-3057

Seattle

Address: Area Director, Century Bldg.,
Rm. 510, 1520 Third Ave., Seattle, WA
98101
Tel.: (206) 442-4482

# APPENDIX E

## CHART OF STATE MINIMUM WAGES

## Comparison Chart — State Minimum Wage

*Most employees are covered by the federal minimum wage standard established by the Fair Labor Standards Act. The standard is $3.80 per hour, effective April 1, 1990, and will rise to $4.25 per hour on April 1, 1991. However, most states also have enacted minimum wage laws.. In some cases, these state laws establish a higher minimum wage than the federal minimum; employers in these states generally are obliged to pay the higher state rate. In other cases, state laws may provide minimum wage protections for groups of employees not covered by the federal law. These laws typically either extend rights to the federal minimum rate to the unprotected groups or establish a lower minimum wage rate that employers must pay. State minimum wage requirements are established either by state legislatures or by wage boards authorized by the legislatures. Wage board orders most often set wage rates for particular industries or occupations.*

| STATE | REQUIREMENTS AND PROVISIONS |
| --- | --- |
| **Alabama** | **Minimum Wage** — No state requirements. |
| **Alaska** | **Minimum Wage Established by State Law** — $4.30 an hour effective 4/1/90; $4.75 an hour effective 4/1/91. (At least 50 cents greater than federal minimum wage.)<br>**Wage Board Orders** — None.<br>**Subminimum Wage** — Less than minimum wage for handicapped, apprentices, learners, and those employed in work therapy in certain residential drug or alcohol treatment programs if approved by Commissioner.<br>**Employees Covered** — All employees, except: those in agriculture; babysitters and domestic workers; federal employees; voluntary workers for nonprofit charitable, cemetery, or educational organizations; newspaper deliverers; watchmen or caretakers for property not in productive use for four or more months; those in bona fide executive, administrative, or professional capacity; outside salespersons on commission; prospectors searching for placer or hard rock minerals; certain employees of nonprofit educational or childcare facility serving as live-in parents.<br>**Meals and Lodging** — No provision.<br>**Tips and Gratuities** — May not be applied toward the minimum wage. |

## Comparison Chart — State Minimum Wage — Contd.

| STATE | REQUIREMENTS AND PROVISIONS |
|---|---|
| Arizona | **Minimum Wage Established by State Law** — Minimum rate for minors under 18 to be set by a wage board for any substantial number of minors receiving unfair wages and wages that do not meet minimum cost of living necessary for health.<br>**Wage Board Orders** — None.<br>**Subminimum Wage** — Less than experienced minors' wage for minor learners and handicapped minors if recommended by a wage board. Less than minimum fair rate for handicapped minors, with license from Industrial Commission.<br>**Employees Covered** — All minor employees under 18, except part-time employees who are: students, domestic workers, or agricultural workers.<br>**Meals and Lodging** — No provision.<br>**Tips and Gratuities** — No provision. |
| Arkansas | **Minimum Wage Established by State Law** — $3.35 an hour effective 9/1/89.<br>**Wage Board Orders** — None.<br>**Subminimum Wage** — Less than minimum wage for learners, apprentices, full-time students, and those handicapped by lack of skill, age, physical deficiency or injury, or otherwise, with special license from Labor Board. At least 85 percent of minimum wage for full-time students of state-accredited school working 20 hours or less during school session or 40 hours during vacation.<br>**Employees Covered** — All employees of employer of four or more workers, except: those working in bona fide executive, administrative, or professional capacity; outside salespersons on commission; employees of federal, state, or local government, except public schools and educational, charitable, religious, or non-profit school districts where no employer-employee relationship exists; independent contractors; workers for agricultural employers not using more than 500 worker-hours of agricultural labor in any quarter of preceding year; members of agricultural employer's immediate family; certain hand-harvest laborers; those in range production of livestock; and certain forestry and lumber workers.<br>**Meals and Lodging** — No provision.<br>**Tips and Gratuities** — Tips may be applied to no more than 50 percent of minimum wage. |

## Comparison Chart — State Minimum Wage — Contd.

| STATE | REQUIREMENTS AND PROVISIONS |
|---|---|
| California | **Minimum Wage Established by State Law** — None.<br><br>**Wage Board Orders** — Minimum wage of $4.25 an hour effective 7/1/88, for the following industries and occupations: manufacturing; personal service; canning, freezing, preserving; professional, technical, clerical, mechanical, and similar occupations; public housekeeping; laundry, linen supply, dry cleaning, and dyeing; mercantile; farm products, after harvest; transportation; amusement and recreation (except full-time ride operators of traveling carnivals); broadcasting; motion picture industry; on-farm preparation of agricultural products for market; agricultural occupations (except sheepherding); and household occupations.<br><br>**Subminimum Wage** — $3.60 for first 90 days of employment for minors under age 18; $3.80 thereafter. Learners under age 20 may be paid $3.60 for first 160 hours, and $3.80 thereafter; learners over age 20 must be paid at least $3.80. After 160 hours, both must be paid the full state minimum wage of $4.25. Physically and mentally handicapped workers, including minors, may also be employed at less than minimum wage with license from Commissioner. At least 85 percent of minimum wage allowed for student employees and counselors of organized camp, regardless of hours worked.<br><br>**Employees Covered** — All employees covered by wage board orders, including minors, except: those in administrative, executive, or professional capacity paid at least $900 a month ($1,150 per month in manufacturing; professional, technical, clerical, mechanical, and similar occupations; public housekeeping; and amusement and recreation occupations) or who are licensed or certified by state in certain occupations; federal, state, or local government employees; outside salespersons; employer's parent, spouse, child, or legally adopted child; and persons exempted by individual order.<br><br>**Meals and Lodging** — Wage board orders provide that meals and lodging may be credited toward minimum wage for covered employees, with voluntary written agreement, up to the following limits: room occupied alone, $20 per week; shared room, $16.50 per week; apartment, ⅔ ordinary rental value, up to $240 per month; for couple who are both employed, ⅔ ordinary rental value up to $355 per month; breakfast, $1.50; lunch, $2.10; dinner, $2.80.<br><br>**Tips and Gratuities** — May not be credited toward minimum wage. |
| Colorado | **Minimum Wage Established by State Law** — None.<br><br>**Wage Board Orders** — A minimum wage of $3.00 an hour for all employees in the laundry and dry cleaning, retail trades, public housekeeping, beauty services, food and beverage, medical profession, and janitorial industries.<br><br>**Subminimum Wage** — Unemancipated minors under 18, and handicapped workers with certificate from Director, may be paid 15 percent below regular minimum.<br><br>**Employees Covered** — All employees, including emancipated minors under 18, except: certain medical occupations; teachers; supervisors; resident managers; outside salespersons; employees of federal, state, or local government; student employees in college dormitory or club; students enrolled in work experience study (special education) program; and unpaid workers in institutional laundry.<br><br>**Meals and Lodging** — For employees covered by wage board orders, deductions from wages may be made for: reasonable cost of fair market value of employee's full maintenance on seven-day-a-week basis; reasonable cost or fair market value (but not employer profit) of meals; or reasonable cost of lodging not exceeding $15 per week.<br><br>**Tips and Gratuities** — May be credited for up to 40 percent of minimum wage if employee regularly receives more than $30 per month in tips, with written report from employee. |

## Comparison Chart — State Minimum Wage — Contd.

| STATE | REQUIREMENTS AND PROVISIONS |
|---|---|
| Connecticut | **Minimum Wage Established by State Law** — $4.25 an hour effective 10/1/88, or highest federal minimum wage plus 0.5 percent, whichever is higher.<br>**Wage Board Orders** — Wage orders for specific industries in effect for beauty shops; laundry, cleaning, and dyeing; mercantile; and restaurant and hotel.<br>**Subminimum Wage** — At least 85 percent of minimum wage for learners, beginners, and minors under 18 for first 200 hours, then regular wage rate, except for institutional training programs exempted by Labor Commissioner. At least 85 percent of minimum wage for minors age 14–18 working in agriculture, but 70 percent if working for employer with eight or fewer workers during preceding calendar year. Less than minimum wage for physically or mentally handicapped and for learners and apprentices in established programs, with permission of Commissioner.<br>**Employees Covered** — All employees, except: those working in camps or resorts open no more than six months a year; domestic workers; those in bona fide executive, administrative, or professional capacity; federal employees; volunteers in activities of educational, charitable, literary, or nonprofit organization without employer-employee relationship; head resident or resident assistant of college or university; outside salespersons; and employees of nonprofit theater operating no more than seven months in calendar year.<br>**Meals and Lodging** — Costs of $0.85 for a full meal, up to $2.55 per day or $0.45 for a light meal, up to $0.90 per day, and cost of lodging, up to $4 for private or $3 for shared room, may be deducted from minimum wage. Lesser of actual cost of maintenance of uniforms or $1.50 per week may also be deducted.<br>**Tips and Gratuities** — May be credited for up to 23 percent of the minimum wage for hotel employees receiving at least $10 per week in tips (at least $2 per day for part-time employees); for other employees customarily receiving tips, credit may be not more than $0.35 per hour, when recorded on weekly basis. |
| Delaware | **Minimum Wage Established by State Law** — $3.80 per hour, effective 4/1/90; $4.25 per hour effective 4/1/91.<br>**Wage Board Orders** — None.<br>**Subminimum Wage** — Less than minimum wage for handicapped, learners, and apprentices, with permission of Department of Labor. Employees 18 years old or younger may be paid less than the minimum wage for the first 90 days of employment, but not less than $3.35.<br>**Employees Covered** — All employees, except: agricultural and domestic workers; those in bona fide executive, administrative, or professional capacity; outside salespersons on commission; volunteers of educational, charitable, religious, or nonprofit organization; federal employees; those working in fish and seafood industry up through first processing; and minor under 18 employed as junior counselor or counselor in training in nonprofit organization's summer camp.<br>**Meals and Lodging** — No provision.<br>**Tips and Gratuities** — May be credited up to one-third of minimum wage for employees regularly receiving more than $30 a month in gratuities and tips. |

## Comparison Chart — State Minimum Wage — Contd.

| STATE | REQUIREMENTS AND PROVISIONS |
|---|---|
| District of Columbia | **Minimum Wage Established by State Law** — None.<br><br>**Wage Board Orders** — $3.35-$4.85 an hour, depending on industry and employee status. $3.35 per hour for: minors under 18 in beauty culture; clerical and semitechnical occupations; child day care center aides and homemaker aides. $3.50 per hour for casual yard workers; babysitters; companions; learners with less than 60 days experience in laundry and dry cleaning. $3.70 per hour for experienced workers in laundry and dry cleaning; adult learners in wholesale trade, manufacturing, printing and publishing. $3.90 per hour for nonexempt employees in private households; clerical and semitechnical workers over 18. $3.95 per hour for workers in manufacturing; wholesale trade; and printing and publishing. $4.25 per hour for adult learners in building service occupations in specified industries. $4.30 an hour for adult learners in building services in buildings subject to rent control. $4.45 per hour for apartment building employees in rent-controlled buildings; and adult learners in hotel, restaurant, and allied occupations. $4.50 per hour for employees in retail trade; beauty culture. $4.75 per hour for workers in hotel, restaurant, apartment building services, and allied occupations; building service employees in specific occupations. $4.85 per hour for machine trade occupations; bench workers; structural workers; parking attendants; car wash employees; guards; ticket takers and ushers; furniture movers; bus, truck, and taxi drivers; lifeguards; and nonclerical temporary help employees.<br>**Subminimum Wage** — Less than minimum wage rate for handicapped with certificate from U.S. Department of Labor.<br>**Employees Covered** — All employees, except: U.S. and D.C. government workers; unpaid volunteers with educational, charitable, religious, or nonprofit organizations; lay members in religious activities within religious organizations; casual babysitters; those in bona fide executive, administrative, or professional capacity; outside salespersons; and those in home newspaper delivery.<br>**Meals and Lodging** — Meal credits permitted up to one meal in four hours, two meals if over four hours, and three meals per day for residential employees. Private household workers: meal credits of up to $0.75 for breakfast, $1 for lunch and $1.25 for dinner up to a maximum of $3 per day. Lodging credit of up to $15 per week. Credits for other facilities with written consent of employee and approval of Wage-Hour Board. Retail trade: meal credits of $2.10 per meal. Lodging credit up to $36 per week or actual rental value, whichever is lower. Laundry and dry cleaning: meal credit of $1.48 per meal. Lodging credit of not more than 80 percent of rental value. Clerical and semi-technical occupations: With written consent of employee, meal credits of $1.32 per meal. Lodging credit of up to 80 percent of rental value. Hotel, restaurant, apartment building and allied occupations: meal credits of $2.06 per meal. Lodging credit up to 80 percent of rental value. Building services (other than workers covered by other wage orders): meal credits of $1.40 per meal. Lodging credits of up to $19 per week for single room; $9.50 per week for shared room. If furnished, not more than 75 percent of rental value.<br>**Tips and Gratuities** — Credits of up to $0.35 per hour for boot blacks; $0.50 per hour in beauty culture occupations; and $2.60 per hour for waiter/waitress, bus person, bartender, bell hop, hotel doorkeeper, and hat checker; $0.20 per hour for parking attendant. |
| **Florida** | **Minimum Wage** — No state requirements. |

## Comparison Chart — State Minimum Wage — Contd.

| STATE | REQUIREMENTS AND PROVISIONS |
|-------|------------------------------|
| Georgia | **Minimum Wage Established by State Law** — $3.25 an hour.<br>**Wage Board Orders** — None.<br>**Subminimum Wage** — Less than minimum wage to certain organizations and businesses to employ handicapped and others who cannot compete effectively, with authorization of Commissioner of Labor.<br>**Employees Covered** — All employees, except: those of employers with five or fewer workers; farm owners, share croppers, and land renters; domestic workers; those working for employers with sales of $40,000 or less a year; those paid wholly or partially in tips; high school and college students; and newspaper carriers.<br>**Meals and Lodging** — No provision.<br>**Tips and Gratuities** — Employees compensated wholly or partially by tips are not covered by minimum wage law. |
| Hawaii | **Minimum Wage Established by State Law** — $3.85 an hour, effective 1/1/88.<br>**Wage Board Orders** — None.<br>**Subminimum Wage** — Less than minimum wage for learners, apprentices, those impaired by old age or physical or mental handicap, certain students, and paroled wards of state youth correctional facility, with rule provided by Director of Labor and Industrial Relations.<br>**Employees Covered** — All employees, except: those with guaranteed monthly salary of $1,000; workers in coffee harvesting operations; agricultural workers if employer has fewer than 20 employees; domestic workers; houseparents in charitable organizations; employer's relatives (brother, sister, brother-in-law, sister-in-law, son, daughter, spouse, parent, parent-in-law); those employed in bona fide executive, administrative, supervisory, or professional capacity; outside salespersons or collectors; those in fish or aquatic farming industry prior to first processing; seafarers; on-call, fixed stand vehicle drivers; golf caddies; student employees of nonprofit school; seasonal employees of certain nonprofit youth camps; and automobile or truck salespersons for licensed dealer.<br>**Meals and Lodging** — Credits permitted for reasonable cost, as determined by the department, of furnishing employee with meals, lodging, and other facilities customarily furnished by employer.<br>**Tips and Gratuities** — Twenty cents an hour less than minimum wage allowed for employees regularly receiving more than $20 a month in tips, if combined wages and tips are at least 50 cents an hour more than minimum wage. |
| Idaho | **Minimum Wage Established by State Law** — $3.80 an hour effective 4/1/90; $4.25 effective 4/1/91. Commissions may be deducted.<br>**Wage Board Orders** — None.<br>**Subminimum Wage** — Less than minimum wage for handicapped, learners, and apprentices, with license from Director of Labor and Industrial Services.<br>**Employees Covered** — All employees, except: employees of federal, state, or local government; of any labor organization (other than when acting as employer); those in bona fide executive, administrative, or professional capacity; agricultural and domestic workers; outside salespersons; minors under 16 working part-time or at odd jobs not exceeding four hours per day with one employer; and seasonal employees of nonprofit camp.<br>**Meals and Lodging** — Employer may deduct $60 per week for full board and lodging; $40 per week for meals; $20 per week for lodging; $3 per day for lodging; and $2 per day for meals ($1.50 per meal for hotel and restaurant workers.)<br>**Tips and Gratuities** — Tips may be applied for up to 25 percent of minimum wage for employees regularly receiving more than $30 per month in tips. Shared or pooled tips may not be applied to minimum wage. |

## Comparison Chart — State Minimum Wage — Contd.

| STATE | REQUIREMENTS AND PROVISIONS |
|---|---|
| Illinois | **Minimum Wage Established by State Law** — $3.80 an hour, effective 4/1/90; $4.25 an hour, effective 4/1/91. May not be less than federal minimum wage.<br>**Wage Board Orders** — None.<br>**Subminimum Wage** — At least 70 percent of minimum wage for learners up to six months of learning. Minimum of $2.85 per hour for minors under 18. Minimum wage for minors under 18 years is 50 cents less than adult minimum ($3.30 per hour, effective 4/1/90). Less than minimum wage for handicapped, with permit from Director after public hearing.<br>**Employees Covered** — All employees, except: those working for employers with fewer than four employees exclusive of parent, spouse, child, or immediate family member; certain agricultural workers; domestic workers; outside salespersons; members of religious corporations or organizations; certain camp counselors; certain aquacultural workers; and students of accredited Illinois colleges and universities employed under FLSA provisions.<br>**Meals and Lodging** — No provision.<br>**Tips and Gratuities** — May be credited for up to 40 percent of minimum wage, with evidence to Director that employee received tips. |
| Indiana | **Minimum Wage Established by State Law** — $2.00 per hour; $3.35 per hour, effective 7/1/90.<br>**Wage Board Orders** — None.<br>**Subminimum Wage** — At least 50 percent of minimum wage for those with age, mental, or physical handicap, with rate to be determined by wage adjustment board.<br>**Employees Covered** — All employees whose employers employ at least two individuals, except self-employed persons; those performing services not in course of employing unit's business; those working on commission; persons employed by parent, spouse, or child; individuals less than 16 years of age; members or volunteers of religious order or charitable organization; student nurses; apprentice funeral directors and embalmers; hospital interns and residents; students working for their school; physically or mentally handicapped persons working for nonprofit organizations; insurance agents on commission; those working in camping, recreation or guidance facilities run by charitable, religious, or educational nonprofit organizations; those in executive, administrative, or professional capacity earning $150 a week; outside salespersons; those not employed for more than four weeks in any four consecutive three-month periods; those subject to Motor Carrier Act or to state public service commission regulations; and certain agricultural workers.<br>**Meals and Lodging** — Reasonable value of board, lodging, apparel, or other items regularly furnished by employer may be credited in amount determined by board but not more, when combined with credits for tips, than 50 percent of minimum rate.<br>**Tips and Gratuities** — May be credited for up to 40 percent of minimum wage for employees receiving more than $30 per month in tips. Employer must be able to support amount of tip credit through reported tips. |

## Comparison Chart — State Minimum Wage — Contd.

| STATE | REQUIREMENTS AND PROVISIONS |
|---|---|
| **Iowa** | **Minimum Wage Established by State Law** — $3.85 per hour effective 1/1/90; $4.25 per hour effective 1/1/91; $4.65 per hour effective 1/1/92.<br>**Wage Board Orders** — None.<br>**Subminimum Wage** — Payable to employee with fewer than 90 calendar days of employment. $3.35, effective 1/1/90; $3.85, effective 1/1/91; $4.25, effective 1/1/92.<br>**Employees Covered** — All except those exempted from coverage by the FLSA. However, the FLSA exemption for certain retailers applies only to retail or service establishments with annual gross income less than 60 percent of the FLSA limit, excluding excise taxes at the retail level that are separately stated.<br>**Meals and Lodging** — No provision.<br>**Tips and Gratuities** — May be credited for up to 40 percent of minimum wage for employees receiving at least $30 per month in tips. |
| **Kansas** | **Minimum Wage Established by State Law** — $2.65 an hour effective 7/1/88.<br>**Wage Board Orders** — None.<br>**Subminimum Wage** — At least 80 percent of minimum wage for learners and apprentices upon hiring, 90 percent after two months, and full minimum wage after three months, with permit from Secretary of Human Resources. At least 85 percent of minimum wage for handicapped and patient laborers at state institutions or hospitals, with one-year permit from Secretary.<br>**Employees Covered** — All employees, except: agricultural and domestic workers; those in bona fide executive, administrative, or professional capacity; outside salespersons on commission; federal employees; unpaid volunteers for nonprofit organization; part-time workers age 18 or under and age 60 or over; and students under 18 working between academic terms.<br>**Meals and Lodging** — No provision.<br>**Tips and Gratuities** — May be credited for up to 40 percent of minimum wage for employees customarily receiving and retaining them. |
| **Kentucky** | **Minimum Wage Established by State Law** — $3.35 per hour; $3.80 per hour, effective 7/15/90; $4.25 per hour, effective 7/15/91.<br>**Wage Board Orders** — None.<br>**Subminimum Wage** — Less than minimum wage for handicapped or for sheltered workshop employees upon certificate from Commissioner. At least 85 percent of minimum wage for students for maximum of 20 hours a week, then minimum wage for hours over 20.<br>**Employees Covered** — All employees, except: agricultural workers; those in bona fide executive, administrative, supervisory, or professional capacity; outside salespersons or collectors as defined by Commissioner; federal employees; domestic workers; employees of retail stores, service industries, hotels, motels, and restaurants with average annual sales less than $95,000 for preceding five years; employer's parent, spouse, child, or immediate family member; babysitter or live-in companion to sick or elderly if principal duties not housekeeping; newspaper deliverers; certain emergency employees; those in nonprofit camp or religious or nonprofit educational conference center operating no more than seven months a year.<br>**Meals and Lodging** — No provision.<br>**Tips and Gratuities** — May count for up to 50 percent of minimum wage for employees regularly receiving more than $20 a month in tips, if weekly records show employees retained tips and wages plus tips equals or exceeds minimum. |

## Comparison Chart — State Minimum Wage — Contd.

| STATE | REQUIREMENTS AND PROVISIONS |
|---|---|
| Louisiana | **Minimum Wage** — No state requirements. |
| Maine | **Minimum Wage Established by State Law** — $3.85 an hour effective 1/1/90. If federal minimum increases, state minimum will increase to the same level.<br>**Wage Board Orders** — None.<br>**Subminimum Wage** — Less than minimum wage for physically handicapped by age or otherwise and for learners and apprentices for fixed period of time, with license from Director of Labor and Industry. At least 75 percent of minimum for students under 19 years of age.<br>**Employees Covered** — All employees, except: agricultural workers, as defined by state law and FUTA (but not including those working on farms with over 300,000 laying birds); domestic workers; unsupervised sales persons on commission; those in nonpolitical public-supported or educational nonprofit organization; summer camp counselors, or employees under 19 in camps operated by or belonging to non-capital stock corporations under state law; those in fish and seafood industry up through first processing; switchboard operators in public telephone exchange with less than 750 stations; unsupervised homeworkers; family members who live with or are dependent upon employer; those in bona fide executive, administrative, or professional capacity earning $175 weekly; taxicab drivers.<br>**Meals and Lodging** — Board and lodging may be credited at follows: Full board and room — single occupancy: weekly, $25; daily, $3.75; multiple occupancy: weekly, $20; daily, $3. Meals — weekly: $15: daily: breakfast, $0.60; lunch, $0.60; dinner, $1. Lodging — single: weekly, $10; daily, $1.50; multiple occupancy: weekly, $5; daily, $0.75.<br>**Tips and Gratuities** — May be credited toward minimum wage up to $2.01 effective 1/1/90, for employees receiving at least $20 per month in tips. |
| Maryland | **Minimum Wage Established by State Law** — $3.80 an hour, effective 4/1/90; $4.25 an hour, effective 4/1/91. (Defined as highest federal minimum wage in effect.)<br>**Wage Board Orders** — None.<br>**Subminimum Wage** — Training wage permitted under commission regulations, subject to the conditions and limits prescribed by FLSA. Less than minimum wage for physically or mentally handicapped, with certificate from Commissioner of Division of Labor and Industry or from U.S. Department of Labor if filed within 10 days of receipt.<br>**Employees Covered** — All employees, except: those in bona fide executive, administrative, or professional capacity; minors under 16 employed by one or more employers less than 20 hours a week, or employees 62 or over not working more than 25 hours a week; volunteers in educational, charitable, religious, or nonprofit organization where no employer-employee relationship exists; those in establishment selling food and drink for consumption on premises with annual gross income of $250,000 or less; employees of movie theaters; those processing or packaging poultry, seafood, or fresh produce or horticultural commodities; outside salespersons and those on commission; employer's parent, spouse, child, or other immediate family member; students in public school special education programs for mentally, emotionally, or physically handicapped employed as part of training; non-administrative day camp personnel; and certain agricultural workers.<br>**Meals and Lodging** — Credit permitted for reasonable cost, as determined by commissioner, of board, lodging and other facilities customarily furnished by employer, except where excluded under a bona fide collective bargaining agreement.<br>**Tips and Gratuities** — May count for up to 45 percent, effective 4/1/90 (50 percent, effective 3/31/91), of minimum wage for employees regularly receiving more than $30 a month in tips, if they retain tips and are informed of rules. |

## Comparison Chart — State Minimum Wage — Contd.

| STATE | REQUIREMENTS AND PROVISIONS |
|---|---|
| Massachusetts | **Minimum Wage Established by State Law** — $3.75 an hour effective 7/1/88.<br><br>**Wage Board Orders** — At least 80 percent of minimum wage for inexperienced workers (those in retail, merchandising, or laundry occupations with less than 80 hours experience; those in personal service occupations required to be licensed with less than 1,040 hours of experience); student employees, with permit from Commissioner; apprentices and learners enrolled in vocational or technical course and employed part-time pursuant to the program, for period fixed by Commissioner; students employed by school or summer camp; those employed at school, hospital, or other training establishment as part of formal training; and high school minors working in hospital ward or school dining hall or dormitory, if ratio of one minor to five adult employees.<br><br>**Subminimum Wage** — Less than minimum wage for those handicapped by age or physical or mental deficiency, with certificate from Commissioner of Labor and Industries. Wages set less than minimum rate: $1.25 an hour for ushers, ticket sellers, and ticket takers; $36 a week for janitors and caretakers of residences when furnished living quarters; certain rates for golf caddies; $1.60 an hour for agricultural employees, except minors under 18 and employer's parent, spouse, child, or other immediate family member.<br><br>**Employees Covered** — All employees, except: minors under 18 in domestic service in employer's home; those being rehabilitated or trained in charitable, educational, or religious institutions; members of religious orders; agricultural, floricultural, and horticultural workers; those in professional service; and outside sales persons not reporting to or visiting office daily.<br><br>**Meals and Lodging** — Credits for meals ($1 for breakfast, $1.75 for lunch, $1.75 for dinner) and for lodging ($30 a week single, $25 double, $20 triple occupancy) may be deducted from wages, but no deduction for uniforms. (However, state law says Commissioner may set board and lodging rates for agricultural workers and other defined classes.)<br><br>**Tips and Gratuities** — May be credited for up to 40 percent of the minimum wage for employees receiving more than $20 a month in tips (except service employees in mercantile occupations and public housekeeping — wage board orders), unless employee challenges. |
| Michigan | **Minimum Wage Established by State Law** — $3.35 an hour.<br><br>**Wage Board Orders** — Certain rates for agricultural piecework are set by the Wage Deviation Board.<br><br>**Subminimum Wage** — Less than minimum wage for those under 18 or over 64 years of age. Less than minimum wage for handicapped covered by blanket wage deviation certificate.<br><br>**Employees Covered** — All employees of employers with two or more employees within calendar year, except: those employed in summer camps not more than four months; employees of fruit, pickle, or tomato growers, or other agricultural workers contracting for harvest on piecework basis.<br><br>**Meals and Lodging** — Meals and lodging may be credited, with employee written consent, up to 25 percent of wage rate provided these credits, together with credits for tips, do not exceed 25 percent of the minimum.<br><br>**Tips and Gratuities** — May be credited, but only if tip credit plus board and lodging credit do not exceed 25 percent of minimum wage; tips are proven by employee's declaration for FICA purposes; and employee has been informed of provision. |

**Comparison Chart — State Minimum Wage — Contd.**

| STATE | REQUIREMENTS AND PROVISIONS |
|---|---|
| Minnesota | **Minimum Wage Established by State Law** — $3.95 an hour effective 1/1/90 for employees over 18 covered by FLSA; $3.80 an hour for employees over 18 covered by state minimum wage law. For minors under 18: $3.56 an hour effective 1/1/90 if covered by FLSA; $3.42 for minors covered by state. minimum wage law. Effective 1/1/91, large employers (annual gross volume of sales or business of at least $362,500, exclusive of excise taxes at retail level separately stated) will pay $4.25; small employers will pay $4.00. |
| | **Wage Board Orders** — Minimum wage of $2.07 an hour for apprentices and learners for first 300 hours. At least 50 percent of minimum wage for handicapped, with permit from Labor Standards Division. |
| | **Subminimum Wage** — Department may permit employment of handicapped at lower rate, but not less than 50 percent of minimum. |
| | **Employees Covered** — All employees, except: certain agricultural workers; seasonal staff members of licensed nonprofit children's camp; those in bona fide executive, administrative, or professional capacity, meeting certain criteria; salespersons with at least 80 percent sales off premises; volunteers for nonprofit organizations; taxicab drivers; elected officials or volunteer workers for any political subdivision; police or firefighters; public employees ineligible to participate in public retirement association; babysitters; seasonal workers in carnival, circus, fair, or ski facility; state conservation officers; those with qualifications and hours under control of U.S. Department of Transportation; seafarers, as defined; employees supervising children in single facility residence that is extension of county home school; and those in religious orders. |
| | **Meals and Lodging** — Credit for $1.15 per meal and $1.50 per night's lodging may be deducted from the minimum wage. |
| | **Tips and Gratuities** — No credit allowed. |
| Mississippi | **Minimum Wage** — No state requirements. |
| Missouri | **Minimum Wage Established by State Law** — $3.80 per hour, effective 8/28/90; $4.25, effective 4/1/91. (Equal to federal minimum.) |
| | **Wage Board Orders** —None. |
| | **Subminimum Wage** — Training wage equal to federal training wage may be paid to learners and apprentices, as defined, but for no longer than three months (six months with director's approval). Employees of an amusement or recreation business, as defined, may be paid training wages for 90 working days. Wages lower than minimum may be paid to individuals whose earning capacity is impaired by physical or mental deficiency, with Director's approval. |

## Comparison Chart — State Minimum Wage — Contd.

| STATE | REQUIREMENTS AND PROVISIONS |
|---|---|
| **Missouri, contd.** | **Employees Covered** — All employees except: those in agriculture; those in bona fide executive, administrative, or professional capacity; those engaged in activities of an educational, charitable, religious, or nonprofit organization where the employer-employee relationship does not exist or services are render voluntarily; individuals providing foster care; individuals employed less than four months per year in a residential or day camp for children, or an educational conference center operated by an educational, charitable, or nonprofit organization; individual employed by an educational organization, where labor is in lieu of payment for tuition, housing, or other fees; occasional workers in a private residence for six hours or less on each occasion; handicapped persons in sheltered workshop; casual employees in domestic service, including babysitters and companions; individuals whose employers are covered by Interstate Commerce Act; golf caddies; newspaper deliverers; salespersons compensated primarily by commission and not under employer's substantial control; individuals covered by federal law or working in government position as defined; individuals employed by retail or service business with gross volume of business of less than $500,000; inmates of penal institutions; employees of certain newspapers. <br><br> **Meals and Lodging** — Employer may credit the fair market value of goods and services provided to employees if incidental to employment and employee is not required to exercise any discretion to receive goods and services. Fair market value to be computed weekly. <br><br> **Tips and Gratuities** — May be credited for up to 50 percent of the minimum wage. |
| **Montana** | **Minimum Wage Established by State Law** — $3.80 an hour, effective 4/1/90; $4.00 per hour, effective 4/1/91. State minimum equals federal minimum, but no higher than $4.00 per hour. <br><br> **Wage Board Orders** — None. <br><br> **Subminimum Wage** — Less than minimum wage for apprentices and learners, with commissioner's approval, for no more than 30 days. $635 a month for agricultural workers. $750 a month for firefighters, except during probationary or training period. At least 50 percent of minimum wage for learners under 18 performing farm work for up to 180 days. New hires may be paid $3.35 per hour for first 120 days. <br><br> **Employees Covered** — All employees, except: students in distributive education program of accredited agency; those performing menial chores in private home; caretakers of children directly employed by household head; employer's relatives dependent on employer for half or more support; to training or evaluation program or who are severely impaired and unable to compete; those in bona fide executive, administrative, or professional capacity; federal employees; and retired or semi-retired residential employees working part-time. <br><br> **Meals and Lodging** — Deductions for board, lodging, or other facilities furnished employee may not exceed 40 percent of total wages paid. <br><br> **Tips and Gratuities** — May not be included in the computation of employees' wages. |

## Comparison Chart — State Minimum Wage — Contd.

| STATE | REQUIREMENTS AND PROVISIONS |
|---|---|
| Nebraska | **Minimum Wage Established by State Law** — $3.35 an hour effective 8/1/87.<br><br>**Wage Board Orders** — None.<br>**Subminimum Wage** — At least 75 percent of minimum wage for student learners employed as part of bona fide vocational training program.<br>**Employees Covered** — All employees, except: those working for employers with 3 or fewer workers (not including seasonal workers of 20 or fewer weeks in calendar year); agricultural workers; babysitters in private home; those in bona fide executive, administrative, professional, or supervisory capacity; employees of federal, state or local government; those engaged in activities of educational, charitable, religious, or nonprofit organization where services voluntarily given or no employer-employee relationship exists; apprentices and learners; primary and secondary students working after school or on vacation; veterans in training under Veterans Administration supervision; employer's child or parent; physically or mentally disabled person employed in rehabilitation program and receiving government aid or welfare.<br>**Meals and Lodging** — No provision.<br>**Tips and Gratuities** — $2.01 minimum wage for tipped employees. Wages plus tips must equal or exceed minimum. |
| Nevada | **Minimum Wage Established by State Law** — $3.80 an hour, effective 4/1/90. (Rate set by commissioner).<br>**Wage Board Orders** — None.<br>**Subminimum Wage** — At least 85 percent ($3.23) of minimum wage for minors age 17 or under.<br>**Employees Covered** — All employees age 18 and older, except: casual babysitters; live-in domestic workers; outside salespersons on commission; agricultural workers for employer who used no more than 500 worker-hours of labor in any quarter of preceding calendar year; taxicab and limousine drivers; and certain handicapped workers.<br>**Meals and Lodging** — No more than $1.50 a day for meals may be credited toward minimum wage (agricultural workers excluded), with employee consent.<br>**Tips and Gratuities** — May not be credited toward minimum wage. |
| New Hampshire | **Minimum Wage Established by State Law** — $3.80 per hour effective 4/1/90; $3.85 effective 1/1/91; and $3.95 effective 1/1/92.<br>**Wage Board Orders** — None.<br>**Subminimum Wage** — At least 75 percent of minimum wage for employees with less than six months experience and for minors 16 years or under, if application filed with Labor Commissioner within 10 days of hire. Less than minimum wage for those with earnings impaired by age or by physical or mental handicap, including those in sheltered workshop, with rate set by Commissioner. Less than minimum, or no rate, for students in work-study programs, with rate set by Commissioner if circumstances warrant.<br>**Employees Covered** — All employees, except: employer's child, grandchild, or ward; spouse working on voluntary basis; agricultural and domestic workers; outside salespersons; newscarriers; employees of summer camp for minors; and nonprofessional ski patrols or golf caddies.<br>**Meals and Lodging** — Meals and lodging may be credited as follows: no more than $6.45 a day or $45 a week for room and board; $1.88 per meal or $39.45 per week for meals; $1.80 per day or $10.88 per week for lodging.<br>**Tips and Gratuities** — May be credited for up to 50 percent of minimum wage for workers paid more than $20 a month in tips. |

## Comparison Chart — State Minimum Wage — Contd.

| STATE | REQUIREMENTS AND PROVISIONS |
|---|---|
| New Jersey | **Minimum Wage Established by State Law** — $3.80 an hour, effective 4/1/90; $4.25, effective 4/1/91; $5.05, effective 4/1/92. |
| | **Wage Board Orders** — Exempt from minimum wage: those in executive, administrative, or professional capacity, as defined; volunteer firefighters, rescue workers, and other public protectors; volunteers caring for sick, aged, destitute, etc., in religious, educational, charitable, hospital, etc., activities; and patients in charitable programs receiving inconsequential pay. Minimum wage of $3.10 per hour for following occupations: first processing of farm products; seasonal amusement occupations except employees in retail, eating, or drinking concessions, camps, swimming facilities, theaters, athletic events, professional entertainment, pool halls, circuses and outdoor shows, country clubs, bowling alleys, or race tracks; hotel and motel occupations, except certain camps and country clubs; restaurant occupations, all employees including minors; air carrier industry. |
| | **Subminimum Wage** — Less than minimum wage for learners, apprentices, and students, and for those with earning capacity impaired by age or by physical or mental handicap, with permit from Office of Wage and Hours Compliance. At least 85 percent of minimum wage for full-time students working for their colleges or universities. |
| | **Employees Covered** — All employees, except: minors under 18 not possessing special vocational graduate permit; those working for nonprofit or religious summer camp, conference, or retreat; part-time child caretakers in employer's home; outside salespersons; motor vehicle salespersons; volunteers working at agricultural fair for nonprofit or religious organization and receiving only incidental benefits. |
| | **Meals and Lodging** — In hotel and motel occupations, for chambermaids, credits for tips, food, and lodging may not exceed 16 percent of minimum rate; for chambermaids in seasonal hotels and motels, credit for tips, food, and lodging may not exceed 25 percent of minimum rate. In restaurant industry, minimum wage after credit for tips, meals, and lodging must not be less than $1.86, with agreement of employee. |
| | **Tips and Gratuities** — Cash gratuities are included in "wages;" value is based on employee statements or formula, with approval of commissioner. For food service and other occupations in the hotel and motel industry where tips are customary, total credits cannot exceed 40 percent of minimum rate; for chambermaids, credits for tips may not exceed 11 percent of minimum rate; for chambermaids in seasonal hotels and motels, credit for tips may not exceed 20 percent of minimum rate. For employees in restaurant industry, wages must be not less than $1.86 per hour after crediting tips, food, and lodging, with agreement of employee. In beauty culture industry, tips shall not be credited against minimum. |
| New Mexico | **Minimum Wage Established by State Law** — $3.35 an hour. |
| | **Wage Board Orders** — None. |
| | **Subminimum Wage** — Less than minimum for handicapped employees with special certificate, but not less than 50 percent of minimum. |
| | **Employees Covered** — All employees, except: those in executive, administrative, professional, or supervisory capacity; domestic workers; public employees; volunteers working for educational, charitable, religious, or nonprofit organization; salespersons and employees on commission, piecework, or flat-rate schedule; apprentices and learners; employees of ambulance services; non-college students working after school or during vacation; persons under 18 who are not students or high school graduates; G.I. bill trainees; certain agricultural workers; resident employees of charitable, religious, or nonprofit group home for mentally, emotionally, or developmentally disabled; and certain seasonal employees of youth camps, with certificate from Labor Commissioner. |
| | **Meals and Lodging** — Reasonable value of room, board, utilities, and supplies may be deducted from wages of agricultural workers. |
| | **Tips and Gratuities** — $2.01 for employees receiving more than $40 a month in tips. |

## Comparison Chart — State Minimum Wage — Contd.

| STATE | REQUIREMENTS AND PROVISIONS |
|---|---|
| New York | **Minimum Wage Established by State Law** — $3.80 per hour, effective 4/1/90; $4.25 per hour, effective 4/1/91, for non-agricultural workers. $3.35 per hour for agricultural workers, rising to $3.80 per hour, effective 1/1/91, and $4.25 per hour, effective 1/1/92.<br>**Wage Board Orders** — Less than minimum wage for handicapped in rehabilitation program approved by Commissioner (except wage orders covering farm workers). Students not deemed working if obtaining supervised experience in another institution to fulfill curriculum requirements. Restaurant, hotel, miscellaneous, and nonprofit orders require minimum of $3.80 per hour, eff. 4/1/90, $4.25 per hour, eff. 4/1/91. Beauty service employees working 30 hours or less per week receive $4.00 per hour eff. 4/1/90; no part-time rate after 4/1/91. Building service industry employees: Janitors, $2.55 per unit per week, effective 4/1/90; $2.85 per unit per week, eff. 4/1/91. Maximum weekly rate for janitors, $161.65, eff. 4/1/90; $181.80, eff. 4/1/91. Other building service employees receive $3.80 per hour, eff. 4/1/90; $4.25 per hour, eff. 4/1/91.<br>**Subminimum Wage** — May be permitted by order for service employees. Nonprofit organizations may pay less than minimum wage for first six months of organization's existence.<br>**Employees covered** — All employees, except: babysitters and live-in companions; farm workers; those in bona fide executive, administrative, or professional capacity; outside salespersons; taxicab drivers; volunteers, learners, apprentices, students, or handicapped working for nonprofit religious, charitable, or educational institution; those whose work is incidental to charitable aid received from charitable or religious organization and not under contract of hire; members of religious orders; employees of summer camp or conference of religious, charitable, or educational institution not more than three months a year; counselors in children's camp; students employed by nonprofit group in college or university; and public employees.<br>**Meals and Lodging** — Credits for meals (per meal): restaurant, nonresort hotel, miscellaneous, non-profitmaking orders allow $1.30, eff. 4/1/90, $1.45, eff. 4/1/91; resort hotel employees, $1.70, eff. 4/1/90; $1.90, eff. 4/1/91. Lodging allowance: restaurant employees, $0.95 per day ($5.95 per week), eff. 4/1/90; $1.05 per day ($6.65 per week), eff. 4/1/91; nonresort hotel employees, $0.15 per hour, eff. 4/1/90; $0.20 per hour, eff. 4/1/91; all others covered by wage orders, except building service, $1.60 per day, eff. 4/1/90; $1.80 per day, eff. 4/1/91; employees of non-profitmaking subject to wage orders, $2.25 per day ($4.75 per day for house or apartment with utilities, $0.15 per hour in children's camp), eff. 4/1/90; $2.50 per day ($5.30 per day for house or apartment with utilities, $0.20 per hour in children's camp), eff. 4/1/91. Building service employees: apartment allowance is based on rentals in effect June 1, 1975; utility allowance, with refrigerator, is $10.65 per month, eff. 4/1/90, $11.90 per month, eff. 4/1/91; utility allowance, without refrigerator, is $7.70 per month, eff. 4/1/90; $8.60 per month, eff. 4/1/91. Uniform credits (all employees covered by wage orders): working over 30 hours per week, $4.75 per week eff. 4/1/90; $5.30 per week eff. 4/1/91; working more than 20 up to 30 hours per week, $3.70 per week, eff. 4/1/90; $4.15 per week, eff. 4/1/91; working 20 hours or less per week, $2.25 per week, eff. 4/1/90; $2.50 per week, eff. 4/1/91.<br>**Tips and Gratuities** — Restaurant and nonresort hotel employees: credit ranges from $0.85 to $1.20 per hour, eff. 4/1/90; $0.95 to $1.35 per hour, eff. 4/1/91. Resort hotel employees (except chambermaids): credit of $1.50 per hour, eff. 4/1/90; $1.70 per hour, eff. 4/1/91. Chambermaid in resort hotel: credit ranges from $0.60 to $1.20 per hour, eff. 4/1/90; $0.65 to $1.35 per hour, eff. 4/1/91. Other employees covered by wage orders: $0.60 to $0.95 per hour, eff. 4/1/90; $0.65 to $1.05 per hour, eff. 4/1/91. No tip credit allowed for employees of non-profitmaking employers subject to wage orders. |

## Comparison Chart — State Minimum Wage — Contd.

| STATE | REQUIREMENTS AND PROVISIONS |
|---|---|
| North Carolina | **Minimum Wage Established by State Law** — $3.35 an hour.<br>**Wage Board Orders** — None.<br>**Subminimum Wage** — At least 90 percent of minimum wage for full-time students, apprentices, learners, and handicapped workers. At least 85 percent of minimum wage for no more than 52 weeks for those unemployed for at least 15 weeks and receiving aid to families with dependent children or supplementary social security benefits, with eligibility certificate from Employment Security Commission. At least 85 percent of minimum wage for seasonal employees, as defined.<br>**Employees Covered** — All employees, except: agricultural and domestic workers; babysitters; pages in state legislature and governor's office; bona fide volunteers in medical, educational, religious, or nonprofit organization where no employer-employee relationship; those confined in public penal, correctional, or mental institution; performers for TV, radio, or film; employees of outdoor drama theaters except ushers, ticket takers, and parking attendants; those working in children's summer camp or seasonal religious or nonprofit educational conference center; employees in seafood industry through first sale; employer's spouse, child, parent, or qualified dependent under state tax laws; those in bona fide executive, administrative, professional, or outside sales capacity; and public employees, including those in seasonal recreation program.<br>**Meals and Lodging** — Reasonable cost of furnishing meals and lodging computed as 50 percent of establishment retail rate.<br>**Tips and Gratuities** — Tips may count for up to 50 percent of minimum wage; no employee's tips may be reduced more than 15 percent when pooled. |
| North Dakota | **Minimum Wage Established by State Law** — A minimum of $350 a month for full-time state employees.<br>**Wage Board Orders** — Effective 8/14/89, general minimum wage of $3.40 per hour for all nonexempt employment, except: minimum wage of $3.25 per hour, plus tips, for workers in public housekeeping.<br>**Subminimum Wage** — Training wage of 80 percent of general minimum ($2.72 per hour; 2.60 per hour, plus tips, for public housekeeping employees) for the lesser of 240 hours or 60 days, effective 8/14/89. $1.70 per hour for student learners in authorized programs.<br>**Employees Covered** — All employees in occupations covered by wage board orders, except outside salespersons on commission; workers providing companion services to the elderly or disabled; or workers physically defective by age or otherwise, apprentices, or learners, with license.<br>**Meals and Lodging** — In other than public housekeeping, reasonable cost or fair value of board, lodging, and other facilities customarily furnished by employer for employee's benefit may be considered part of wages up to $10 per day, with written agreement.<br>**Tips and Gratuities** — May not be considered part of employees' wages for public housekeeping employees. Employees must be allowed to keep tips. |
| Ohio | **Minimum Wage Established by State Law** — $2.30 an hour. $1.50 for non-tipped employees ($1.00 for tipped employees) of employer with less than $150,000 in gross annual sales.<br>**Wage Board Orders** — None.<br>**Subminimum Wage** — At least 80 percent of minimum wage for learners for no more than 90 days, and for students at state-approved cooperative vocational education programs for no more than 180 days. At least 85 percent of minimum wage for apprentices for no more than 90 days, with license from Director of Industrial Relations. Less than minimum wage for those with earning capacity impaired by physical or mental deficiencies or injuries, with license from Director. |

### Comparison Chart — State Minimum Wage — Contd.

| STATE | REQUIREMENTS AND PROVISIONS |
|---|---|
| Ohio, contd. | **Employees Covered** — All employees, except: hand harvest laborers on piecework basis or under 16 and working for parents, under certain conditions; federal employees; babysitters or live-in companions; those delivering newspapers to consumers; outside salespersons on commission; those in bona fide executive, administrative, or professional capacity; agricultural workers for employer using no more than 500 worker-hours during any calendar quarter of preceding calendar year; employer's parent, spouse, child, or other immediate family member; volunteers providing personal services in health institution; police and firefighters; students working part-time or seasonally for state political subdivision; employees of camp or recreational area for minors owned and operated by non-profit organization.<br>**Meals and Lodging** — No provision.<br>**Tips and Gratuities** — Tips may count for up to 50 percent of minimum wage for workers given more than $20 a month in tips; notice of policy required on menus. |
| Oklahoma | **Minimum Wage Established by State Law** — $3.80 an hour, effective 4/1/90; $4.25 an hour, effective 4/1/91. State minimum equals federal minimum, except employers with 10 or fewer employees grossing less than $100,000 per year pay a minimum of $2.00 per hour.<br>**Wage Board Orders** — None.<br>**Subminimum Wage** — Commissioner may permit subminimum wage for: learners, apprentices, and messengers; individuals whose earning capacity is impaired by age or physical or mental deficiency; employees of state or local governments or instrumentalities; or for students at institution of higher learning.<br>**Employees Covered** — All employees, except: minors under 18; employees of state, or of concessionaire; farm workers connected with raising or harvesting any farm commodity or with operating or managing a farm; domestic workers; federal employees; volunteers working for charitable, religious, or nonprofit organization; newspaper vendors or carriers; employees of any carrier subject to Part I of Interstate Commerce Act; those in bona fide executive, administrative, or professional capacity; outside salespersons; those under 18 not graduates of vocational or high school; students under 22; employees of feed store operated primarily for farmers and ranchers; and reserve force deputy sheriffs.<br>**Meals and Lodging** — Meals and lodging may be credited toward minimum wage, but may not exceed 50 percent of minimum wage when combined with tip credit. Reasonable cost of uniforms supplied by employer may be credited toward minimum wage.<br>**Tips and Gratuities** — Credit toward minimum wage for tips not to exceed 50 percent of minimum when combined with credit for meals and lodging. |

## Comparison Chart — State Minimum Wage — Contd.

| STATE | REQUIREMENTS AND PROVISIONS |
|---|---|
| Oregon | **Minimum Wage Established by State Law** — $4.25 per hour effective 1/1/90; $4.75 per hour effective 1/1/91. $1.95 to $4.46 per hour for individuals providing in-home care. Commissions and bonuses may be credited, if commission or bonus plus wage equals or exceed minimum wage.<br>**Wage Board Orders** — None.<br>**Subminimum Wage** — At least 75 percent of minimum wage for student-learners in vocational training programs, with authorization of Commissioner. Less than minimum wage for handicapped and aged, with permit from Bureau of Labor. Less than minimum wage for specific employees, including, but not limited to, mentally and physically handicapped who cannot perform all of job within entry level time, with authorization of Commissioner. Blanket approval for less than minimum wage for handicapped in sheltered workshops, etc., under certain conditions.<br>**Employees Covered** — Agricultural employees under 18, and all employees over 18, except: those donating services to public employer or religious, charitable, educational, public service, or similar nonprofit organization; certain agricultural workers; domestic workers; those in administrative, executive, or professional capacity earning more than $650 a month salary; federal employees; students working for their school; outside salespersons; taxicab operators; those employed in own home; those domiciled at place of employment to be available for emergencies or occasional duties; those paid to be available for duty during specific hours; those domiciled at multi-unit accommodation designed to provide other people with lodging for purpose of maintenance, management, or assistant management; seasonal employees of camp with gross annual income less than $275,000; and those employed at nonprofit conference ground or center operated for charitable or religious purposes.<br>**Meals and Lodging** — Fair market value may be credited for room, board, facilities, and services. No credit allowed for tools, equipment, or uniforms supplied/maintained by employer and required to be used, or for other items required by the employer to be used or worn as a condition of employment.<br>**Tips and Gratuities** — No credit allowed. |
| Pennsylvania | **Minimum Wage Established by State Law** — $3.80 per hour, effective 4/1/90. Increases tied to federal minimum wage.<br>**Wage Board Orders** — None.<br>**Subminimum Wage** — At least 85 percent of minimum wage for learners and students, with certificate from Secretary. Less than minimum wage for handicapped with license from Secretary.<br>**Employees Covered** — All employees, except: farm laborers; domestic workers; newspaper deliverers to consumers; employees of weekly, semiweekly, or daily publication with circulation under 4,000; those in executive, administrative, or professional capacity, including academic administrative personnel and elementary and secondary teachers; outside sales personnel, including certain retail and service personnel; voluntary workers for educational, charitable, religious, or nonprofit organization; certain seasonal workers; students working in nonprofit educational institution where enrolled; employees of public amusement or recreational establishment, organized camp, or religious or nonprofit educational conference center, under certain conditions; golf caddies; telephone company switchboard operators; and employees not subject to civil service laws: elected office holders and their personal staff and advisors.<br>**Meals and Lodging** — Credit allowed, with employee agreement, for reasonable cost as determined by the Secretary, of board, lodging, and other facilities customarily furnished by employer except where deductions are excluded under a bona fide collective bargaining agreement.<br>**Tips and Gratuities** — May count for up to 45 percent of minimum wage, provided employees informed of provision, customarily receive more than $30 a month in tips, and retain own tips or pool tips among selves. |

## Comparison Chart — State Minimum Wage — Contd.

| STATE | REQUIREMENTS AND PROVISIONS |
|---|---|
| Puerto Rico | **Minimum Wage Established by State Law** — None.<br><br>**Wage Board Orders** — Minimum wage rates from $0.24 to $4.00 an hour for 40 industries set by Minimum Wage Board, revised every two years; last amended in June, 1989. However, FLSA amendments of 1989 provide for phasing in the federal minimum wage. Regulations from the Employment Standards Administration divide Puerto Rico employers into four tiers, each having a different effective date for the federal minimum wage. The minimum wages are as follows (effective dates in parentheses). Tier 1 (average industry wage more than $4.64) must pay $3.80 (4/1/90); $4.25 (4/1/91 — 4/1/96). Tier 2 (average industry wage at least $4.00 but not more than $4.64) must pay $3.55 (4/1/90); $3.70 (4/1/91); $3.90 (4/1/92); $4.05 (4/1/93); $4.25 (4/1/94 — 4/1/96). Tier 3 (most employers with average industry wage less than $4.00) must pay $3.50 (4/1/90); $3.65 (4/1/91); $3.80 (4/1/92); $3.95 (4/1/93); $4.10 (4/1/94); $4.25 ((4/1/95 — (4/1/96). Tier 4 (Certain commonwealth, municipality, or other political entity employees earning less than $4.00 per hour) must pay $3.50, (4/1/90); $3.60 (4/1/91); $3.75 (4/1/92); $3.85 (4/1/93); $4.00 (4/1/94); $4.10 (4/1/95); $4.25 (4/1/96). Wage Board may continue to set rates for specific industries that are higher than the federal minimum in effect.<br><br>**Subminimum Wage** — At least 50 percent of minimum wage for apprentices, except those whose rate is fixed by Apprenticeship Council, with permit from Secretary of Labor. At least 50 percent of minimum wage for those with earning capacity impaired by age, physical disability, injury, or other reason, with permit from Secretary.<br><br>**Employees Covered** — All employees in 40 specified industries, except: domestic workers (except chauffeurs); federal, commonwealth, capital, and municipal employees (except those working for commonwealth agencies operating as private enterprises); and managers, executives, and professionals.<br><br>**Meals and Lodging** — Credits permitted for meals and lodging in certain industries.<br><br>**Tips and Gratuities** — Not included in wages. |
| Rhode Island | **Minimum Wage Established by State Law** — $4.25 an hour, effective 8/1/89.<br><br>**Wage Board Orders** — None.<br><br>**Subminimum Wage** — At least 75 percent of minimum wage for minors age 14-15 working 24 hours or less a week; full minimum wage for those working over 24 hours. At least 90 percent of minimum wage for full-time students under 19 working for nonprofit organization. Less than minimum wage for learners for first 90 days and for handicapped, with license from Director of Labor.<br><br>**Employees Covered** — All employees, except: agricultural and domestic workers; volunteers for educational, charitable, religious, or nonprofit organization; news carriers for home delivery; shoe shiners; golf caddies; bowling alley pin setters; ushers in theaters; outside salespersons; employer's parent, spouse, or child under 18; and employees of resort establishments open less than six months annually (May to October) and serving meals to the public.<br><br>**Meals and Lodging** — No provision.<br><br>**Tips and Gratuities** — Tips may count for up to 35 percent of minimum wage, except for bus boys (unless directly tipped by customers) and taxi drivers. |
| South Carolina | **Minimum Wage** — No state requirements except for Sunday work. |
| South Dakota | **Minimum Wage Established by State Law** — $3.80 an hour effective 4/1/90; $4.25 an hour, effective 4/1/91.<br><br>**Wage Board Orders** — None.<br><br>**Subminimum Wage** — Training wage as described in FLSA payable to minors age 18 or 19. Less than minimum wage for apprentices, on-the-job learners, mentally or physically deficient employees with permit from Department of Labor.<br><br>**Employees Covered** — All except: babysitters and outside salespersons. |

## Comparison Chart — State Minimum Wage — Contd.

| STATE | REQUIREMENTS AND PROVISIONS |
|---|---|
| **South Dakota, contd.** | **Meals and Lodging** — Room and board are not considered part of minimum wage.<br><br>**Tips and Gratuities** — Tips may be credited for up to 40 percent of minimum wage (50 percent, effective 4/1/91) for employees regularly receiving more than $30 a month ($35, effective 4/1/91) in tips and other considerations, with consent of employee. |
| **Tennessee** | **Minimum Wage Established by State Law** — $3.80 per hour, effective 4/1/90; $4.25 per hour 4/1/91. (Federal minimum.)<br>**Wage Board Orders** — None.<br>**Subminimum Wage** — No provision.<br>**Employees Covered** — Blind employees paid by the state.<br>**Meals and Lodging** — No provision.<br>**Tips and Gratuities** — No provision. |
| **Texas** | **Minimum Wage Established by State Law** — $3.35 an hour effective 9/1/87.<br>**Wage Board Orders** — None.<br>**Subminimum Wage** — Less than minimum wage for hand harvesters, as set by Commissioner. At least 60 percent of minimum wage for handicapped and those over 65, except agricultural workers, with medical certificate. Less than minimum wage for Department of Mental Health and Mental Retardation clients working in institution as part of therapy or being trained in sheltered workshop.<br>**Employees Covered** — All employees, including agricultural employees, except: agricultural employees engaged in production of livestock; agricultural hand harvesters paid by piece rate; members of religious orders and Christian Science readers on duty; those under 18 not vocational or high school graduates; students under 20, except those in agriculture; those in bona fide executive, administrative, or professional capacity; outside salespersons and collectors on commission; switchboard operators in certain independent companies; babysitters and domestic workers; those in jail; volunteers for nonprofit organization where no employer-employee relationship exists; family members; certain handicapped workers under 21; employees of certain amusement or recreational establishments; those working for Boy or Girl Scouts of America, or nonprofit camp; employees of dairy farm; agricultural workers not covered by state unemployment compensation act; and employee and spouse working for nonprofit educational organization as residential parents to children and receiving room and board without cost.<br>**Meals and Lodging** — Reasonable cost of meals and lodging may be deducted from wages if customarily furnished and stated separately on earnings statement.<br>**Tips and Gratuities** — May be counted for up to 50 percent of minimum wage if employee receives at least $20 per month in tips. |
| **Utah** | **Minimum Wage Established by State Law** — $3.80 per hour, effective 4/1/90. May not exceed federal minimum wage.<br>**Wage Board Orders** — None.<br>**Subminimum Wage** — Learner (other than a minor) may be paid $0.25 per hour less than the state minimum hourly wage for adult employees for the first 160 hours of employment. Minors may be paid at 85 percent of the minimum wage for adults.<br>**Employees Covered** — All employees except outside salespersons; employer's immediate family; casual, domestic, and companionship service employees; certain seasonal employees; federal employees; prisoners employed through penal system; apprentices or students employed by educational institution in which they are enrolled; agricultural employees in some circumstances; and handicapped individuals.<br>**Meals and Lodging** — No provision.<br>**Tips and Gratuities** — Tips may be credited for up to 45 percent of the minimum wage provided the employee receives at least $30 per month in tips. Credit may not exceed tips actually received. Employees must retain all tips, except under pooling arrangement. |

## Comparison Chart — State Minimum Wage — Contd.

| STATE | REQUIREMENTS AND PROVISIONS |
|---|---|
| Vermont | **Minimum Wage Established by State Law** — $3.85 an hour, effective 4/1/90; $4.25 an hour effective 4/1/91. (Federal minimum applies if it is higher than legislated state minimum.)<br>**Wage Board Orders** — Minimum wage of $3.65 an hour for employees who have worked more than 90 days in hotel, motel, restaurant, tourist, retail, wholesale, and service occupations.<br>**Subminimum Wage** — Handicapped workers in hotel, motel, tourist, restaurant, retail, wholesale, or service establishments may be paid less than minimum with work permit from Commissioner. Learners in retail, wholesale, service establishments may be paid $3.05 per hour for 30 days or 240 hours; learners may not exceed 10 percent of employer's workforce.<br>**Employees Covered** — All employees of employer with two or more workers, except: agricultural and domestic workers; federal or state employees; those in public-supported nonprofit organization, except laundry workers, nurses' aides, or practical nurses; those in bona fide executive, administrative, or professional capacity; home deliverers of newspapers or advertising; taxicab drivers; outside salespersons; and students working during school year or vacation.<br>**Meals and Lodging** — Employer may credit amounts for board, lodging, apparel, rent, utilities, or other items. For employees covered by wage board orders, credit may be taken of $1 for breakfast; $1.25 for lunch; $1.50 for dinner. In hotel, motel, tourist place, and restaurant industry, credit for lodging of $1.75 per night; $10.50 per week for room; $22.50 per week for full board; $33 per week for full room and board.<br>**Tips and Gratuities** — May be credited up to $1.46 against minimum wage, if employee in hotel, motel, tourist, or restaurant industry customarily receives more than $30 per month in tips. |
| Virginia | **Minimum Wage Established by State Law** — $2.65 an hour.<br>**Wage Board Orders** — None.<br>**Subminimum Wage** — No provision.<br>**Employees Covered** — All employees of employers with at least four workers (excluding employer's spouse, parent, or child), except: employees under 16 or over 64; persons whose earning capacity is impaired by physical or mental deficiency; students and apprentices in bona fide educational or apprenticeship programs; county or municipal employees; farm laborers or employees; domestic workers; those working in primarily public-supported charitable institutions; volunteers in educational, charitable, religious, or nonprofit organization where no employer-employee relationship exists; newspaper carriers; shoe shiners; golf caddies; babysitters; theater ushers, cashiers, and concession and door attendants; outside salespersons on commission; taxicab drivers and operators; employer's child or ward under 18; those confined in state or local penal, corrective, or mental institutions; employees of children's summer camp; those employed on piece-rate basis; full-time students under 18 not employed more than 20 hours a week; students of any age enrolled in full-time work study program or equivalent at educational institution; and minors under 18 under jurisdiction of a juvenile and domestic relations district court.<br>**Meals and Lodging** — Reasonable cost of meals and lodging may be deducted, if customarily furnished.<br>**Tips and Gratuities** — Amount deducted from wages for tips shall be determined by employer, unless employee able to show actual amount is less. |

## Comparison Chart — State Minimum Wage — Contd.

| STATE | REQUIREMENTS AND PROVISIONS |
|---|---|
| **Washington** | **Minimum Wage Established by State Law** — $4.25 an hour, effective 1/1/90. Nursing homes under contract to state, $5.15, effective 1/1/89. Rates apply to workers over age 16. Minimum wage rates for minors may be established by industry wage order.<br>**Wage Board Orders** — For seasonal recreational camp, minimum wage of $2.00 per hour for kitchen helpers working more than 27 hours per week, camp cooks, and all non-counselor employees in seasonal recreational camps; $1.75 for other employees. Nonresident counselors receive from $36 to $66 per week; resident counselors $21 to $51 per week.<br>**Subminimum Wage** — Higher of federal minimum or 85 percent of state minimum wage for minors under 16. Less than minimum wage for handicapped, with permit from Director. See also wage board orders.<br>**Employees Covered** — All workers over age 18 except: hand harvest labor paid on piece-work basis; casual labor in/around private home; individuals in bona fide professional, executive, or administrative capacity; outside salespersons as defined; volunteer for educational, charitable, religious, state or local governmental body or agency, or nonprofit organization, where employer-employee relationship does not exist; newspaper vendors or carriers; carriers subject to ICC regulation; forest protection or fire prevention workers; employees of charitable childcare institutions; workers on-call; residents of correctional, detention, treatment, or rehabilitative institutions; elected or appointed public officials; Washington state ferry workers; and seafarers on non-American vessels.<br>**Meals and Lodging** — Resident counselors' wages cannot be credited with lodging or meals.<br>**Tips and Gratuities** — May not be credited toward minimum wage |
| **West Virginia** | **Minimum Wage Established by State Law** — $3.35 an hour.<br>**Wage Board Orders** — None.<br>**Subminimum Wage** — No provision.<br>**Employees Covered** — All employees of employers with six or more workers in one location or establishment, unless 80 percent of workers covered by FLSA, except: federal employees; volunteers in educational, charitable, religious, fraternal, or nonprofit organization with no employer-employee relationship; workers 62 years or older receiving social security old age or survivor's benefits; newspaper carriers; shoe shiners; golf caddies; bowling alley pin setters and chasers; outside salespersons; employer's spouse, parent, or child; those in bona fide professional, executive, or administrative capacity; on-the-job trainees; severely physically and mentally handicapped employed in nonprofit sheltered workshop; employees of children's camp; agricultural workers, as defined by FLSA; state firefighters; theater ushers; students working part-time; employees of motorbus carriers; and certain employees of state legislature.<br>**Meals and Lodging** — $1.00 a day for meals allowed for full-time workers (no credit when employee is under bona fide medical care for dietary problems or during leave). Reasonable deductions allowed for board and lodging, as provided in regulations by Commissioner of Labor.<br>**Tips and Gratuities** — May count for 20 percent of minimum wage. |

## Comparison Chart — State Minimum Wage — Contd.

| STATE | REQUIREMENTS AND PROVISIONS |
|---|---|
| Wisconsin | **Minimum Wage Established by State Law** — None.<br><br>**Wage Board Orders** — $3.80 an hour, effective 4/1/90, for nonagricultural employees age 18 and over; $3.45 an hour, effective 4/1/90, for employees 17 and under. Minimum of $3.60 an hour, effective 4/1/90, for agricultural employees age 18 and over; $3.25 an hour, effective 4/1/90, for agricultural employees age 17 and under.<br><br>**Subminimum Wage** — Less than minimum for handicapped and student workers, with license from department. Probationary wage for first 60 days of employment; 60 days may be spread over three years. For nonagricultural workers over 18 the subminimum is $3.50 an hour, effective 4/1/90; for those 17 and under, the wage is $3.25 an hour, effective 4/1/90. Effective 4/1/90, no probationary wage applies to agricultural workers. Employers covered by FLSA must pay the greater of the federal minimum or the state minimum. Special rates for camp counselors and golf caddies.<br><br>**Employees Covered** — All employees, except: those in home newspaper delivery; those in direct retail sales to consumers; real estate agents and salespersons strictly on commission; casual domestic workers employed 15 hours or less a week; and certain live-in companions who spend less than 15 hours per week on general work.<br><br>**Meals and Lodging** — Board and lodging allowances for nonagricultural workers (probationary rates in parentheses) are: meals only, 18 years and over: $45.60 ($42.00) per week, $2.15 ($2.00) per meal; meals only, 17 years or less: $41.40 ($39.00) per week, $1.95 ($1.85) per meal; lodging, age 18 or over: $30.40 ($28.00) per week, $4.35 ($4.00) per day; lodging, age 17 or under: $27.60 ($26.00) per week, $3.95 ($3.70) per day. For agricultural workers the rates are: meals only, 18 and over: $43.20 per week, $2.05 per meal; 17 and under, $39.00 per week, $1.85 per meal; lodging, age 18 and over: $28.80 per week, $4.10 per day; 17 and under, $26.00 per week, $3.70 per day. No credit may be given for board or room for seasonal nonresident agricultural employees that would result in an hourly rate less than the minimum.<br><br>**Tips and Gratuities** — Effective 4/1/90, minimum wage for tipped workers is 55 percent of established minimum wage. |
| Wyoming | **Minimum Wage Established by State Law** — $1.60 an hour.<br><br>**Wage Board Orders** — None.<br><br>**Subminimum Wage** — No provision.<br><br>**Employees Covered** — All employees 18 years and over, except: agricultural workers; those in executive, administrative, or professional capacity; public employees; those in educational, charitable, religious, or nonprofit organization where no employer-employee relationship exists or on voluntary basis; outside salespersons solely on commission; drivers of ambulances or other vehicles on call at any time; and part-time and piece workers working 20 hours a week or less.<br><br>**Meals and Lodging** — No provision.<br><br>**Tips and Gratuities** — Employer may credit up to 50 percent of tips toward the minimum wage of employees customarily receiving more than $20 a month in tips, so long as wages paid are not less than $1.10 an hour. |

# APPENDIX F

## COEFFICIENT TABLE FOR COMPUTING OVERTIME

## Coefficient Table for Computing Overtime

The coefficient table below (WH-134) was prepared by Wage-Hour and Public Contracts Divisions to simplify overtime computations. The accompanying text is the official explanation of how the table was constructed and how it may be used.

In determining the extra half-time that is due for overtime pay, the method of calculation commonly used is to divide the straight-time earnings by the total number of hours worked and multiply the results by the number of overtime hours divided by two. For instance, in weeks in which overtime is due after 40 hours, the computation would be :

$$\text{for } 47\tfrac{3}{4} \text{ hours, } \frac{\text{Earnings}}{47\tfrac{3}{4}} \times \frac{7\tfrac{3}{4}}{2} ;$$

$$\text{for } 48 \text{ hours, } \frac{\text{Earnings}}{48} \times \frac{8}{2} ; \text{ and}$$

$$\text{for } 50 \text{ hours, } \frac{\text{Earnings}}{50} \times \frac{10}{2} .$$

The following tables contain the decimal equivalents of the fraction, $\dfrac{\text{O.T. Hours}}{\text{Total Hrs.} \times 2}$ .

For example, the decimal for :

$$47\tfrac{3}{4} \text{ hours } \frac{7\tfrac{3}{4}}{47\tfrac{3}{4} \times 2} = \frac{7.75}{95.5} = .081 ;$$

$$\text{for } 48 \text{ hours is } \frac{8}{48 \times 2} = \frac{1}{12} = .083 ; \text{ and}$$

$$\text{for } 50 \text{ hours it is } \frac{10}{50 \times 2} = \frac{1}{10} = .1 .$$

**U.S. DEPARTMENT OF LABOR**
EMPLOYMENT STANDARDS ADMINISTRATION
WAGE AND HOUR DIVISION

## COEFFICIENT TABLE FOR COMPUTING EXTRA HALF-TIME FOR OVERTIME

This Form has been prepared for use by employers who may find the coefficient table to be a time-saver when computing the extra half-time for hours worked over 40 in a workweek.

| Hours 40 | Even | 1/4 | 1/2 | 3/4 | 1/10 | 2/10 | 3/10 | 4/10 | 6/10 | 7/10 | 8/10 | 9/10 |
|---|---|---|---|---|---|---|---|---|---|---|---|---|
| 40 | | 0.003 | 0.006 | 0.009 | 0.0012 | 0.0025 | 0.0037 | 0.0049 | 0.0074 | 0.0086 | 0.0098 | 0.0110 |
| 41 | 0.012 | .015 | .018 | .021 | .0134 | .0146 | .0157 | .0169 | .0192 | .0204 | .0215 | .0227 |
| 42 | .024 | .027 | .029 | .032 | .0249 | .0261 | .0272 | .0283 | .0305 | .0316 | .0327 | .0338 |
| 43 | .035 | .038 | .040 | .043 | .0360 | .0370 | .0381 | .0392 | .0413 | .0423 | .0434 | .0444 |
| 44 | .045 | .048 | .051 | .053 | .0465 | .0475 | .0485 | .0495 | .0516 | .0526 | .0536 | .0546 |
| 45 | .056 | .058 | .060 | .063 | .0565 | .0575 | .0585 | .0595 | .0614 | .0624 | .0633 | .0643 |
| 46 | .065 | .068 | .070 | .072 | .0662 | .0671 | .0680 | .0690 | .0708 | .0717 | .0726 | .0736 |
| 47 | .074 | .077 | .079 | .081 | .0754 | .0763 | .0772 | .0781 | .0798 | .0807 | .0816 | .0825 |
| 48 | .083 | .085 | .088 | .090 | .0842 | .0851 | .0859 | .0868 | .0885 | .0893 | .0902 | .0910 |
| 49 | .092 | .094 | .096 | .098 | .0927 | .0935 | .0943 | .0951 | .0968 | .0976 | .0984 | .0992 |
| 50 | .100 | .102 | .104 | .106 | .1008 | .1016 | .1024 | .1032 | .1047 | .1055 | .1063 | .1071 |
| 51 | .108 | .110 | .112 | .114 | .1086 | .1094 | .1101 | .1109 | .1124 | .1132 | .1139 | .1146 |
| 52 | .115 | .117 | .119 | .121 | .1161 | .1169 | .1176 | .1183 | .1198 | .1205 | .1212 | .1219 |
| 53 | .123 | .124 | .126 | .128 | .1234 | .1241 | .1248 | .1255 | .1269 | .1276 | .1283 | .1289 |
| 54 | .130 | .131 | .133 | .135 | .1303 | .1310 | .1317 | .1324 | .1337 | .1344 | .1350 | .1357 |
| 55 | .136 | .138 | .140 | .141 | .1370 | .1377 | .1383 | .1390 | .1403 | .1409 | .1416 | .1422 |
| 56 | .143 | .144 | .146 | .148 | .1435 | .1441 | .1448 | .1454 | .1466 | .1473 | .1479 | .1485 |
| 57 | .149 | .151 | .152 | .154 | .1497 | .1503 | .1510 | .1516 | .1528 | .1534 | .1540 | .1546 |
| 58 | .155 | .157 | .158 | .160 | .1558 | .1564 | .1569 | .1575 | .1587 | .1593 | .1599 | .1604 |
| 59 | .161 | .162 | .164 | .165 | .1616 | .1622 | .1627 | .1633 | .1644 | .1650 | .1656 | .1661 |
| 60 | .167 | .168 | .169 | .171 | .1672 | .1678 | .1683 | .1689 | .1700 | .1705 | .1711 | .1716 |
| 61 | .172 | .173 | .175 | .176 | .1727 | .1732 | .1737 | .1743 | .1753 | .1759 | .1764 | .1769 |
| 62 | .177 | .179 | .180 | .181 | .1779 | .1785 | .1790 | .1795 | .1805 | .1810 | .1815 | .1820 |
| 63 | .183 | .184 | .185 | .186 | .1830 | .1835 | .1840 | .1845 | .1855 | .1860 | .1865 | .1870 |
| 64 | .188 | .189 | .190 | .191 | .1880 | .1885 | .1890 | .1894 | .1904 | .1909 | .1914 | .1918 |
| 65 | .192 | .193 | .195 | .196 | .1928 | .1933 | .1937 | .1942 | .1951 | .1956 | .1960 | .1965 |
| 66 | .197 | .198 | .199 | .200 | .1974 | .1979 | .1983 | .1988 | .1997 | .2001 | .2006 | .2010 |
| 67 | .201 | .203 | .204 | .205 | .2019 | .2024 | .2028 | .2033 | .2041 | .2046 | .2050 | .2054 |
| 68 | .206 | .207 | .208 | .209 | .2063 | .2067 | .2072 | .2076 | .2085 | .2089 | .2093 | .2097 |
| 69 | .210 | .211 | .212 | .213 | .2106 | .2110 | .2114 | .2118 | .2126 | .2131 | .2135 | .2139 |
| 70 | .214 | .215 | .216 | .217 | .2147 | .2151 | .2155 | .2159 | .2167 | .2171 | .2175 | .2179 |
| 71 | .218 | .219 | .220 | .221 | .2187 | .2191 | .2195 | .2199 | .2207 | .2211 | .2214 | .2218 |
| 72 | .222 | .223 | .224 | .225 | .2226 | .2230 | .2234 | .2238 | .2245 | .2249 | .2253 | .2257 |
| 73 | .226 | .227 | .228 | .229 | .2264 | .2268 | .2271 | .2275 | .2283 | .2286 | .2290 | .2294 |
| 74 | .230 | .231 | .232 | .232 | .2301 | .2305 | .2308 | .2312 | .2319 | .2323 | .2326 | .2330 |
| 75 | .233 | .234 | .235 | .236 | .2337 | .2340 | .2344 | .2347 | .2354 | .2358 | .2361 | .2365 |
| 76 | .237 | .238 | .239 | .239 | .2372 | .2375 | .2379 | .2382 | .2389 | .2392 | .2396 | .2399 |
| 77 | .240 | .241 | .242 | .243 | .2406 | .2409 | .2413 | .2416 | .2423 | .2426 | .2429 | .2433 |
| 78 | .244 | .244 | .245 | .246 | .2439 | .2442 | .2446 | .2449 | .2455 | .2459 | .2462 | .2465 |
| 79 | .247 | .248 | .249 | .249 | .2472 | .2475 | .2478 | .2481 | .2487 | .2491 | .2494 | .2497 |
| 80 | .250 | .251 | .252 | .252 | .2503 | .2506 | .2509 | .2512 | .2519 | .2522 | .2525 | .2528 |
| 81 | .253 | .254 | .255 | .255 | .2534 | .2537 | .2540 | .2543 | .2549 | .2552 | .2555 | .2558 |
| 82 | .256 | .257 | .258 | .258 | .2564 | .2567 | .2570 | .2573 | .2579 | .2582 | .2585 | .2587 |
| 83 | .259 | .260 | .261 | .261 | .2593 | .2596 | .2599 | .2602 | .2608 | .2611 | .2613 | .2616 |
| 84 | .262 | .263 | .263 | .264 | .2622 | .2625 | .2628 | .2630 | .2636 | .2639 | .2642 | .2644 |
| 85 | .265 | .265 | .266 | .267 | .2650 | .2653 | .2655 | .2658 | .2664 | .2666 | .2669 | .2672 |

**TO CONVERT INTO WEEKLY EQUIVALENT:** Multiply SEMIMONTHLY salary by 0.4615; MONTHLY salary by 0.2308; ANNUAL salary by 0.01923.

**TO CONVERT INTO STRAIGHT-TIME HOURLY EQUIVALENT FOR 40 HOURS:** Multiply WEEKLY salary by 0.025; SEMIMONTHLY by 0.01154; MONTHLY by 0.00577; ANNUAL by 0.00048.

**TO CONVERT INTO TIME AND ONE-HALF HOURLY RATE BASED ON 40 HOUR WEEK:** Multiply WEEKLY salary by 0.0375; SEMIMONTHLY by 0.0173; MONTHLY salary by 0.00866; ANNUAL by 0.000721.

**CAUTION:** Be sure straight-time earnings are not below legal minimum

(SEE INSTRUCTIONS ON REVERSE SIDE)

Form WH-134
(Rev. Aug. 1974)

# APPENDIX G

## CHART OF STATE MAXIMUM HOURS-OVERTIME

## State Maximum Hours and Overtime Laws — Comparison Chart

| STATE | REQUIREMENTS AND PROVISIONS |
|---|---|
| Alabama | **Maximum Hours before Overtime** — No general provision.<br>**Overtime Pay** — No general provision.<br>**Employees Covered** — No general provision.<br>**Special Occupations** — Truckdrivers: 10-hour day followed by 8-hour rest, plus certain provisions. State Law Enforcement Officers: 1½ times regular pay or compensatory time for hours in excess of 8-hour day or 40-hour week.<br>**Day of Rest** — No minor, apprentice, or servant may be required to perform any labor on Sunday, except customary domestic duties or works of charity; merchants, shopkeepers, druggists excepted, may not keep stores open on Sunday. Certain other specific operations exempted.<br>**Meal and Rest Periods** — No general provision. |
| Alaska | **Maximum Hours before Overtime** — 8-hour day, 40-hour week; 10-hour day, 40-hour week for workers with flexible work hour plan if part of collective bargaining agreement or signed employer-employee agreement filed with state Department of Labor.<br>**Overtime Pay** — 1½ times regular pay for hours in excess of maximum.<br>**Employees Covered** — All employees, except: those of employer with fewer than 4 workers; those in executive, administrative, or professional capacity; outside salespersons, as defined; those employed in making dairy products and handling or preparing for market agricultural or horticultural products; agricultural employees; those employed in certain newspapers with circulation under 1,000; certain switchboard operators; taxicab employees; certain retail or service workers handling telegraphic, telephone or radio messages; seafarers; forestry and lumbering workers of firms with 12 or fewer workers; small mining operations with fewer than 12 employees, provided that hours do not exceed 12 per day or 56 per week during mining season, as defined; outside buyers of raw poultry or dairy products; casual employees, as defined; and nonprofit hospital workers.<br>**Special Occupations** — Underground Mines: 8-hour day in all underground mines or workings, excluding days on which shifts are changed; emergencies, meal periods, or time spent in going to or from actual place of work.<br>**Day of Rest** — No general provision.<br>**Meal and Rest Periods** — No general provision. |
| Arizona | **Maximum Hours before Overtime** — No general provision.<br>**Overtime Pay** — No general provision.<br>**Employees Covered** — No general provision.<br>**Special Occupations** — Law enforcement officers and security personnel in municipal correctional institution must receive 1½ times regular pay for hours in excess of 40 per week. Laundries: 8-hour day and 48-hour week, with certain exceptions. Mines: 8-hour day for workers in underground mines or workings; open cut or pit workings in connection with operation of smelters, reduction works, stamp mills, concentrating mills, chlorination processes, cyanide processes, cement works, rolling mills, rod mills, coke ovens, and blast furnaces (except in emergencies and during shift changes if not more than once in two weeks). Public Works Contractors: 8-hour day for manual or mechanical laborers, except in emergencies. Motor Transportation: 10-hour day (or 10-hour aggregate in any 24 hours, followed by 8 hours off) for truck and bus operators and their helpers, except for unforeseen delays and emergencies. Railroads: 16 hours followed by 9 hours rest, except for emergencies and actual necessity.<br>**Day of Rest** — No general provision.<br>**Meal and Rest Periods** — No general provision. |

## Comparison Chart — State Hours Laws — Contd.

| STATE | REQUIREMENTS AND PROVISIONS |
|---|---|
| Arkansas | **Maximum Hours before Overtime** — 40-hour week; 48-hour week for employees of hotel, motel, restaurant, and tourist attraction with annual sales volume less than $362,500.<br>**Overtime Pay** — 1½ times regular pay for hours in excess of maximum.<br>**Employees Covered** — All employees, except agricultural workers.<br>**Special Occupations** — Motor Transportation: 12 consecutive hours followed by 8 hours rest for drivers, except when wrecks or washouts. Highway Construction: 8-hour day.<br>**Day of Rest** — On Sunday, unlawful for any person to sell, offer for sale, or employ others to sell certain specified goods. Law inapplicable to sale of goods for charitable or governmental purposes, or the advertising for sale of personal property. Person who conscientiously observes a day other than Sunday as a day of rest and abstains on that day from the sale of items prohibited also exempted.<br>**Meal and Rest Periods** — No general provision. |
| California | **Maximum Hours before Overtime** — 8-hour day unless contract specifies otherwise; for state employees, 8-hour day, 40-hour week, unless governor determines that 40 hours be performed in 4 days.<br>**Overtime Pay** — 1½ times regular pay for hours in excess of maximum. Hospitals: Twice the regular pay for hospital workers, under certain conditions. Agriculture: Twice the regular rate for agricultural workers in excess of 8 hours on seventh day. manufacturing; personal service; canning, freezing, and preserving; professional, technical, clerical, mechanical, and similar occupations; laundry, linen supply, dry cleaning, and dyeing; mercantile occupations; farm products, after harvest; amusement and recreation; broadcasting; and preparing agricultural products for market, on the farm: 1½ times regular rate for hours in excess of 40 per week or eight per day; twice the regular pay for hours in excess of 12 hours a day and eight hours on seventh day. For alternative schedules, 1½ times regular pay for hours beyond schedule, up to twelve per day or 40 per week; twice the regular pay for hours in excess of twelve; for employees with 4-day week, 10-hour day agreement, 1½ times regular rate for first 8 hours of additional workday, twice regular rate for additional hours.<br>**Employees Covered** — All employees except those subject to specific hours, i.e., workers in a manufacturing establishment in operation 24 hours per day, 7 days per week; pharmacists; workers in motor vehicle or railroad transportation; apprentices; workers in the seasonal ski industry; employees of licensed hospitals; workers subject to wage board orders covering hours to be worked (see special occupations).<br>**Special Occupations** — By Law: Manufacturing operations continuously working for 24 hour per day, 7 days per week: three 12-hour days per week, or two week period of three 12-hour days in first week and four 12-hour days in second. Mines: Not more than eight hours within any 24, unless collective bargaining agreement expressly provides for up to 12 hours within 24. Pharmacies: Nine-hour day or 108 hours/12 days within two consecutive weeks. Motor Vehicle Transportation: 10 consecutive hours, or 10 hours within 15 consecutive hours, if transporting people; 12 hours in 15 consecutive hours if transporting merchandise, freight, materials, or other property. 8 hours of rest for all drivers. Railroad Transportation: 12 consecutive hours off duty after 12 consecutive hours or work, or 8 hours off in 24. Persons directing trains in towers, offices, places, and stations operated continuously day and night, 9 hours within 24; 13 hours within 24 if operating only by day. Four additional hours on no more than three days in any week if emergency warrants. Seasonal ski industry: regularly established workweek of up |

## Comparison Chart — State Hours Laws — Contd.

| STATE | REQUIREMENTS AND PROVISIONS |
|---|---|
| **California, Contd.** | to 56 hours, provided employees working more than 56 hours are paid 1½ times regular rate. Hospital employees: regular workweek of no more than three 12-hour days permitted, provided employer tries to find alternate employment for workers unable to work 12 consecutive hours. Apprentices: hours as prescribed by law for person of apprentice's age and sex. Hospitals: no more than three 12-hour days per week. By Order: common provisions: no more than 8-hour day, six-day week for minors, with 1½ times regular pay for hours over 40. 8-hour day, 40-hour week for: manufacturing; personal service; canning freezing, preserving industry; professional, technical, clerical, mechanical, and similar occupations; public housekeeping; laundry, linen supply, dry cleaning, and dyeing; mercantile occupations; transportation; amusement and recreation industry; broadcasting industry; motion picture industry; agricultural product preparation for market (on the farm). Ten-hour day, six-day week for agricultural employees age 18 and over; 8-hour day, six-day week for minors. At least 12 consecutive off-duty hours for live-in employee in household occupation. **Day of Rest** — All employees are entitled to one day's rest in seven, except: in emergencies; work performed in necessary care of animals, crops, or agricultural lands; work required to prevent loss of life or property; common carriers connected with movement of train; however, if nature of work requires seven or more consecutive days, days of rest may be accumulated and equivalent time off allowed during calendar month. Work on seventh day may be permitted if total hours of employment do not exceed six per day or 30 per week. **Meal and Rest Periods** — One-half hour between third and fifth hour of each day's shift for employees of plants or mills that process or manufacture any lumber or allied wood products. Thirty minute meal period after five consecutive hours, unless employee works six-hour day, and 10 minute rest period for each four hours working time for employees in: manufacturing; personal service; canning, freezing, and preserving; professional, technical, clerical, mechanical, and similar occupations; laundry, linen supply, dry cleaning, and dyeing; mercantile occupations; farm products, after harvest; amusement and recreation; broadcasting; and preparing agricultural products for market, on the farm. |
| **Colorado** | **Maximum Hours before Overtime** — No general provision. **Overtime Pay** — 1½ times regular pay for hours in excess of 40 per workweek or 12 per day for employees in: laundry and dry cleaning; food and beverage services; beauty services; public housekeeping; medical profession (including office support personnel); janitorial services. 1½ times regular rate for hours in excess of 8 per day or 40 per week for minors. **Employees Covered** — By Order: employees in laundry and dry cleaning; retail trade; public housekeeping; beauty services; food and beverage services; medical profession (including office support personnel); janitorial services. **Special Occupations** — Cement and plaster factories: 8-hour day, except in emergencies; two periods of 8 hours each, separated by 8-hour rest period, not more than once per week during shift change. Municipal firefighters may not work more than aggregate of 12 hours per day, except in emergency; workers in underground mines may work more than 8 hours in 24 under agreement and with reasonable notice. Railroad employees who have worked 16 consecutive hours must have 10 hours rest before resuming work. Motor vehicle dealers may not stay open on Sundays. **Day of Rest** — No general provision; motor vehicle dealers forbidden to stay open on Sundays for purposes of selling vehicles. **Meal and Rest Periods** — At least 30 minute meal period after five hours of work (optional if workday is six hours or less) and 10 minute rest period every four hours for employees in: laundry and dry cleaning; public housekeeping; beauty services; retail trade; food and beverage services; janitorial occupations; and medical profession, including office support. If nature of work requires it, meal may be eaten "on-the-job," in which case employee must be paid for meal time. |

## Comparison Chart — State Hours Laws — Contd.

| STATE | REQUIREMENTS AND PROVISIONS |
|---|---|
| **Connecticut** | **Maximum Hours before Overtime** — Nine-hour day, 48-hour week in manufacturing/mechanical establishments for workers under 18 or over 66, handicapped persons, and disabled veterans. Ten-hour day, 55-hour week during emergencies or peak demand, with commissioner's permission, for limited period of time; for workweek of less than 5 days, daily hours may be extended provided weekly hours do not exceed limits. Nine-hour day (10 hours on one day per week), six-day, 48-hour week for employees under 18 or over 66, handicapped persons, and disabled veterans in: public restaurant, cafe, dining room, barber shop, hairdressing or manicuring establishment; amusement or recreational establishment; bowling alley; shoe shining establishment; billiard or pool room, or photographic gallery. Hotels exempt. Eight hour day, 48-hour, six-day week for workers under 18 or over 66, handicapped workers, and disabled veterans working in mercantile establishments.<br>**Overtime Pay** — 1½ times regular pay for hours in excess of maximum.<br>**Employees Covered** — All except: drivers or helpers with hours set by Interstate Commerce Commission; employees subject to Railroad Labor Act; seafarers; announcers, news editors, and chief engineers of TV/radio stations; bona fide executive, administrative, or professional employees; outside salespersons; inside salespersons working up to 54 hours/week whose regular pay exceeds two times the minimum wage or whose monthly compensation is more than half from commissions; taxicab drivers paid 40 percent or more of meter fares; milk and bakery route salespersons; automobile salespersons; agricultural employees; permanent municipal police and firefighters; firefighters employed by private nonprofit firm under contract with municipality; beer delivery truck driver not paid on hourly basis; mechanics employed by sellers of motor vehicles or farm equipment provided the mechanics' actual pay exceeds the sum of regular pay for all hours worked plus ½ times regular rate for all hours in excess of 40.<br>**Special Occupations** — Workweek limited to 40 hours for workers in: beauty shops; laundries; cleaning and dyeing; mercantile trade; 48-hour week for employees in hotel and restaurant services.<br>**Day of Rest** — Employer may not compel employee engaged in commercial occupation or industrial process to work more than six days in calendar week. No person who conscientiously believes that a particular day of week ought to be observed as the Sabbath may be required by employer to work on such day. No person, firm, or corporation shall engage or employ others in work, labor, or business on Sunday except charitable, religious, or service organization; federal, state, municipal or local governmental agency; person, firm, or corporation performing acts necessary for public safety or health; or person who observes another day as the Sabbath. Inapplicable to certain specified business operations; the sale or furnishing of specified articles, if they are sold in ordinary course of business; or to isolated or occasional sales by persons not engaged in the sale, transfer, or exchange of property as a business.<br>**Meal and Rest Periods** — At least 30 consecutive minutes for employee working 7½ or more consecutive hours; meal period must occur after the first two hours of work and before the last two hours. Exemptions may be granted by commission. |
| **Delaware** | No state requirements. |
| **District of Columbia** | **Maximum Hours before Overtime** — 40-hour week for most employees. Automobile washers are exempt, if paid 1½ times their regular rate for hours in excess of 160 hours during any 4-week period.<br>**Overtime Pay** — 1½ times regular pay for hours in excess of maximum.<br>**Employees Covered** — All employees working in: private households; retail trade; laundry and dry cleaning establishments; beauty culture; manufacturing, wholesale trade, printing, and publishing; clerical and semi-technical occupations; building services; and miscellaneous occupations including machine trade, benchwork, and structural work occupations, parking and car wash attendants, guards, ushers, ticket takers, furniture movers, bus, truck, and cab drivers, lifeguards, and temporary help employees. Workers in bona fide executive, administrative, or professional capacity are exempt.<br>**Special Occupations** — No provision.<br>**Day of Rest** — No general provision.<br>**Meal and Rest Periods** — No general provision. |

## Comparison Chart — State Hours Laws — Contd.

| STATE | REQUIREMENTS AND PROVISIONS |
|---|---|
| Florida | **Maximum Hours before Overtime** — No general provision.<br>**Overtime Pay** — No general provision.<br>**Employees Covered** — No general provision.<br>**Special Occupations** — Manual Labor: 10-hour day; extra pay required for additional hours. Railway Employees: 8-hour rest after 13 consecutive hours, except when behind schedule or in emergencies.<br>**Day of Rest** — No general provision.<br>**Meal and Rest Periods** — No general provision. |
| Georgia | **Maximum Hours before Overtime** — No general provision.<br>**Overtime Pay** — No general provision.<br>**Employees Covered** — No general provision.<br>**Special Occupations** — Motor Carriers: 10-hour day followed by 10 hour rest for drivers of motor contract and common carriers, except in emergencies. Railroads: 13-hour day followed by 10 hour rest, except in case of casualty. Cotton or woolen manufacturer employees: 10-hour day, 60-hour week for all employees except engineers; firefighters; guards; mechanics; teamsters; yard employees; clericals; and repair employees.<br>**Day of Rest** — Pursuit of business or work of ordinary calling forbidden on Lord's day, except works of necessity or charity. The operation of any business involved in sales, with some exceptions, on both the two consecutive days of Saturday and Sunday is a public nuisance and subject to penalty. Counties may exempt themselves by referendum.<br>**Meal and Rest Periods** — No general provision. |
| Hawaii | **Maximum Hours before Overtime** — 40-hour week.<br>**Overtime Pay** — 1½ times regular pay for hours in excess of maximum.<br>**Employees Covered** — All employees except: those with guaranteed monthly salary of $1,000; agricultural work in any week when employer with fewer than 20 employees or engages in coffee harvesting; domestic workers; houseparents in charitable organizations; employer's relatives; bona fide executive, administrative, supervisory, or professional employees; outside salespersons or collectors; those in fish or aquatic farming industry prior to first processing; seafarers; on-call, fixed stand vehicle drivers; golf caddies; student employees of nonprofit school; seasonal employees of certain nonprofit youth camps; and automobile or truck salespersons for licensed dealer.<br>**Special Occupations** — Employers in certain industries may select 20 work-weeks per year during which they shall be exempt from the overtime compensation requirement, although they must pay 1½ times the regular rate for hours in excess of 48 per week. These industries are: agriculture; first processing of dairy products; processing of sugar cane molasses or sugar cane; first processing or canning or packing any agricultural or horticultural commodity; handling, slaughtering, or dressing poultry or livestock; agriculture and processing of agricultural products seasonally; or first processing or, canning or packing seasonal fresh fruits.<br>**Day of Rest** — No general provision.<br>**Meal and Rest Periods** — Lunch period of 45 minutes allowed all government employees. |
| Idaho | **Maximum Hours before Overtime** — 40 hours per seven-day week.<br>**Overtime Pay** — 1½ times regular rate for hours in excess of maximum.<br>**Employees Covered** — All whose employers are not exempted or excepted from the FLSA overtime provisions.<br>**Special Occupations** — Mines: 8-hour day for workers in or upon underground mines and workings, and 10-hour day for workers in or upon surface mines and workings. Work over 10 hours per day in emergency only. Eight hour day, with extension to 10 hours permitted, in smelters, ore reduction works, stamp mills, concentrators, and other places where metalliferous ores are treated, except when life or property in imminent danger. Time worked in excess of 10 hours per day or 40 hours per week shall be paid at 1½ regular rate. |

## Comparison Chart — State Hours Laws — Contd.

| STATE | REQUIREMENTS AND PROVISIONS |
|---|---|
| **Idaho, Contd.** | **Day of Rest** — No general provision.<br>**Meal and Rest Periods** — No general provision. |
| **Illinois** | **Maximum Hours before Overtime** — 40-hour week. 8-hour day in all mechanical trades and other labor by the day except farm employment, if no agreement to the contrary.<br>**Overtime Pay** — 1½ times regular pay for hours in excess of maximum.<br>**Employees Covered** — All employees, except: those working for employer with fewer than 4 employees; salespersons or mechanics in nonmanufacturing firm primarily selling or servicing automobiles, trucks, farm implements, boats, or aircraft; agricultural workers; government employees; those in bona fide executive, administrative, or professional capacity; commissioned employees, as defined by FLSA; domestic workers; outside salespersons; members of religious corporation or organization; certain camp counselors; and employees working in another employee's stead as part of worktime exchange agreement.<br>**Special Occupations** — Motor Transportation: 10 hours followed by 8 hours off duty and 60 hours in seven days for operators unless emergency permission from Department of Law Enforcement, except for: public utility operators in emergency or temporary necessity, drivers connected with packing and preserving perishable fruits and vegetables, those hauling materials to and from construction site within 50-mile radius, and driver-salespersons within 50 miles of principal business. Municipal firefighters: 56 hours in any week of month for firefighters in towns over 10,000 in population.<br>**Day of Rest** — At least 24 consecutive hours of rest in every calendar week in addition to regular period of rest allowed at the close of each working day. Inapplicable to part-time employees who work fewer than 20 hours per week; workers needed in case of breakdown of machinery or equipment, or other emergency requiring immediate services of experienced labor; agricultural and coal mining employees; watchmen or security guards; employees in bona fide executive, administrative, or professional capacity; outside salespersons; workers engaged for 20 or fewer weeks per calendar year in canning and processing of perishable products. Before operating on Sunday, employer must post in conspicuous place schedule containing list of employees required or allowed to work on Sunday, and designating day of rest for each. No employees shall be required to work on their designated day of rest.<br>**Meal and Rest Periods** — At least 20 minutes for meal period beginning no later than five hours after the start of work period for employees working for 7½ continuous hours or longer. Inapplicable to employees for whom meal periods are established through collective bargaining. |
| **Indiana** | **Maximum Hours before Overtime** — No general provision.<br>**Overtime Pay** — No general provision.<br>**Employees Covered** — No general provision.<br>**Special Occupations** — Railroads: 12-hour day followed by 10 hours off duty, or 12 hours aggregate in 24 hours followed by 8 hours off duty for employees engaged in movement of passenger or freight trains. Motor Transportation: Part 395 of federal Motor Carrier Safety Regulations adopted as Indiana law.<br>**Day of Rest** — Common labor or pursuit of usual vocation on Sunday forbidden to persons age 14 and over, except for work of charity and necessity. Nothing shall be construed to affect those who observe conscientiously the Sabbath, those engaged in conveying travelers, toll bridge and gate keepers, ferry operators, newspaper employees, baseball and hockey players, after 1 p.m. and at least 1,000 feet from any established house of worship or public or private hospitals.<br>**Meal and Rest Periods** — No general provision. |

## Comparison Chart — State Hours Laws — Contd.

| STATE | REQUIREMENTS AND PROVISIONS |
|---|---|
| Iowa | **Maximum Hours before Overtime** — No provision.<br>**Overtime Pay** — No general provision.<br>**Employees Covered** — No general provision.<br>**Special Occupations** — Motor Transportation: 12 hours followed by 10 hours off duty, or 12 aggregate hours in 24 hours followed by 8 hours off duty. 12 hours in 24 hours for urban transit drivers; driver on split shift shall have at least 1 hour off between shifts. Railroads: 16 hours followed by 10 hours of rest, or 16 aggregate hours in 24 hours, for employees connected with movement of trains unless to protect life or property, except employees of sleeping car companies.<br>**Day of Rest** — No general provision.<br>**Meal and Rest Periods** — No general provision. |
| Kansas | **Maximum Hours before Overtime** — 46-hour week.<br>**Overtime Pay** — 1½ times regular pay for hours in excess of maximum.<br>**Employees Covered** — All employees, except: employees primarily selling motor vehicles for nonmanufacturing retail firm; prisoners; those covered by FLSA; agricultural and domestic workers; those in bona fide executive, administrative, or professional capacity; outside salespersons on commission; federal employees; unpaid volunteers for nonprofit organization; part-time workers age 18 or under and age 60 or over; and students under 18 working between academic terms.<br>**Special Occupations** — 258 hours in 28-day period (or equivalent hour/day ratio for periods from seven to 27 days) for firefighters, law enforcement personnel, and security personnel in correctional institution unless covered under FLSA. 8-hour day for employees in lead and zinc mines, except in emergencies. Railroads: 16 hours followed by 8 hours of rest, except in case of washout, wreck, or unavoidable blockade; inapplicable to train crews handling livestock or perishable freight; sleeping car, baggage, and express employees. Motor Transportation: Hours fixed by Public Utilities Commission.<br>**Day of Rest** — Sunday labor prohibited except works of necessity or charity; not applicable to persons observing a different Sabbath.<br>**Meal and Rest Periods** — No general provision. |
| Kentucky | **Maximum Hours before Overtime** — 40-hour week.<br>**Overtime Pay** — 1½ times regular pay for hours in excess of maximum. 1½ times regular pay for hours worked on seventh day of week.<br>**Employees Covered** — All employees, except for: those whose primary duty is to direct or supervise; employees of telephone exchanges with less than 500 subscribers; stenographers; bookkeepers; technical assistants of licensed professions; employees subject to Federal Railway Labor Act; seafarers and those operating on navigable streams; those icing railroad cars; and employees of common carriers under supervision of bureau of vehicle regulation.<br>**Special Occupations** — Motor Transportation: 12 hours followed by 8 hours off duty, or 16 hours in any 24 hours followed by 10 hours off duty, for motor vehicle drivers, except in emergencies or for those under collective bargaining agreement. |

## Comparison Chart — State Hours Laws — Contd.

| STATE | REQUIREMENTS AND PROVISIONS |
|---|---|
| Kentucky, Contd. | **Day of Rest** — Fines will be levied on any person who works on Sunday or employs any other person in labor or other business, whether for profit or amusement, unless work or the employment of others is in the course of ordinary household duties, a necessity or charity, or required in the maintenance or operation of public service, utility, or system. Inapplicable to religious society which observes another day as Sabbath, certain specified operations, or employers using continuous work scheduling that permits at least one day of rest each calendar week for each employee. **Meal and Rest Periods** — Employers, except those subject to federal Railway Labor Act, shall grant employees a reasonable period for lunch, which shall be as close to the middle of the employee's scheduled shift as possible. Employee shall not be required to take lunch period sooner than three hours or later than five hours from commencement of shift; provision does not negate any provision of collective bargaining or mutual agreement between employer and employee. Rest period of 10 minutes during each four hours worked, except employees subject to FRLA. |
| Louisiana | **Maximum Hours before Overtime** — No general provision. **Overtime Pay** — No general provision. **Employees Covered** — No general provision. **Special Occupations** — No provision. **Day of Rest** — No store or business opposed to being open on Sunday shall be required to open on Sunday, unless required by lease agreement. New or used car or truck dealers may not be open on Sunday. **Meal and Rest Periods** — No general provision. |
| Maine | **Maximum Hours before Overtime** — 40-hour week. **Overtime Pay** — 1½ times regular pay for hours in excess of maximum. **Employees Covered** — All employees, except: those processing, marketing, or storing agricultural products, meat, fish, and other perishable goods; seafarers; employees of hotel, motel, eating establishment, nursing home, or hospital; public employees except firefighters, who are covered; automobile mechanics or salespersons. **Special Occupations** — No provision. **Day of Rest** — No place of business shall be kept open on Sunday except for work of necessity, emergency, or charity; operation or maintenance of common contract or private carriers; taxicabs; airplanes; newspapers; radio and television stations; hotels, motels, rooming houses, tourist and trailer camps; restaurants; garages and auto service stations; retail monument dealers; automatic laundries; pharmacies; greenhouses; seasonal stands selling produce; public utilities; industries in continuous operation; agricultural processing plants; ship chandlers; marinas; establishments selling boats, sporting equipment, souvenirs, or novelties; motion picture theaters; sports and athletic events; musical concerts; lectures; scenic, historic, recreational, and amusement facilities; real estate brokers; salespersons; stores employing fewer than 5 persons; vending machines; bowling alleys; fireworks displays; mobile homes salespersons; public dancing. Isolated transactions by persons not engaged in sale, transfer, or exchange of property as a business are exempt. **Meal and Rest Periods** — In absence of collective bargaining or other agreement, worker may be employed or permitted to work for no more than six consecutive hours at one time without at least 30 consecutive minutes of rest time, except in cases of emergency in which there is danger to property, life, public safety, or health. Rest time may be used as meal time. Inapplicable to place of employment where fewer than three employees are on duty at one time, and nature of work allows employees frequent breaks during work day. |

## Comparison Chart — State Hours Laws — Contd.

| STATE | REQUIREMENTS AND PROVISIONS |
|---|---|
| Maryland | **Maximum Hours before Overtime** — 40-hour week.<br><br>**Overtime Pay** — 1½ times regular pay for hours in excess of maximum.<br><br>**Employees Covered** — All employees, except: employees of amusement or recreational establishments operating less than seven months in calendar year and with average receipts for any six months are less than ⅓ of average receipts for other six months; those covered by Federal Motor Carrier Act or Part I of Interstate Commerce Act; employees of hotel, motel, or restaurant, or institution other than hospital engaged in care of the sick, the aged, or the mentally ill who are paid for work in excess of 48 hours in any week at 1½ regular rate; salespersons, partspersons, or mechanics primarily selling or servicing automobiles, trailers, trucks, or machinery in nonmanufacturing firm; gasoline service station employees; bowling establishment employees paid 1½ times regular rate for hours in excess of 48 per week; taxicab drivers; country club employees; those working for nonprofit employer furnishing temporary at-home services for sick, aged, mentally ill, or handicapped; agricultural workers exempted by FLSA.<br><br>**Special Occupations** — Agricultural workers: 60-hour week. Railroads: 8-hour day for telephone and telegraph operators handling train movements under "block system," except when fewer than nine passenger or 20 freight trains each way in 24 hours. Cotton and Wool Manufacturing: 10-hour day for employees manufacturing cotton or woolen yarns, fabrics, or domestics, except during repairs, improvements, firing up, and readying machinery. Tobacco Warehouses (Baltimore only): hours from 7 a.m. to 12 noon and 1 p.m. to 6 p.m. for tobacco warehouse employees.<br><br>**Day of Rest** — Retail establishment may operate on Sunday, provided that all employees other than managerial, professional, or part-time employees (fewer than 25 hours per week) are permitted to choose either Sunday or employee's Sabbath as day of rest. State law lists exceptions and special rules for each county.<br><br>**Meal and Rest Periods** — No general provision. |
| Massachusetts | **Maximum Hours before Overtime** — 40-hour week.<br><br>**Overtime Pay** — 1½ times regular pay for hours in excess of maximum; commissions, drawing accounts, bonuses, or other incentive pay based on sales or production are excluded in computing regular rate and overtime pay. 1½ times regular rate for Sunday labor in retail establishments, except for employer with fewer than seven employees including proprietor, and workers in bona fide executive, administrative, or professional capacity earning over $200 a week. Employees in retail establishments required to work on the second Monday in October (Columbus Day) must be paid 1½ times their regular rate.<br><br>**Employees Covered** — All employees, except: caretakers of residential property if furnished living quarters and paid at least $36 a week; golf caddies, news carriers, or child performers; those in bona fide executive, administrative, or professional capacity or training for such positions and earning more than $80 a week; outside salespersons and buyers; learners, apprentices, or handicapped, with special license; those catching or taking aquatic animal or vegetable life; public telephone switchboard operators; drivers and helpers under Interstate Commerce Commission or Railway Labor Act; those employed in business determined seasonal by Commissioner and existing not more than 120 days in any year; seafarers; employees of passenger motor carrier, as defined; hotel, motel, and restaurant employees; garage and gasoline station workers; those working in hospital, home for the aged, nonprofit school or summer camp; agricultural laborers; employees in amusement park operating not more than 150 days a year. |

## Comparison Chart — State Hours Laws — Contd.

| STATE | REQUIREMENTS AND PROVISIONS |
|---|---|
| **Massachusetts, Contd.** | **Special Occupations** — Railways: 9-hour day within 11 consecutive hours for employees of street, electric, or elevated railways. Motor Transportation: 12-hour day followed by 8 hours off duty, or 16 hours followed by 10 hours off duty, with 3 hours or more breaking continuity, for motor vehicle drivers.<br>**Day of Rest** — For each seven consecutive days worked, employees must have 24 consecutive hours of rest, including unbroken period between 8 a.m. and 5 p.m., except in emergency for employees in workshop or manufacturing, mechanical, or mercantile establishments. Employees working on Sunday must be allowed 24 consecutive hours without work in the six days following, except employees in manufacture or distribution of gas, electricity, milk, or water; hotels, transportation, sale, or delivery of food by establishments other than restaurants; railroads or railways; janitors; employees whose only Sunday duties are: setting sponges in bakeries, caring for live animals, caring for machinery, maintaining fires, preparing, printing, publishing, or delivery of newspapers, farm or personal services, pharmacists in drug stores, or any labor called for by an emergency. Sunday labor prohibited, except works of necessity or charity, or employment specifically exempted.<br>**Meal and Rest Periods** — No person shall be required to work for more than six hours a day without an interval of at least 30 minutes for a meal, with certain specified exceptions. |
| **Michigan** | **Maximum Hours before Overtime** — 40-hour week. Ten hours a day in factories, workshops, salt blocks, saw-mills, logging or lumber camps, booms or drivers, mines or other places used for mechanical or manufacturing purposes.<br>**Overtime Pay** — 1½ times regular pay for hours in excess of maximum.<br>**Employees Covered** — All employees, except: those in bona fide executive, administrative, or professional capacity; elected and appointed government officials; workers in amusement or recreational establishment operating not more than seven months in calendar year; employees in all branches of agriculture; employees not subject to minimum hourly wage provisions.<br>**Special Occupations** — 216 hours in 28 days (or equivalent hour/day ratio for periods from seven to 27 days) for public fire protection and law enforcement employees, including security personnel in correctional institution. Motor Transportation: 10 hours in any 15 consecutive hours followed by 8 hours off duty for drivers of motor trucks and truck tractors, except those operating government vehicles or operating within 50-mile radius of domicile, unless emergency, as defined.<br>**Day of Rest** — Barber shops and pawn shops must be closed on Sunday.<br>**Meal and Rest Periods** — No general provision. |

## Comparison Chart — State Hours Laws — Contd.

| STATE | REQUIREMENTS AND PROVISIONS |
|---|---|
| **Minnesota** | **Maximum Hours before Overtime** — 48-hour week.<br><br>**Overtime Pay** — 1½ times regular pay for hours in excess of maximum. State and political subdivisions may grant time off at a rate of 1½ hours per hour worked in excess of 48 per week to public employees. Health care facility may agree with employees to accept work period of 14 days, with overtime pay due for workers who work more than 80 hours in 14 days or 8 hours in one day.<br><br>**Employees Covered** — All employees, except: those subject to agreement under Sec. 7(b)(2) of FLSA; executive, administrative, professional employees; outside salespersons; elected officials; taxi drivers; seasonal camp or ski resort employees; sugar beet hand laborers on piece rate basis, when hourly pay exceeds minimum wage by 40 cents; salespersons, partspersons, and mechanics on commission or incentive basis for retail employer selling or servicing automobiles, trailers, trucks, or farm implements; those employed in farm silo construction or installing appurtenant equipment on unit or piece rate basis, when pay exceeds minimum wage; caretakers and other employees of residential building living on-site when available but not performing duties; companions of aged or infirm, under certain conditions.<br><br>**Special Occupations** — Motor Transportation: 12 hours for truck drivers, unless transporting own products or fresh vegetables between farms, canneries, and viner stations. Railroads: 14 hours followed by 9 hours rest (less if worker requests). 16 hours out of 24, followed by 8 hours rest for those engaged in movement of trains, except in defined emergencies.<br><br>**Day of Rest** — All trades, manufacturing, and mechanical employments are prohibited on Sunday, with certain specified exceptions. Violations are misdemeanors, but it is sufficient defense that another day of the week is kept uniformly as holy time and that the act complained of was done in such a manner as not to disturb others in observance of the Sabbath.<br><br>**Meal and Rest Periods** — Adequate time within each four consecutive hours of work to visit nearest convenient restroom. Employee working 8 hours or more must have sufficient time to eat a meal; meal time need not be paid. |
| **Mississippi** | **Maximum Hours before Overtime** — No general provision.<br><br>**Overtime Pay** — No general provision.<br>**Employees Covered** — No general provision.<br>**Special Occupations** — No provision.<br>**Day of Rest** — Sunday work prohibited except for necessary household work; labor on railroads, steamboats, and common and contract motor vehicle carriers; telegraph or telephone lines; street railways; newspapers; livery stables; ice houses; garages and gasoline stations; meat markets; manufacturing operations which operate continuously; church or religious societies.<br>**Meal and Rest Period** — No general provision. |
| **Missouri** | **Maximum Hours before Overtime** — 40 hours per week.<br><br>**Overtime Pay** — 1½ times regular rate for hours in excess of maximum.<br>**Employees Covered** — All except agricultural employers.<br>**Special Occupations** — Mining: 8 hours within 24 for workers engaged in mining or crushing rocks, or in reducing, roasting, refining, or smelting minerals in ores for mechanical, chemical, manufacturing, or smelting company. Public Works: 8-hour day in 24 hours for laborers and mechanics on public works in second class city. Railroads: 9-hour day in 24 hours for employees operating interlocking tower. Amusement or recreation business employees (as defined in FLSA): 52-hour week before overtime.<br>**Day of Rest** — It is unlawful to sell or expose for sale at retail on Sunday a number of specified articles. County with population over 400,000 may exempt itself by referendum; many counties and the City of St. Louis have done so.<br>**Meal and Rest Periods** — No general provision. |

## Comparison Chart — State Hours Laws — Contd.

| STATE | REQUIREMENTS AND PROVISIONS |
|-------|------------------------------|
| Montana | **Maximum Hours before Overtime** — 8 hours per day; 40 hours per week. 48-hour week for students employed by seasonal amusement or recreational area who are furnished with board, lodging, or other facilities.<br>**Overtime Pay** — 1½ times regular pay for hours in excess of maximum.<br>**Employees Covered** — All employees, except: farming and stock raising employees; those subject to U.S. Department of Transportation or Part I of Interstate Commerce Act; outside buyers of raw dairy and poultry products; salespersons, partspersons, or mechanics on commission or contract selling or servicing automobiles, trucks, mobile homes, recreational vehicles, or farm implements for retail establishment; salespersons selling trailers, boats, or aircraft to ultimate purchaser; drivers and helpers making local deliveries and paid on delivery payment plan, with permit; agricultural workers; those engaged in supplying and storing water for agriculture; employees of country elevators with no more than five workers; taxicab drivers; spouses employed by nonprofit educational institution as resident children's parents and receiving board, lodging, and $10,000 a year; workers planting, tending, cruising, surveying, felling, or transporting trees or forestry products to mill, plant, or transportation terminal, if employed by employee with eight or fewer workers; municipal or county employees with collectively bargained workweek of 40 hours in 7-day period; public firefighters with collective bargaining agreement; police officers in third class city or police department employees in first or second class city working under chief's schedule; sheriff's or public safety employees working under established work period; students in distributive education program of accredited agency; domestic workers; caretakers of children directly employed by household head; certain hospital employees; employer's relatives dependent on employer for at least half their support; volunteers in nonprofit organization; handicapped whose work is incidental to training or evaluation program or who are severely impaired and unable to compete; those in executive, administrative, or professional capacity; and federal employees.<br>**Special Occupations** — Mining: 8-hour day for workers in underground and strip mines or workings, except in emergencies. 8 hours in 24 hours for hoisting engineers, under certain conditions. Motor Transportation: 8-hour day followed by 12 hours rest in every 24 hours for drivers and attendants, except in emergencies. Railroads: 12 consecutive hours, or 16 aggregate hours in 24, followed by 8 hours off duty, except during emergencies. Public Amusements: 8 hour day, 48 hour week for persons employed or working in any carnival, circus, derby show, walkathon, marathon dance, race, or walk, or other endurance contest. Retail stores: 8-hour day and 48-hour week. Telephone operators: Nine hours in 24 hour period. State and Municipal Governments and School Districts: 8-hour day, except firefighters with work period established by collective bargaining agreement. 40-hour workweek of four consecutive 10-hour days for employees of road and bridge departments. 8-hour days for workers in cement plants, quarries, and hydroelectric dams, except in emergency. Sugar refineries: 8-hour day except in emergency. Restaurants: 8-hour day, 48-hour week.<br>**Day of Rest** — No general provision.<br>**Meal and Rest Periods** — No general provision. |

## Comparison Chart — State Hours Laws — Contd.

| STATE | REQUIREMENTS AND PROVISIONS |
|---|---|
| Nebraska | **Maximum Hours before Overtime** — No general provision.<br>**Overtime Pay** — No general provision.<br>**Employees Covered** — No general provision.<br>**Special Occupations** — Motor Transportation: 12 hours in 24 hours for motor carrier employees (passenger or freight), except taxicab drivers within city or village and in emergencies. Railroads: 16 consecutive hours followed by 10 continuous hours of rest, or 16 hours aggregate in 24-hour period followed by 8 hours of rest. 9-hour work period for employees in places operating day and night, and 13 hours in places operating during day only, except in certain emergencies allowing up to 4 more hours three times a week.<br>**Day of Rest** — No general provision.<br>**Meal and Rest Periods** — Employees in assembly plant, workshop, or mechanical establishments are required to have at least one-half hour lunch period between 12 noon and 1 p.m. without having to remain on premises, unless establishment operates in three 8-hour shifts each 24-hour period. |
| Nevada | **Maximum Hours before Overtime** — 8-hour day, 40-hour week, unless mutually agreed 10-hour day, 4-day week.<br>**Overtime Pay** — 1½ times regular pay for hours in excess of maximum.<br>**Employees Covered** — All employees, except: those not covered by state minimum wage provisions; those paid not less than 1½ times the minimum wage; outside buyers; retail salespersons on commission if regular rate more than 1½ times the minimum rate and half of compensation comes from commissions; those in executive, administrative, or professional capacity; employees covered by collective bargaining agreement; motor carrier drivers, drivers' helpers, loaders, and mechanics subject to Motor Carrier Act; air carrier and railroad employees; drivers and helpers making local deliveries and paid on trip-rate or other delivery plan basis; taxicab and limousine drivers; agricultural workers; employees of businesses with annual gross sales less than $250,000; salespersons and mechanics primarily selling or servicing automobiles, trucks, or farm equipment.<br>**Special Occupations** — Mining: 8 hours in 24-hour period for employees in underground and surface mines, except: in emergencies; when employee voluntarily agrees to more hours; when maintenance crew needs to complete work; or if no qualified worker available for relief. Smelting: 8-hour day in smelters and other places reducing or refining ore, except in emergencies or when employee voluntarily agrees to more hours. Cement: 8-hour day, except in emergencies. Railroads: 16 hours followed by 10 hours off duty, or 16 hours aggregate in 24 hours followed by 8 hours off duty. 8 hours, followed by 16 hours off duty, for employees handling orders for movement of trains. Motor Transportation: Maximum hours subject to order of public service commission.<br>**Day of Rest** — No general provision.<br>**Meal and Rest Periods** — At least one-half hour for meal for a continuous work period of eight hours. Rest periods of 10 minutes for every 4 hours worked. |

Comparison Chart — State Hours Laws — Contd.

| STATE | REQUIREMENTS AND PROVISIONS |
|---|---|
| New Hampshire | **Maximum Hours before Overtime** — 8-hour day, 40-hour week.<br>**Overtime Pay** — 1 ½ times regular pay for hours in excess of maximum.<br>**Employees Covered** — All employees, except: those working in amusement, seasonal, or recreational establishment operating no more than seven months in calendar year or that received at least 75 percent of income during any six months of previous year; and employees covered by FLSA.<br>**Special Occupations** — 10-hour day, 48-hour week for manual or mechanical labor in manufacturing. Regular employees in mercantile establishments during the seven-day period immediately preceding Christmas Day may work overtime, but weekly average for year may not exceed 54 hours. Laundry workers may be employed up to 10 ¼ hours per day, 60 hours per week, for up to three months of the year, with special license from commissioner.<br>**Day of Rest** — Employers in manufacturing or mercantile establishments are required to give all employees a 24-hour rest period every 7 days. Employers in commercial, industrial, transportation, or communication establishments permitted to operate on Sunday are required to allow employees 24 hours' rest during the 6-day period thereafter, except for employers in manufacture or distribution of gas, electricity, milk, or water; hotels, restaurants, drug stores, livery stables, garages; transportation, sale, or delivery of food; janitors, guards, firefighters, or caretakers; employees whose Sunday duties include setting sponges in bakeries, caring for live animals, caring for machinery and plant equipment; preparation, printing, publication, sale, or delivery of newspapers; farm labor or personal services; labor due to emergency; theaters or motion picture houses, canning of perishable goods, telegraph and telephone offices. Employers may be exempt from Sunday provisions where mutual employer-employee agreements are reached, approval is given by the Commissioner, and it appears to be in the best interests of all concerned.<br>**Meal and Rest Periods** — Employer may not require employee to work more than five consecutive hours without granting one-half hour lunch or eating period, unless it is feasible for employee to eat during performance of work and employer permits worker to do so. |
| New Jersey | **Maximum Hours before Overtime** — 40-hour week.<br>**Overtime Pay** — 1 ½ times regular pay for hours in excess of maximum.<br>**Employees Covered** — All employees, except: farm workers; hotel employees; those employed by passenger bus company; those raising or caring for livestock; employees in bona fide executive, administrative, or professional capacity; those working for nonprofit or religious summer camp, conference, or retreat.<br>**Special Occupations** — Motor Transportation: 12 continuous hours (or 12 hours in aggregate of 16 hours) followed by 8 hours off duty. Street and Elevated Railways: 12 consecutive hours, except in emergencies. First Process of Farm Products: 1 ½ times regular rate for hours in excess of 48 per week, or 10 per day, for a period not to exceed 10 weeks; 1 ½ times regular rate for hours in excess of 50 per week or 10 per day for a period up to 10 weeks.<br>**Day of Rest** — It is unlawful on Sunday for any person to engage in the business of selling, either at retail, wholesale, or by auction, certain specified articles except as works of necessity and charity or as isolated transactions not in the usual course of business.<br>**Meal and Rest Periods** — No general provision. |
| New Mexico | **Maximum Hours before Overtime** — 10-hour day, 70-hour, 7-day week for hotels, restaurants, and eating houses.<br>**Overtime Pay** — 1 ½ times regular pay for hours in excess of maximum.<br>**Employees Covered** — All employees in hotels, restaurants, and eating houses, except: workers in interstate commerce, whose working hours are regulated by federal law; employees of hospitals or sanitariums, registered or practical nurses, midwives, domestic employees. |

## Comparison Chart — State Hours Laws — Contd.

| STATE | REQUIREMENTS AND PROVISIONS |
|---|---|
| New Mexico, Contd. | **Special Occupations** — Motor Vehicle drivers: 10 hours, following 8 consecutive hours off duty; 60 hours in any seven consecutive days. Cotton Ginning Workers: exempt, if employed for 14 or fewer weeks of the year. Railroad Transportation: 10 consecutive hours rest following 16 consecutive hours work. 8 hours off after 16 hours aggregate work in 24 hours for workers in the movement of rolling stock, engines, or trains, except crews of wrecking or relief trains and sleeping car employees.<br>**Day of Rest** — No general provision.<br>**Meal and Rest Periods** — Not less than one-half hour excluded from working day. |
| New York | **Maximum Hours before Overtime** — 40-hour week for most employees; 44-hour week for resident employees.<br>**Overtime Pay** — 1½ times regular pay for hours in excess of maximum.<br>**Employees Covered** — All employees, except part-time babysitters and live-in companions; farmworkers; bona fide executives, administrators, and professionals; outside salespersons; taxi-cab drivers, volunteers for nonprofit organization; members of religious order; sextons; learners and trainees in nonprofit institution, under certain conditions; and counselors and employees in children's summer camp.<br>**Special Occupations** — Motor Transportation: 8 hours off-duty after 15 hours in 24-hour period, or 10 hours in 15-hour period. No more than 60 hours per week. Pharmacies: No more than 70 hours per week, except 6 hours overtime may be worked if succeeding week is shortened so that aggregate hours for two weeks does not exceed 132; 54 hours per week, or two-week aggregate of 108 hours in cities over 1,000,000 population. Public Work Contractors: 8-hour day, 5-day week for laborers, workers, and mechanics, except in extraordinary emergency. Railroads: Employee operating trains may not exceed 16 hours, followed by 10 hours off duty, or aggregate of 16 hours in 24, with 8 hours off duty. Street or Elevated Railways: 10 consecutive hours in any day, including ½ hour for dinner. Brickyards: 10 hour day, no work prior to 7 a.m. Work in compressed air limited by board orders.<br>**Day of Rest** — At least 24 consecutive hours of rest in each calendar week must be allowed employees by factory, mercantile establishments, hotel, restaurant, freight or passenger elevator in any building or place, including janitors, superintendents, supervisors, managers, and guards in warehouses, storage houses, offices, dwellings, apartments, lofts, and other buildings and structures; projectionists; firefighters; employees in places where legitimate stage productions are presented. Employers operating on Sunday must post notices listing employees scheduled to work and designating day of rest for each of them. All labor on Sunday is prohibited, except works of charity and necessity. All trades, manufacturing, agricultural, or mechanical employments on Sunday are prohibited, except when the same are works of necessity. All manner of public selling or offering for sale of any property is prohibited with certain specified exceptions; provision is inapplicable to those who uniformly keep another day of the week as holy time. One day a week may be set aside for rest and relaxation by owner of business or commercial enterprise. However, retail or merchant association or organization shall not have right to determine a day of rest and relaxation for its members. No provision of law shall be construed to prohibit any owner from doing business seven days a week where any other law, rule, or regulation does not specifically prohibit such activity.<br>**Meal and Rest Periods** — Person employed in mercantile or other covered establishments and occupations shall be allowed at least 45 minutes and person employed in factories shall be allowed at least 60 minutes for a noon day meal. Employees on a shift starting before noon and continuing later than 7 p.m. allowed an additional meal period of at least 20 minutes between 5 p.m. and 7 p.m. Commissioner may grant permits for shorter meal periods. |

## Comparison Chart — State Hours Laws — Contd.

| STATE | REQUIREMENTS AND PROVISIONS |
|---|---|
| North Carolina | **Maximum Hours before Overtime** — 45-hour week. 8-hour day and 80 hours in 14-day period for hospital and nursing home employees, if employees notified in advance.<br>**Overtime Pay** — 1½ times regular pay for hours in excess of maximum.<br>**Employees Covered** — All employees, except: those working for an employer with fewer than 3 employees; drivers, drivers' helpers, loaders, and mechanics, as defined by FLSA; taxicab drivers; seafarers; railroad and air carrier employees; salespersons and mechanics employed by automotive, truck, farm implement, trailer, boar, or aircraft dealer; child care or other live-in workers in home for dependent children; radio/TV announcers, performers, news editors, and chief engineers; agricultural and domestic workers; babysitters; pages in state legislature and governor's office; volunteers in medical, educational, religious, or non-profit organization where no employer-employee relationship; those confined in public penal, correctional, or mental institution; employees of outdoor drama theaters except ushers, ticket takers, and parking attendants; those working in children's summer camp or seasonal religious or nonprofit educational conference center; employees in seafood industry through first sale; employer's spouse, child, parent, or qualified dependent under state tax laws; those in bona fide executive, administrative, professional, or outside sales capacity; employee of employer with two or fewer workers in any workweek; and public employees, including those in seasonal recreation program.<br>**Special Occupations** — Railroads: 16 consecutive hours followed by 10 hours rest, or 16 aggregate hours in 24 hours followed by 8 hours rest. 9-hour day for employees handling movement of trains by telegraph or telephone in place operating day and night, and 13-hour day in place operating during day only, with 4 more hours a day not over three times a week in emergencies. State Institutions: 12 hours in any 24 hours or 84 hours in one week for employees of state correctional institution and Dorothea Dix, Broughton, and Cherry Hill Hospitals (unless emergency determined by superintendent), except for: state prison, institution controlled by Commissioner of Highways and Public Works, and hospital doctors and superintendents.<br>**Day of Rest** — Board of county commissioners has power to regulate sale of merchandise on Sundays in certain designated counties.<br>**Meal and Rest Periods** — No general provision. |
| North Dakota | **Maximum Hours before Overtime** — 40 hours per week. 8-hour day, 56-hour week, for city employees except: elected public officers, police officers, firefighters, city department heads. Maximum of 140 hours in any two week period, except fire department chief in any city with population of 20,000 or more.<br>**Overtime Pay** — 1½ times regular pay for hours in excess of maximum.<br>**Employees Covered** — All employees except those in domestic service; professional, technical, clerical, and similar occupations, earning $250 or more per week; management and management trainees spending more than 50 percent of their time in management duties; or employment exempted by state legislature, judicial decision, or federal preemption.<br>**Special Occupations** — Railroads: 12 hours, followed by 10 hours of rest.<br>**Day of Rest** — It is forbidden on Sunday to conduct business or labor for profit as usual or to operate a business open to the public, or to cause, direct, or authorize employee or agent to do so, with some exceptions. Not applicable to person who in good faith observes day other than Sunday as the Sabbath.<br>**Meal and Rest Periods** — 30 minute uninterrupted meal time between third and fifth hours of each shift. |

## Comparison Chart — State Hours Laws — Contd.

| STATE | REQUIREMENTS AND PROVISIONS |
|-------|------------------------------|
| Ohio | **Maximum Hours before Overtime** — 40-hour week. 8-hour day in mechanical, manufacturing, and mining businesses, unless contract otherwise specifies.<br>**Overtime Pay** — 1½ times regular pay in excess of maximum.<br>**Employees Covered** — All employees, except: agricultural workers; individual working for employer with annual gross sales of less than $150,000; federal employees; babysitters and companions; outside salespersons; newspaper deliverers; and employees exempt under FLSA.<br>**Special Occupations** — Motor Transportation: 14 consecutive hours (or 14 aggregate hours in 24 hours) followed by 8 hours off duty. Railroads and Railways: 15 hours, followed by 8 hours of rest (regulated so that employee has 8 consecutive hours off in each 24 hours).<br>**Day of Rest** — No general provision.<br>**Meal and Rest Periods** — No general provision. |
| Oklahoma | **Maximum Hours before Overtime** — No general provision.<br>**Overtime Pay** — No general provision.<br>**Employees Covered** — No general provision.<br>**Special Occupations** — No provision.<br>**Day of Rest** — It is unlawful to do any servile work or to work at any trade, manufacturing, or mechanical employment on Sunday, except for works of charity or necessity and other specified exemptions.<br>**Meal and Rest Periods** — No general provision. |
| Oregon | **Maximum Hours before Overtime** — 10-hour day and 40-hour week. Waiting and on-call time may be considered hours worked.<br>**Overtime Pay** — 1½ times regular pay, or 1½ times regular price for piece work, for hours in excess of maximum.<br>**Employees Covered** — Employees in mill, factory, or manufacturing establishment, except those subject to collective bargaining agreement where employer and labor organization have agreed on hours and overtime, engaged as watch personnel, in necessary repairs, or in emergencies where life or property in imminent danger; and employees in cannery, drier, or packing plant that primarily processes products on farm, except agricultural workers.<br>**Special Occupations** — Lumber: 8-hour day and 48-hour week for workers in saw, planing, and shingle mills and logging camps with 3 hours overtime permitted, except for: logging train crews; watch personnel; firefighters; those engaged in necessary repairs, emergencies, or transporting workers; and certain other personnel. Mining: 8 consecutive hours for those working in underground metal mines, excluding those in first stage of mine development.<br>**Day of Rest** — No general provision.<br>**Meal and Rest Periods** — Employees shall receive meal period of not less than 30 minutes within first five hours and one minute of reporting for work. Where employees cannot be relieved of all duties, a period in which to eat while continuing to work is permitted, provided time is not deducted from employees' hours. Employer may apply for exemption. Rest period of at least 10 minutes per four hours worked, except for employees covered by collective bargaining agreement. For workers employed 24 hours or more at a time, meal and sleeping time may be excluded by agreement. |

## Comparison Chart — State Hours Laws — Contd.

| STATE | REQUIREMENTS AND PROVISIONS |
|---|---|
| Pennsylvania | **Maximum Hours before Overtime** — 40-hour week. 10-hour day, 48-hour, 6-day week for seasonal farm workers.<br>**Overtime Pay** — 1½ times regular pay for hours in excess of maximum.<br>**Employees Covered** — All employees, except: students in seasonal occupations excluded by regulation; seafarers; salespersons, partspersons, and mechanics primarily selling or servicing automobiles, trailers, trucks, farm implements, or aircraft for retail dealer; taxicab drivers; certain radio/TV station employees; nonseasonal farm labor; domestic workers; newspaper deliverers; executive, administrative, professional employees; outside salespersons; golf caddies; employees processing maple sap; movie theater employees.<br>**Special Occupations** — Agriculture: 10-hour day, 48-hour, 6-day week for seasonal farm workers, regardless of number of employers. Mining: 8 hours within 24 hours for hoisting engineers in anthracite mines. Railway Transportation: 12-hour day. Bakeries: 6-day week (between 6 p.m. Sunday and 6 p.m. Saturday) for bakery and confectionery workers. Compressed Air: Certain hours, as defined.<br>**Day of Rest** — Worldly employment or business on Sunday is prohibited, except for works of necessity and charity and wholesome recreation. Special provisions for particular types of selling activity, sports, etc. Motion picture places must allow each employee one calendar day of 24 consecutive hours of rest in each calendar week.<br>**Meal and Rest Periods** — No seasonal farm worker shall be permitted to work more than five hours continuously without meal or rest period of at least 30 minutes, which shall not be considered part of labor hours. No period of less than 30 minutes shall be deemed to interrupt a continuous work period. |
| Puerto Rico | **Maximum Hours before Overtime** — 8-hour day, 40-hour week.<br>**Overtime Pay** — Twice the regular pay for hours in excess of maximum, except: 1½ times the regular pay for employees covered by FLSA. Board order or collective bargaining agreement may fix other working or compensation standards.<br>**Employees Covered** — All employees, except those in executive, administrative, or professional capacity; traveling agents and mobile salespersons; labor union officers and organizers, when acting as such; domestic workers (who are entitled to one day of rest a week); government employees, except those engaged in proprietary endeavors; workers in continuous operation commercial establishments, if exempted by Secretary of Labor; and drivers and chauffeurs on commission.<br>**Special Occupations** — No provision.<br>**Day of Rest** — No general provision.<br>**Meal and Rest Periods** — At least one hour must be allowed for meals unless shorter period is fixed for convenience of employee, stipulated by employee and employer and approved by Secretary of Labor. Employee who works during mealtime shall receive double-time. |

## Comparison Chart — State Hours Laws — Contd.

| STATE | REQUIREMENTS AND PROVISIONS |
|---|---|
| **Rhode Island** | **Maximum Hours before Overtime** — 40-hour week.<br>**Overtime Pay** — 1½ times regular pay for hours in excess of maximum and for Sunday or holiday work.<br>**Employees Covered** — All employees except: those working in summer camp open no more than six months a year; state employees on "non-standard" work schedule; municipal police and firefighters; executive, administrative, or professional employees; salaried employees of nonprofit national voluntary health agency who elect to take time off for hours worked in excess of 40 hours; agricultural workers; domestic employees; drivers, drivers' helpers, loaders, and mechanics of motor carrier under hour regulation of U.S. Department of Transportation.<br>**Special Occupations** — Motor Transportation: 12 hours followed by 8 hours off duty, or 16 aggregate hours in 24 hours followed by 10 hours off duty, except in emergencies. Street Railways: 12 consecutive hours followed by 10 hours off duty during 24 hours for conductors and motormen, except for emergencies or holidays when extra compensation must be paid.<br>**Day of Rest** — No person may engage in gainful activities in any store, mill, or factory; in commercial occupations; in work of transportation or communication; or in industrial processes on Sundays, except work of necessity and charity and in licensed athletic meets and contests. Unlawful for employer to require or permit employee to work on Sunday except work of absolute necessity. "Employee" does not include individuals employed in certain specified trades. Town councils may grant licenses for certain retail sales on Sundays; certain other retail and service businesses may be carried on without a license. Retail employees who work on Sunday are compensated at no less than time and one-half and must be guaranteed at least four hours of employment, except for retail establishments that prepare or sell bakery products and pharmacies.<br>**Meal and Rest Periods** — At least 20 minutes must be allowed for meals after 6 consecutive hours of work, except telephone operators who are not required to operate switchboard continuously but are able to sleep during considerable part of the night. Work period of 6½ hours allowed if employment ends no later than 1 p.m. and worker is dismissed for the day. Work period of 7½ hours allowed if employment ends no later than 2 p.m. and worker has sufficient opportunity to eat on the job. |
| **South Carolina** | **Maximum Hours before Overtime** — No general provision.<br>**Overtime Pay** — No general provision.<br>**Employees Covered** — No general provision.<br>**Special Occupations** — No provision.<br>**Day of Rest** — It is unlawful to employ others to work on Sunday except certain works of necessity or charity and in certain specified businesses and services; sale of certain specified items also prohibited. Not applicable to any business or service that was lawful prior to April 7, 1962. Moving pictures, athletic sports, and musical concerts lawful after 2 p.m. on Sunday, but not between 7 p.m. and 9 p.m. Sunday work exemptions granted to manufacture and finishing of textile products and operation of machine shops provided no person is required to work who is conscientiously opposed to Sunday work. Sunday work prohibited in manufacturing or mercantile establishments, except cafeterias and restaurants, with certain exceptions.<br>**Meal and Rest Periods** — No general provision. |

## Comparison Chart — State Hours Laws — Contd.

| STATE | REQUIREMENTS AND PROVISIONS |
|---|---|
| South Dakota | **Maximum Hours before Overtime** — 8 hours per day for adult employees in manufacturing or mechanical establishment, unless agreement to contrary. 10 hours per day for all employees, unless agreement to contrary. <br> **Overtime Pay** — No general provision. <br> **Employees Covered** — No general provision. <br> **Special Occupations** — 10-hour day unless express agreement to contrary. 8-hour day for employees in manufacturing or mechanical establishment unless express agreement to contrary, except those employed by week, month, or year. Railroads: 16 hours followed by 10 hours off duty, or 16 aggregate hours in 24 hours followed by 8 hours off duty. Municipal firefighters: 212 hours in 28-day period or 204 hours during 27 day work period, as agreed. <br> **Day of Rest** — No general provision. <br> **Meal and Rest Periods** — No general provision. |
| Tennessee | No state provision. |
| Texas | **Maximum Hours before Overtime** — No general provision. <br> **Overtime Pay** — No general provision. <br> **Employees Covered** — No general provision. <br> **Special Occupations** — Railroads: 16 hours, followed by 10 hours of rest. <br> **Day of Rest** — Employer may not require employee to work seven consecutive days in retail establishment and may not deny employee at least 24 consecutive hours off for rest or worship in seven-day period. Employer must accommodate employee's religious practices unless it can be shown that to do so would constitute undue business hardship, and may not require employee to work during period employee requests to be off to attend one regular worship service a week of employee's religion. No employer may compel employee to sell or offer for sale motor vehicle on both consecutive Saturday and Sunday. <br> **Meal and Rest Periods** — No general provision. |
| Utah | **Maximum Hours before Overtime** — No general provision. <br> **Overtime Pay** — No general provision. <br> **Employees Covered** — No general provision. <br> **Special Occupations** — Mining: 8-hour day for underground miners and those reducing or refining ores or metals, except in emergencies or with written certificate from industrial commission. 8½-hour day for hoisters and pumpers on underground pumps in continuous operation. Public Works: 40 hour workweek for state, county, or municipal works. 1½ times regular rate for all hours over 40 per week. <br> **Day of Rest** — No general provision. <br> **Meal and Rest Periods** — No general provision. |

## Comparison Chart — State Hours Laws — Contd.

| STATE | REQUIREMENTS AND PROVISIONS |
|---|---|
| Vermont | **Maximum Hours before Overtime** — 40-hour week.<br>**Overtime Pay** — 1½ times regular pay for hours in excess of maximum.<br>**Employees Covered** — All employees of employers with two or more workers, except: those in amusement or recreation industry not operating more than seven months in calendar year, or whose average receipts for any six months in preceding year not more than 1/3 of average receipts for other six months; employees of hotel, motel, restaurant; hospital, public health center, nursing and maternity home, therapeutic community residence, and community care home workers, provided employer pays biweekly, employee elects to be covered, and employee receives 1½ times regular rate for work in excess of 8 hours per day or 80 hours per biweekly period; transportation employees covered by FLSA; state employees.<br>**Special Occupations** — No provision.<br>**Day of Rest** — No general provision.<br>**Meal and Rest Periods** — No general provision. |
| Virginia | **Maximum Hours before Overtime** — No state provision.<br>**Overtime Pay** — No provision.<br>**Employees Covered** — No provision.<br>**Special Occupations** — No provision.<br>**Day of Rest** — No person shall engage in work, labor, or business or employ others to engage in same on Sunday, with certain exceptions; inapplicable to works of charity conducted solely for charitable purposes by any person or nonprofit organization. Except in emergency, employer shall allow employee at least 24 consecutive hours of rest in each calendar week in addition to regular rest periods normally allowed or legally required in each work day. Nonmanagerial employee upon written notice is entitled to choose Sunday as a day of rest; however, nonmanagerial employee who conscientiously believes that the seventh day of the week ought to be observed as a Sabbath and actually refrains from all secular business and labor on that day shall be entitled to choose the seventh day of the week as a day of rest. Provision not applicable to persons engaged in certain specified industries or businesses.<br>**Meal and Rest Periods** — No general provision. |

## Comparison Chart — State Hours Laws — Contd.

| STATE | REQUIREMENTS AND PROVISIONS |
|---|---|
| **Washington** | **Maximum Hours before Overtime** — 40-hour week.<br>**Overtime Pay** — 1½ times regular pay, or 1½ times regular piece work rate (unless specifically exempted), for hours in excess of maximum.<br>**Employees Covered** — All employees, except: seasonal hand harvest labor; casual labor about private home; bona fide executives, administrators, professionals, or outside salespersons; services for educational, charitable, religious, state or local governmental or nonprofit organization performed by non-employees; voluntary services by public employees; newspaper vendors or carriers; carriers regulated by Interstate Commerce Commission; employees in forest protection and fire prevention activities; charitable child care workers; resident, inmate, or patient of public correctional or rehabilitation institution; elected or appointed public officials; seafarers; workers requesting time off in lieu of overtime pay; seasonal workers at concessions and recreational establishments at agricultural fair employed not more than 14 days; agricultural workers;<br>**Special Occupations** — Firefighters and Law Enforcement Personnel: 240 hours in 28 consecutive days, or tours of duty in period of more than seven but less than 28 days which bear the same ratio to number of consecutive days in work period as 240 hours bears to 28 days. Mining: 8-hour day for coal miners working underground; 10-hour day for mining engineers, rope-riders, motormen, cagers, and others transporting miners in and out of mines, except in emergencies or weekly change of shift. Railroads: 12-hour day followed by 10 hours of rest, or 12 aggregate hours in 24 hours followed by 8 hours of rest, for those connected with movement of trains, except in emergencies. Domestic and Household Employees: 60-hour week, including hours on call, except in emergencies. Motor Carriers subject to rules of utilities and transportation commission.<br>**Day of Rest** — No general provision.<br>**Meal and Rest Periods** — 30 minute meal period beginning no less than two nor more than 5 hours from beginning of shift; additional 30 minute meal period prior to or during overtime period of three or more hours following normal workday, for all employees except volunteers, bona fide executives, administrators, professionals, or outside salespersons; or independent contractors. Rest periods of at least 10 minutes per four hours working time, applicable to same employees as meal periods. |
| **West Virginia** | **Maximum Hours before Overtime** — 40-hour week.<br>**Overtime Pay** — 1½ times regular pay for hours in excess of maximum.<br>**Employees Covered** — All employees except: salespersons, partspersons, or mechanics primarily engaged in selling or servicing automobiles, trailers, trucks, farm implements, or aircraft; employees exempt from the state minimum wage law.<br>**Special Occupations** — Railroads: 8-hour day in any 24 consecutive hours for telephone or telegraph operators spacing or blocking trains, handling train orders, or interlocking switches, except in cases of emergency, when operators may work 13 hours in 24, but for no longer than 2 days; operators may agree to work between 8 and 12 hours.<br>**Day of Rest** — Sunday work prohibited except in household or other work of necessity or charity; work of necessity or charity does not include selling at retail, wholesale, or auction but lengthy list of permitted Sunday activities exists. Exception also made for those who conscientiously observe Saturday as Sabbath as long as they do not compel others to work on Sunday.<br>**Meal and Rest Periods** — Where employee is required to be on duty 24 hours or more, employer and employee may agree on bona fide meal and sleeping periods; if no expressed or implied agreement is made, eight hours' sleeping time and lunch periods shall constitute hours worked. |

Comparison Chart — State Hours Laws — Contd.

| STATE | REQUIREMENTS AND PROVISIONS |
|---|---|
| Wisconsin | **Maximum Hours before Overtime** — 40-hour week; 44-hour week for restaurant employees.<br>**Overtime Pay** — 1½ times regular pay for hours in excess of maximum.<br>**Employees Covered** — Employees in manufacturing, mechanical, or mercantile establishment; beauty parlor; laundry; restaurant; confectionery store; telegraph or telephone office or exchange, or express or transportation company; and hotel. Exceptions: persons employed in farming, as defined; domestic household employees; employees in primarily executive, administrative, or professional capacity; outside salespersons, as defined; commission employees of retail and service establishments if 50 percent of earnings is in commissions, and 1½ times the minimum wage is received for all hours worked; drivers, drivers' helpers, loaders, or mechanics; common rail and air carrier employees; taxicab drivers; automobile, truck, farm implement, trailer, boat, motorcycle, snowmobile, recreational vehicle, or aircraft salespersons, partspersons, or mechanics; employees of recreational or amusement establishments operating seven months or less per year; employees of independent contractors in specified industries; movie theater employees; resident hospital and institution employees under agreement with employer; funeral establishment employees.<br>**Special Occupations** — Railroads: 16 hours followed by 10 hours of rest, or 16 aggregate hours in 24 hours followed by 8 hours of rest, except in specified emergencies. Motor Transportation: Motor Vehicle Department prescribes rules.<br>**Day of Rest** — Employees in factory or mercantile establishments are entitled to at least 24 consecutive hours of rest every seven consecutive days, with certain specified exceptions. Work on seventh day permitted in case of breakdown of machinery or equipment requiring immediate services of experienced and competent labor to prevent serious injury to person, damage to property, or suspension of essential operation.<br>**Meal and Rest Periods** — Employees must receive at least 30 minutes for each meal period reasonably close to usual meal period time or near middle of a shift. Shifts of more than six consecutive hours without a meal period should be avoided; requirements mandatory for minors under 18. |
| Wyoming | **Maximum Hours before Overtime** — No general provision.<br>**Overtime Pay** — No general provision.<br>**Employees Covered** — No general provision.<br>**Special Occupations** — Mining: 8-hour day in all underground mines and workings, except when employer-employee agreement for longer period not to exceed 16 hours in 24 hours.<br>**Day of Rest** — No general provision.<br>**Meal and Rest Periods** — No general provision. |

# APPENDIX H

# CHART OF OVERTIME COMPENSATION RULES FOR STATE AND LOCAL GOVERNMENT EMPLOYEES*

* Source: 52 Fed. Reg. 2012, at 2045 (1987) (to be codified at 29 C.F.R. §§553.230–553.233).

*Following is the text of Overtime Compensation Rules for police personnel and firefighters of state and local governments.*

## Overtime Compensation Rules

§ 553.230   Maximum hours standards for work periods of 7 to 28 days—section 7(k).

(a) For those employees engaged in fire protection activities who have a work period of at least 7 but less than 28 consecutive days, no overtime compensation is required under section 7(k) until the number of hours worked exceeds the number of hours which bears the same relationship to 212 as the number of days in the work period bears to 28.

(b) For those employees engaged in law enforcement activities (including security personnel in correctional institutions) who have a work period of at least 7 but less than 28 consecutive days, no overtime compensation is required under section 7(k) until the number of hours worked exceeds the number of hours which bears the same relationship to 171 as the number of days in the work period bears to 28.

(c) The ratio of 212 hours to 28 days for employees engaged in fire protection activities is 7.57 hours per day (rounded) and the ratio of 171 hours to 28 days for employees engaged in law enforcement activities is 6.11 hours per day (rounded). Accordingly, overtime compensation (in premium pay or compensatory time) is required for all hours worked in excess of the following maximum hours standards (rounded to the nearest whole hour):

| Work period (days) | Maximum hours standards | |
|---|---|---|
| | Fire Protection | Law enforcement |
| 28 | 212 | 171 |
| 27 | 204 | 165 |
| 26 | 197 | 159 |
| 25 | 189 | 153 |
| 24 | 182 | 147 |
| 23 | 174 | 141 |
| 22 | 167 | 134 |
| 21 | 159 | 128 |
| 20 | 151 | 122 |
| 19 | 144 | 116 |
| 18 | 136 | 110 |
| 17 | 129 | 104 |
| 16 | 121 | 98 |
| 15 | 114 | 92 |
| 14 | 106 | 86 |
| 13 | 98 | 79 |
| 12 | 91 | 73 |
| 11 | 83 | 67 |
| 10 | 76 | 61 |
| 9 | 68 | 55 |
| 8 | 61 | 49 |
| 7 | 53 | 43 |

§ 553.231   Compensatory time off.

(a) Law enforcement and fire protection employees who are subject to the section 7(k) exemption may receive compensatory time off in lieu of overtime pay for hours worked in excess of the maximum for their work period as set forth in §553.230. The rules for compensatory time off are set forth in §§553.20 through 553.28.

(b) Section 7(k) permits public agencies to balance the hours of work over an entire work period for law enforcement and fire protection employees. For example, if a firefighter's work period is 28 consecutive days and he or she works 80 hours in each of the first two weeks, but only 52 hours in the third week, and does not work in the fourth week, no overtime compensation (in cash wages or compensatory time) would be required since the total hours worked do not exceed 212 for the work period. If the same firefighter had a work period of only 14 days, overtime compensation or compensatory time off would be due for 54 hours (160 minus 106 hours) in the first 14-day work period.

§ 553.232   Overtime pay requirements.

If a public agency pays employees subject to section 7(k) for overtime hours worked in cash wages rather than compensatory time off, such wages must be paid at one and one-half times the employees' regular rates of pay. In addition, employees who have accrued the maximum 480 hours of compensatory time must be paid cash wages of time and one-half their regular rates of pay for overtime hours in excess of the maximum for the work period set forth in § 553.230.

§ 553.233   "Regular rate" defined.

The rules for computing an employee's "regular rate," for purposes of the Act's overtime pay requirements, are set forth in 29 CFR Part 778. These rules are applicable to employees for whom the section 7(k) exemption is claimed when overtime compensation is provided in cash wages. However, whenever the word "workweek" is used in Part 778, the words "work period" should be substituted.

# APPENDIX I

## DIRECTORY OF U.S. EQUAL EMPLOYMENT OPPORTUNITY COMMISSION ADMINISTRATIVE AND DISTRICT AREA OFFICES

## Equal Employment Opportunity Commission
## Administrative Offices

*Address: 1801 L Street, N.W., Washington, D.C. 20507*
*Public Information Telephone: (202) 663-4900*
*Toll-free: 800-USA-EEOC*

*(Created by Section 705 of Title VII of the 1964 Civil Rights Act)*

**Commissioners**

Evan J. Kemp, Jr. *(Chairman)*
Rosalie Gaull Silberman (Vice-Chairman)
Joy Cherian
Tony Gallegos

**Office of Review & Appeals**

Dolores L. Rozzi, Director

**Office of Legal Counsel**

Thomasina Rogers, Acting Legal Counsel

**Office of Inspector General**

William D. Miller, Inspector General

**Office of Program Operations**

James Troy, Director

**Program Research and Surveys Branch**

Joachim Neckere, Director

**Office of Communications and Legislative Affairs**

James C. Lafferty, Acting Director

**Office of Management**

R. Edison Elkins, Director

**Office of General Counsel**

Donald Livingston, Acting General Counsel

William Ng, Deputy General Counsel

Gwendolyn Reams, Associate General Counsel, Appellate Services

Phillip Sklover, Associate General Counsel, Trial Services

James Finney, Associate General Counsel, Systemic Litigation Services

### EEOC District, Area, and Local Offices

*Following is an alphabetical directory of EEOC's "full-service" district offices and the area and local offices serving those districts.*

**ALBUQUERQUE AREA OFFICE (Phoenix District)**

Western Bank Building, Suite 1105
505 Marquette, N. W.
Albuquerque, New Mexico 87102
(Hours —7:30 a.m. —4:30 p.m. MST)
(505) 766-2061

**ATLANTA DISTRICT OFFICE**

Citizens Trust Building,
75 Piedmont Avenue, N. E., Suite 1100
Atlanta, Georgia 30335
(Hours —8:30 a.m. —5:00 p.m. EST)
(404) 331-6531

**BALTIMORE DISTRICT OFFICE**

111 Market Place, Suite 4000
Baltimore, Maryland 21202
(Hours —9:00 a.m. —5:30 p.m. EST)
(301) 962-3932

**BIRMINGHAM DISTRICT OFFICE**

2121 Eighth Avenue, North, Suite 824
Birmingham, Alabama 35203
(Hours —8:00 a.m. —4:30 p.m. CST)
(205) 731-1166

**BOSTON AREA OFFICE (New York District)**

JFK Building, Room 409-B
Boston, Massachusetts 02203

(Hours —8:30 a.m. —5:00 p.m. EST)
(617) 565-3200

## BUFFALO LOCAL OFFICE (New York District)

Guaranty Building, 28 Church Street
Buffalo, New York 14202
(Hours —8:45 a.m. —5:15 p.m. EST)
(716) 846-4441

## CHARLOTTE DISTRICT OFFICE

5500 Central Avenue
Charlotte, North Carolina 28212
(Hours —8:30 a.m. —5:00 p.m. EST)
(704) 567-7100

## CHICAGO DISTRICT OFFICE

Federal Building, Room 930-A
536 South Clark Street
Chicago, Illinois 60605
(Hours —8:30 a.m. —4:00 p.m. CST)
(312) 353-2713

## CINCINNATI AREA OFFICE (Cleveland District)

Federal Building, Room 7015
550 Main Street
Cincinnati, Ohio 45202
(Hours —8:15 a.m. —5:00 p.m. EST)
(513) 684-2851

## CLEVELAND DISTRICT OFFICE

1375 Euclid Avenue, Room 600
Cleveland, Ohio 44115
(Hours —8:15 a.m. —5:00 p.m. EST)
(216) 522-7425

## DALLAS DISTRICT OFFICE

8303 Elmbrook Drive
Dallas, Texas 75247
(Hours —7:30 a.m. —5:00 p.m. CST)
(214) 767-7015

## DENVER DISTRICT OFFICE

1845 Sherman Street, 2nd Floor
Denver, Colorado 80203
(Hours —8:00 a.m. —5:00 p.m. MST)
(303) 866-1300

## DETROIT DISTRICT OFFICE

Patrick V. McNamara Federal Building
477 Michigan Avenue, Room 1540
Detroit, Michigan 48226
(Hours —8:30 a.m. —5:00 p.m. EST)
(313) 226-7636

## EL PASO LOCAL OFFICE (San Antonio District)

700 East San Antonio St., Suite B-406
El Paso, Texas 79901
(Hours —7:30 a.m. —4:30 p.m. CST)
(915) 543-6550

## FRESNO AREA OFFICE (San Francisco District)

1313 P Street, Suite 103
Fresno, California 93721
(Hours —8:30 a.m. —5:00 p.m. PST)
(209) 487-5793

## GREENSBORO LOCAL OFFICE (Charlotte District)

324 West Market St., Room B-27
Post Office Box 3363
Greensboro, North Carolina 27402
(Hours —8:30 a.m. —5:00 p.m. EST)
(919) 333-5174

## GREENVILLE LOCAL OFFICE (Charlotte District)

Federal Building, Room B-41
300 East Washington St.
Greenville, South Carolina 29601
(Hours —8:30 a.m. —5:00 p.m. EST)
(803) 233-1791

## HOUSTON DISTRICT OFFICE

405 Main Street, Sixth Floor
Houston, Texas 77002
(Hours —8:00 a.m. —5:00 p.m. CST)
(713) 653-3320

## INDIANAPOLIS DISTRICT OFFICE

U.S. Courthouse Building
46 East Ohio Street, Room 456
Indianapolis, Indiana 46204
(Hours —8:00 a.m. —4:30 p.m. EST)
(317) 226-7212

## JACKSON AREA OFFICE (Birmingham District)

McCoy Federal Office Building
100 West Capitol Street, Suite 721
Jackson, Mississippi 39269
(Hours —8:00 a.m. —4:30 p.m. CST)
(601) 965-4537

**KANSAS CITY AREA OFFICE (St. Louis District)**

911 Walnut, 10th Floor
Kansas City, Missouri 64106
(Hours —8:00 a.m. —4:30 p.m. CST)
(816) 426-5773

**LITTLE ROCK AREA OFFICE (Memphis District)**

Savers Building, Suite 621
320 West Capitol Avenue
Little Rock, Arkansas 72201
(Hours —8:00 a.m. —4:30 p.m. CST)
(501) 378-5060

**LOS ANGELES DISTRICT OFFICE**

3660 Wilshire Boulevard, 5th Floor
Los Angeles, California 90010
(Hours—8:30 a.m. —5:00 p.m. PST)
(213) 251-7278

**LOUISVILLE AREA OFFICE (Indianapolis District)**

601 West Broadway, Room 613
Louisville, Kentucky 40202
(Hours —8:00 a.m. —4:30 p.m. EST)
(502) 582-6082

**MEMPHIS DISTRICT OFFICE**

1407 Union Avenue, Suite 621
Memphis, Tennessee 38104
(Hours —8:00 a.m. —4:30 p.m. CST)
(901) 521-2617

**MIAMI DISTRICT OFFICE**

Metro Mall
1 Northeast First Street, 6th Floor
Miami, Florida 33132
(Hours —8:00 a.m. —4:30 p.m. EST)
(305) 536-4491

**MILWAUKEE DISTRICT OFFICE**

310 West Wisconsin Avenue, Suite 800
Milwaukee, Wisconsin 53203-2292
(Hours —8:00 a.m. —4:30 p.m. CST)
(414) 291-1111

**MINNEAPOLIS LOCAL OFFICE (Milwaukee District)**

220 Second Street South, Room 108
Minneapolis, Minnesota 55401-2141
(Hours —8:00 a.m. —4:30 p.m. CST)
(612) 370-3330

**NASHVILLE AREA OFFICE (Memphis District)**

Parkway Towers, Suite 1100
Nashville, Tennessee 37219
(Hours —8:00 a.m. —4:30 p.m. CST)
(615) 251-5820

**NEWARK AREA OFFICE (New York District)**

60 Park Place, Room 301
Newark, New Jersey 07102
(Hours —8:00 a.m. —4:30 p.m. EST)
(201) 645-6383

**NEW ORLEANS DISTRICT OFFICE**

701 Loyola Ave., Suite 600
New Orleans, Louisiana 70113
(Hours —8:00 a.m. —4:30 p.m. CST)
(504) 589-2329

**NEW YORK DISTRICT OFFICE**

90 Church Street, Room 1505
New York, New York 10007
(Hours —8:45 a.m. —5:15 p.m. EST)
(212) 264-7161

**NORFOLK AREA OFFICE (Baltimore District)**

252 Monticello Ave.
Norfolk, Virginia 23510
(Hours —8:30 a.m. —5:00 p.m. EST)
(804) 441-3470

**OAKLAND LOCAL OFFICE (San Francisco District)**

1333 Broadway, Room 430
Oakland, California 94612
(Hours —8:00 a.m. —4:30 p.m. CST)
(415) 273-7588

**OKLAHOMA AREA OFFICE (Dallas District)**

513 Couch St.
First Floor
Oklahoma City, Oklahoma 73102
(Hours —8:30 a.m. —5:00 p.m. CST)
(405) 231-4911

**PHILADELPHIA DISTRICT OFFICE**

1421 Cherry Street, 10th Floor
Philadelphia, Pennsylvania 19102

(Hours —8:00 a.m. —4:30 p.m. EST)
(215) 597-7784

## PHOENIX DISTRICT OFFICE

4520 North Central Avenue, Suite 300
Phoenix, Arizona 85012
(Hours —8:00 a.m. —5:00 p.m. MST)
(602) 261-3882

## PITTSBURGH AREA OFFICE (Philadelphia District)

Federal Building, Room 2038A
1000 Liberty Avenue
Pittsburgh, Pennsylvania 15222
(Hours —8:00 a.m. —4:30 p.m. EST)
(412) 644-3444

## RALEIGH AREA OFFICE (Charlotte District)

127 West Hargett Street, Suite 500
Raleigh, North Carolina 27601
(Hours —8:30 a.m. —5:00 p.m. EST)
(919) 856-4064

## RICHMOND AREA OFFICE (Baltimore District)

400 North 8th Street, Room 7026
Richmond, Virginia 23240
(Hours —8:30 a.m. —5:00 p.m. EST)
(804) 771-2692

## SAN ANTONIO DISTRICT OFFICE

5410 Fredericksburg Rd., Suite 200
San Antonio, Texas 78229-3555
(Hours —8:00 a.m. —5:00 p.m. CST)
(512) 229-4810

## SAN DIEGO LOCAL OFFICE (Los Angeles District)

110 West C Street, Room 1702
San Diego, California 92101
(Hours —8:30 a.m. —5:00 p.m. PST)
(619) 237-7405

## SAN FRANCISCO DISTRICT OFFICE

901 Market St, Suite 500
San Francisco, California 94103
(Hours —8:30 a.m. —5:00 p.m. PST)
(415) 995-5049

## SAN JOSE LOCAL OFFICE (San Francisco District)

U. S. Courthouse & Federal Building
280 South First Street, Room 4150
San Jose, California 95113
(Hours —8:30 a.m. —5:00 p.m. PST)
(408) 291-7352

## SEATTLE DISTRICT OFFICE

Arcade Plaza Building
1321 Second Avenue, 7th Floor
Seattle, Washington 98101
(Hours —8:30 a.m. —5:00 p.m. PST)
(206) 442-0968

## ST. LOUIS DISTRICT OFFICE

625 N. Euclid Street, Fifth Floor
St. Louis, Missouri 63108
(Hours —8:00 a.m. —4:30 p.m. CST)
(314) 425-6585

## TAMPA AREA OFFICE (Miami District)

700 Twiggs Street, Room 302
Tampa, Florida 33602
(Hours —8:00 a.m. —4:30 p.m. EST)
(813) 228-2310

## WASHINGTON FIELD OFFICE

1400 L Street, N.W., Suite 200
Washington, D.C. 20005
(Hours —9:00 a.m. —5:30 p.m. EST)
(202) 275-7377

# APPENDIX J

## Directory of U.S. Department of Defense, Defense Contract Administration Services, Regional Offices

## Defense Contract Administration Services

### Headquarters, Defense Supply Agency

*Address: Cameron Station, Alexandria, Va. 22314*
*Telephone: (703) 274-6241*

*(Listed below are the regional offices under the Defense Contract Administration Services. The regional offices conduct compliance reviews, follow-up reviews, pre-award reviews, and complaint investigations. About 7,000 contractors doing business in approximately 40,000 facilities are covered by the regional offices' functions.)*

## Regional Offices

**Atlanta**
805 Walker Street
Marietta, Georgia 30060
Phone: (404) 429-6000
*Area covered:* Alabama, Caribbean, Central America, Florida, Georgia, Mississippi, North Carolina, South America, South Carolina, and Tennessee.

**Boston**
495 Summer Street
Boston, Massachusetts 02210
Phone: (617) 451-4298
*Area covered:* Connecticut, Maine, Massachusetts, New Hampshire, New York (excluding New York City, Long Island; Orange, Putnam, Rockland, and Westchester Counties), Rhode Island, and Vermont

**Chicago**
O'Hare International Airport
P.O. Box 66475
Chicago, Illinois 60666
Phone: (312) 694-3031
*Area covered:* Indiana, Northern Illinois, and Wisconsin

**Cleveland**
Federal Office Building
1240 East 9th Street
Cleveland, Ohio 44199
Phone: (216) 522-6701
*Area covered:* Commonwealth of Canada, Kentucky, Michigan, Northwestern Pennsylvania (Erie, Crawford, and Mercer Counties), and Ohio

**Dallas**
500 South Ervay Street
Dallas, Texas 75201
Phone: (214) 744-4581
*Area covered:* Arkansas, Louisiana, Mexico (except states of Baja California and Sonora), New Mexico, Oklahoma, and Texas

**Los Angeles**
11099 S. La Cienega Boulevard
Los Angeles, California 90045
Phone: (213) 643-1110
*Area covered:* Alaska, Arizona, California, Hawaii, Idaho, Montana, Nevada, Oregon, Washington, and the Marianas and Marshall Islands

**New York**
60 Hudson Street
New York, New York 10013
Phone: (212) 374-9000
*Area covered:* New Jersey (all counties North of Burlington, Mercer, and Ocean Counties), and New York (New York City and Long Island; Orange, Putnam, Rockland, and Westchester Counties)

**Philadelphia**
2800 South 20th Street
Philadelphia, Pennsylvania 19101
Phone: (215) 952-1110

*Area covered:* Delaware, District of Columbia, Maryland, New Jersey, (Burlington, Mercer, and Ocean Counties), Pennsylvania (except Crawford, Erie, and Mercer Counties), Virginia, and West Virginia

**St. Louis**

1136 Washington Avenue
St. Louis, Missouri 63101
Phone: (314) 263-6510

*Area covered:* Colorado, Illinois (Adams, Brown, Cass, Douglas, Edgar, Macon, Menard, and Sangamon Counties and all counties to the South), Iowa, Kansas, Minnesota, Missouri, Nebraska, North Dakota, South Dakota, Utah, and Wyoming

# APPENDIX K

# TRAINING WAGE REGULATIONS

# Training Wage Regulations

*Text of interim final regulations governing the subminimum training wage provisions of the Fair Labor Standards Amendments of 1989, issued by the Employment Standards Administration (55 FR 7455), effective April 1, 1990, as amended 55 FR 19065.*

## PART 517—TRAINING WAGE PROVISIONS OF THE FAIR LABOR STANDARDS AMENDMENTS OF 1989

**Subpart A—General**
Sec.
517.1   Summary.
517.2   Purpose and scope of regulations.
517.3   Statutory effective and expiration dates of the training wage provisions.
517.4   Training wage rates.
517.5   Definitions.
**Subpart B—Employee Eligibility Requirements**
517.100   General.
517.101   Duration.
517.102   Proof of age required.
517.103   Proof of eligibility for employment at the training wage.
517.104   Good faith defense.
**Subpart C—Employer Requirements**
517.200   General.
517.201   First 90-day period.
517.202   Second 90-day period.
517.203   Maximum hours per month.
517.204   Maximum hours exceeded.
517.205   Notice to employees paid at the training wage.
517.206   Posting, reporting and recordkeeping requirements for the second 90-day period of eligibility.
517.207   Child labor restrictions.
**Subpart D—On-the-Job Training**
517.300   On-the-job training.
**Subpart E—Wage Conditions and Prohibitions**
517.400   Prohibited actions.
517.401   Prohibited layoffs.
517.402   Prohibited displacements.
517.403   Disqualification and enforcement.
**Subpart F—Administrative Proceedings**
General
517.500   Applicability of procedures and rules.
**Procedures Relating to Hearing**
517.501   Written notice of determination required.
517.502   Contents of notice.
517.503   Request for hearing.
**Rules of Practice**
517.504   General.
517.505   Service and computation of time.
517.506   Commencement of proceeding.
**Referral for Hearing**
517.507   Referral to Administrative Law Judge.
517.508   Appointment of Administrative Law Judge and notification of prehearing conference and hearing date.
517.509   Decision and Order of Administrative Law Judge.
517.510   Non-applicability of the Equal Access to Justice Act.
**Appeals to the Secretary**
517.511   Procedures for initiating and undertaking review.
517.512   Notice of the Secretary to review decision.
517.513   Final decision of the Secretary.
517.514   Filing and service.
517.515   Responsibility of the Office of Adminstrative Law Judges.
**Record**
517.516   Retention of official record.
517.517   Certification of official record.
**Appendix A—Notice to Employees About the Training Wage**

Authority: Sec. 6, Pub. L. 101-157, 103 Stat. 938; 29 U.S.C. 201 et seq.

## SUBPART A—General

### Sec. 517.1 Summary.

(a) The Fair Labor Standards Amendments of 1989 (Public Law 101-157) were enacted into law on November 17, 1989. Among other provisions, these amendments to the Fair Labor Standards Act (FLSA) increase the minimum wage in section 6(a)(1) from $3.35 an hour to $3.80 an hour on April 1, 1990, and to $4.25 an hour on April 1, 1991; establish a training wage; and change certain provisions relating to coverage, exemptions, tip credit, and enforcement under the Act.

(b) Sec. 6 of the Amendments permits employers under certain conditions to pay employees under the age of 20 a wage rate of at least 85 percent of the minimum wage prescribed by Section 6(a)(1) of the FLSA (but not less than $3.35 per hour) for up to 90 days. An employee who has been paid the training wage for 90 days also may be employed at the training wage for 90 additional days by different employer(s) if such employer(s) provide(s) on-the-job training in accordance with criteria established by the Secretary of Labor.

### Sec. 517.2 Purpose and scope of regulations.

The purpose of this part is to set forth regulations on the training wage provisions of section 6 of the Amendments to the FLSA. The regulations in this part are divided into six subparts. Subpart A contains provisions that generally pertain to a training wage for eligible workers, including definitions relating to the training wage provisions. Subpart B sets forth rules regarding employees who are eligible for the training wage. Subpart C sets forth the requirements for employer eligibility for the employment of workers at the training wage during the first and second 90-day periods. Subpart D sets forth the criteria which on-the-job training programs must meet for employers to qualify to pay the training wage for the second 90-day period. Subpart E sets forth the prohibitions against displacement of employees (including reductions in hours worked, wages, or employment benefits). Subpart F contains the administrative proceedings for disqualifying employers who have violated the displacement prohibitions from using the training wage.

### Sec. 517.3 Statutory effective and expiration dates of the training wage provisions.

Pursuant to section 6(b) of the amendments, authorization to employ eligible employees at the training wage for the designated periods begins on April 1, 1990, and expires March 31, 1993.

### Sec. 517.4 Training wage rates.

(a) Effective April 1, 1990, the training wage shall be not less than $3.35 an hour.

(b) Effective April 1, 1991, the training wage shall be not less than $3.35 an hour or 85 percent of the wage prescribed by section 6 of the FLSA, *whichever is greater*, for the period ending March 31, 1993. Thus, for employers subject to the minimum wage of $4.25 per hour under section 6(a)(1) of the Act beginning April 1, 1991, the training wage shall be not less than $3.6125 per hour (which, if rounded, must be rounded up to $3.62 per hour).

(c) Different minimum wage rates, and thus different training wage rates apply in American Samoa and Puerto Rico. However, in no event may anyone lawfully be paid a training wage of less than $3.35 per hour, including employees in American Samoa and Puerto Rico.

(d) Under no circumstances may an employer simultaneously employ an individual under both the training wage provisions and the special minimum wage provisions in FLSA section 14 (which provide for employment at wages lower than the section 6(a)(1) minimum under certain circumstances).

### Sec. 517.5 Definitions.

For purposes of this part:

(a) *Act* or *FLSA* means the Fair Labor Standards Act of 1938, as amended (29 U.S.C. 201, et seq.).

(b) *Amendments* or *1989 Amendments* means the Fair Labor Standards Amendments of 1989 (Pub. L. 101-157).

(c) *Secretary* means the Secretary of Labor, or a duly authorized representative of the Secretary.

(d) *Administrator* means the Administrator of the Wage and Hour Division of the Employment Standards Administration, U.S. Department of Labor, or a duly authorized representative of the Administrator.

(e) *Establishment* means a distinct physical place of business. The term is not synonymous with the words "business" or "enterprise" when those terms are used to describe multi-unit operations.

(f) *Employer* includes any person acting directly or indirectly in the interest of an employer in relation to an employee and includes a public agency, but does not include any labor organization (other than when acting as an employer) or anyone acting in the capacity of officer or agent of such labor organization.

(g) *Employee* means any individual employed by an employer, except for those types of individuals excluded by

Sec. 3(e), paragraphs (2), (3), and (4), of the FLSA.

(h) *Workweek* means a fixed and regulatory recurring period of 168 hours—seven consecutive 24-hour periods. It need not coincide with the calendar week but may begin on any day and at any hour of the day. Once the beginning time of an employee's workweek is established, it remains fixed regardless of the schedule of hours worked by that employee. The beginning of the workweek may be changed only if the change is intended to be permanent and is not designed to evade the requirements of the FLSA.

(i) *Ninety Days* or *90 Days* means a total of 90 calendar days in an employment status with one or more employers. Employment status includes the period from the first day after an employee is hired on which the employee performs work, until the employee's termination of employment with the employer, irrespective of the number of hours, days or weeks during such period that the employee actually performs work, but does not include any break of service with an employer (e.g., bona fide layoffs). Normal work absences, such as weekends, holidays, sick or annual leave, do not constitute a break in service.

(j) *On-the-job training* means training that is offered to an individual while employed in productive work that provides training, technical and other related skills, and personal skills that are essential to the full and adequate performance of such employment.

(k) *Migrant agricultural worker* and *seasonal agricultural worker* are defined in accordance with paragraphs (8) and (10) of sec. 3 of the Migrant and Seasonal Agricultural Worker Protection Act (29 U.S.C. 1802 (8) and (10)) (as amplified in the regulations issued thereunder at 29 CFR 500.20), without regard to subparagraph (B) of such paragraphs, as follows:

(1) a *migrant agricultural worker* is an individual who is employed in agricultural employment of a seasonal or other temporary nature and is required to be absent overnight from his or her permanent place of residence;

(2) a *seasonal agricultural worker* is an individual who is employed in agricultural employment of a seasonal or other temporary nature and is not required to be absent overnight from his or her permanent place of residence—

(i) When employed on a farm or ranch performing field work related to planting, cultivating, or harvesting operations; or

(ii) When employed in canning, packing, ginning, seed conditioning or related research, or processing operations, and transported, or caused to be transported, to or from the place of employment by means of a day-haul operation.

(l) *Temporary nonimmigrant agricultural worker* means an alien, admitted to the United States under 8 U.S.C. 1101(a)(15)(H)(ii)(a), having a residence in a foreign country which he or she has no intention of abandoning who has come temporarily to the United States to perform agricultural labor or services, as defined by the Secretary of Labor in 20 CFR 655.100(c), of a temporary or seasonal nature.

**Subpart B—Employee Eligibility Requirements**

**Sec. 517.100 General.**

(a) An employee is eligible to be paid the training wage, for the period(s) described in Sec. 517.101, if such employee—

(1) Has not reached 20 years of age;

(2) Is not a migrant agricultural worker or a seasonal agricultural worker;

(3) Is not a temporary nonimmigrant agricultural worker.

(b) Individuals become ineligible for the training wage on the date on which they become 20 years of age, and, as of that date, they must receive not less than the minimum wage otherwise applicable under the FLSA.

(c) Individuals are not eligible to be paid the training wage in any workweek in which they are employed in industries or occupations in which they cannot be employed legally because of their age as a result of any Federal, State or local child labor law or ordinance or any regulation or hazardous occupation order issued pursuant to such law or ordinance. Similarly, individuals are not eligible to be paid the training wage in any workweek in which hours are worked which are impermissible under such laws, ordinances or regulations. See Sec. 517.207.

### Sec. 517.101 Duration.

(a) An employee is initially eligible to be paid the training wage until the employee has been employed by one or more employers a cumulative total of 90 days at such wage.

(b) An employee who has been employed at the training wage for 90 cumulative days may be employed by one or more other employers for an additional cumulative 90 days if such employer(s) meet(s) the requirements listed in Sec. 517.202 below.

(c) The total period that an employee may be employed at the training wage by any combination of employers may not exceed a cumulative total of 180 days.

(d) Special rules apply to individuals who are employed by an employer on April 1, 1990, or who were employed by an employer on or after March 1, 1990, and who thereafter were laid off on or before April 1, 1990, but are subsequently rehired by that employer:

(1) Individuals who, as of April 1, 1990, have been employed by their current employer for at least 90 days are ineligible for employment at the training wage by such employer.

(2) Individuals who, as of April 1, 1990, have been employed by their current employer for less than 90 days are eligible for employment at the training wage with such employer until they have been employed for a total of 90 days by their current and any subsequent employer. Such employment is subject to all the requirements of this Part with respect to employment at the training wage for the first 90 days.

(3) Individuals ineligible for employment at the training wage by their current employer by virtue of paragraphs (d)(1) or (2) of this section are eligible to be hired for an additional 90 days at the training wage by a different employer provided all the requirements of this Part with respect to employment at the training wage for a second 90 days are met.

### Sec. 517.102 Proof of age required.

An individual may be employed at the training wage only upon presentation to the employer of documentary evidence of age under 20. Acceptable types of documentation include the following:

(a) A birth certificate or similar official statement of the recorded date and place of birth;

(b) A Federal certificate of age;

(c) A State certificate of age (sometimes known as an age, employment or working certificate or permit);

(d) A baptismal record which shows the date of birth;

(e) A driver's license;

(f) A passport, or certificate of arrival in the United States issued by the U.S. Immigration and Naturalization Service (INS), or any other document reviewed by an employer to establish identity or employment eligibility in completing INS Form I-9, provided such document contains the person's date of birth;

(g) A school record of age;

(h) A physician's certificate of physical age of the individual;

(i) A signed statement by a parent or guardian.

[Approved by the Office of Management and Budget under control number 1215-0172]

### Sec. 517.103 Proof of eligibility for employment at the training wage.

(a) *First 90 days of eligibility.* An individual under the age of 20 who is to be employed at the training wage must provide written proof, as specified below, to the employer that he or she has been previously employed at such wage for fewer than 90 days.

(b) *Second 90 days of eligibility.* An individual under the age of 20 who has been employed at the training wage for

90 days and who is to be employed by one or more different employers for an additional 90 days, must provide written proof to the employer(s) of any previous period(s) of employment at the training wage by other employers.

(c) *Nature of proof.* In view of the special rules for current employees set forth in Sec. 517.101(d), the written proof of prior employment shall include any employment on or after January 1, 1990. Where the individual has had no such previous employment, the written proof shall consist of a signed statement to that effect. Where the individual has been previously employed since January 1, 1990, the written proof shall consist of a signed, accurate list prepared by the individual of all of his or her prior employers, the starting and ending dates of employment with each employer, and the wage rate(s) paid. A signed job application form with all the required information accurately entered will meet this requirement. Such written proof shall be retained by the employer for a period of three years from the date such proof is furnished to the employer.
[Approved by the Office of Management and Budget under control number 1215-0172]

### Sec. 517.104 Good faith defense.

Information furnished to the employer pursuant to Sec. 517.103 may be relied on in determining whether an individual is eligible for employment at the training wage. Absent any attempt at evasion or coercion by the employer, a violation of the FLSA with respect to employee eligibility shall not be deemed to exist by virtue of the employment of any person at the training wage for whom the employer has on file the documentation of evidence of such individual's age, or a notation as to the nature of the evidence of date of birth provided by the individual, and, as appropriate, a signed list provided by the individual of previous employers, which shows the starting and ending dates of employment with each employer and the wage rate(s) paid, or a signed statement to the effect that the individu-

al was not previously employed at the training wage, provided such documents indicate compliance with the employee eligibility requirements of this subpart.
[Approved by the Office of Management and Budget under control number 1215-0172]

### Subpart C—Employer Requirements

### Sec. 517.200 General.

(a) Employers covered by the FLSA are eligible to employ workers at the training wage provided they meet the requirements of this part. The requirements differ with respect to workers employed at the training wage for their first 90 days and workers employed at the training wage for a second 90-day period by a different employer.

(b) For the sole purpose of determining whether an individual has been employed by an employer for 90 days, the term "employer" means an employer who is required to withhold payroll taxes for such employee. For all other purposes, the term "employer" shall have the meaning set forth in section 3(d) of the FLSA and Sec. 517.5(f) of these regulations.

### Sec. 517.201 First 90-day period.

To be eligible to employ a worker during his or her first 90 days of employment at the training wage, an employer must:

(a) Ensure that the worker meets the eligibility requirements set forth in subpart B;

(b) Provide the worker with a copy of the notice as required by Sec. 517.205;

(c) Comply with the restrictions on the maximum number of hours that can be paid at the training wage set forth in Sec. 517.203; and

(d) Not commit any of the prohibited acts related to the displacement of workers set forth in subpart E.

It should be noted that the Amendments do not impose any specific training requirements for individuals during their first 90-day period of employment at the training wage.

### Sec. 517.202 Second 90-day period.

In addition to meeting all the requirements in Sec. 517.201, an employer wishing to employ a worker during his or her second 90-day period of employment at the training wage must:

(a) Not have employed the worker during any part of his or her first 90 days of employment at the training wage;

(b) Prepare in writing and retain a training program that outlines the on-the-job training provided workers so employed in accordance with subpart D;

(c) Furnish a copy of the training program to each worker;

(d) Provide training to each worker in accordance with such training program;

(e) Post in a conspicuous place in the establishment(s) in which such workers are employed a notice of the types of jobs for which on-the-job training is being provided pursuant to these regulations (as required by Sec. 517.206(g)); and

(f) Furnish a copy of such notice annually to the Department of Labor (as required by Sec. 517.206(h)).

### Sec. 517.203 Maximum hours per month.

(a) As a condition of using the training wage provisions (both the first and second 90-day periods), Sec. 6(d)(1) of the 1989 Amendments provides that during any month in which employees are employed in an establishment at the training wage, the hours of work for such employees may not exceed a proportion equal to one-fourth of the total hours worked by all employees in that establishment.

(b) In determining the hours worked by all employees of the establishment, the hours worked by full-time "executive, administrative, professional, and outside sales employees" (as these terms are defined and delimited in 29 CFR part 541), who are exempt from the Act's minimum wage and overtime pay provisions under FLSA section 13(a)(1) (and thus from certain recordkeeping requirements in 29 CFR part 516), may be estimated at no more than 40 hours per workweek where no record exists of the actual hours worked by such individuals.

(c) As alternatives to using calendar months in making the calculations, employers may designate a "fiscal month" system, consisting of consecutive 30-day periods, or a "four-workweek" system, consisting of four consecutive seven-day periods or two consecutive 14-day periods. However, where an alternative is selected it must be intended to be permanent, and the alternative selected must be continued in use until such time as no employees have been employed at the training wage for at least thirty days.

### Sec. 517.204 Maximum hours exceeded.

(a) It is the employer's responsibility to ensure that the total number of hours paid at the training wage does not exceed the statutory limitation of one-quarter of the total hours worked by all employees in the establishment. Employers using this provision, therefore, must closely monitor the hours worked by all employees, and not only those paid at the training wage, to avoid any violation of this limit.

(b)(1) If, at the end of a given month (or other period allowable under Sec. 517.203(c)), the number of hours worked by employees paid at the training wage exceeds one-quarter of the total hours worked by all employees at the establishment, the Administrator will not assert the illegality of the use of the training wage for that month if, but only if, the employer promptly pays the difference between the training wage and the minimum wage prescribed by sec. 6(a) of the FLSA for all hours which had been worked and paid at the training wage in excess of the 25% limitation. For purposes of the previous sentence the word "promptly" means no later than 30 days after the last day of the month in question. Once the total amount of additional wages due to make such payment is determined, the total must be prorated among all the employees paid at the training wage during that month based on the number of hours worked by each employee.

(2) For example, assume an employer has two employees paid at a training wage of $3.35 per hour, one of whom works 10 hours per week and the other of whom works 30 hours per week. In addition, the employer employs three full-time employees at or above the FLSA's minimum wage ($3.80 in this example). One of the full-time employees quits towards the end of a given month. Assume that the training wage employees together worked 160 hours and the other employees all together worked 432 hours, so that the total hours worked in the establishment are 592. Thus, employer finds that the number of hours paid at the training wage exceeds one-fourth of the total hours worked by all employees by 12 hours in that month. (25% of 592 = 148. 160 - 148 = 12.) Technically, all hours compensated at $3.35 per hour have been under-compensated. However, no violation will be asserted by the Administrator for that month if the employer promptly pays the total of $5.40 in additional wages due ($3.80 - $3.35 x 12 hours). The trainee who worked 10 of the 40 total hours per week paid at the training wage would be paid an additional $1.35 (10/40 x $5.40), and the trainee who worked 30 of the 40 total hours per week paid at the training wage would be paid an additional $4.05 (30/40 x $5.40). It should be noted that the payment of such make-up pay has no effect on an employee's 90-day period of eligibility for the training wage.

(3) There may be occasions where the 25% limitation is exceeded and employees are paid varying training wage rates. In such situations it will not be possible to simply determine the total amount of back wages due and then prorate that amount among the employees involved. Rather, it will be necessary in such cases first to determine each employee's pro rata share of the hours that exceed the 25% limitation and then multiply that number by the difference between the

minimum wage and the employee's training wage. For example, assume the same facts as in the example in paragraph (b)(2) of this section, except that the employee who worked 10 hours was paid $3.50 per hour instead of $3.35 per hour. That employee would be due 10/40 x 12 x $.30 ($3.80 - $3.50) = $.90. The other employee would be due 30/40 x 12 x $.45 ($3.80 - $3.35) = $4.05. The employer would owe a total of $4.95.

### Sec. 517.205 Notice to employees paid at the training wage.

(a) Sec. 6(e) of the 1989 Amendments requires that employers provide a written notice to each employee who is to be paid at the training wage before the employee begins employment at the training wage. The notice must state the requirements of the training wage provisions and the statutory remedies available for violations.

(b) The Secretary is required by the Amendments to furnish the text of this notice to employers, and the text is set forth in Appendix A to this part. No particular form for the notice is required, and it may consist of a handwritten copy, typed copy, or photocopy of Appendix A. However, the text of the notice provided must be legible and identical to the text of Appendix A (or an accurate translation thereof) with no additions or deletions.
[Approved by the Office of Management and Budget under control number 1215-0172]

### Sec. 517.206 Posting, reporting and recordkeeping requirements for the second 90-day period of eligibility.

(a) As required by sec. 6(h) of the Amendments and as discussed in Sec. 517.202, employers wishing to employ individuals for any portion of a second 90-day period of employment at the training wage must prepare in writing a training program setting forth the on-the-job-training to be provided such individuals.

(b) No particular format for the written training program discussed in paragraph (a) of this section is required.

However, the training program must meet all of the requirements in subpart D.

(c) It is anticipated that the training program may be revised from time to time and that new training programs may be developed for new employees or new positions.

(d) A copy of the applicable written training program must be furnished any job applicant hired for employment at the training wage during any portion of his or her second 90-day period of eligibility for such wage.

(e) The employer must retain the original or a copy of the training program(s), including any revisions, for two years after the last day on which an individual was employed at the training wage pursuant to such training program(s).

(f) Section 6(h)(1) of the Amendments provides that any employer who wishes to employ any individual at the training wage during their second 90-day period of eligibility, must notify the Secretary annually of the positions at which such employees are to be employed at such wage. The Department will accept as compliance with this provision the employer's compliance with the reporting requirements set forth in paragraphs (g) and (h) of this section.

(g) Section 6(h)(5) of the Amendments requires that any employer who wishes to employ any individuals at the training wage during their second 90-day period of eligibility, post in a conspicuous place a notice of the types of positions for which the employer is providing on-the-job training. The notice must include a listing of all positions (vacant or filled) in the establishment in which workers are already employed in the training program or for which they may be hired. The Amendments do not require that the wage rates actually paid or offered to be paid be identified for such positions in the notice. No employer may hire any worker at the training wage during any portion of his or her second 90-day period of eligibility for employment at the training wage, unless the type of position

to be occupied is identified on the posted notice.

(h) Section 6(h)(6) of the Amendments requires that employers send a copy of the notice in paragraph (g) of this section to the Secretary on an annual basis. Provided that the employer complies with the requirements in paragraph (g) of this section, the requirements of paragraph (f) and this section may be simultaneously met as follows: Prior to employing individuals at the training wage during any portion of their second 90-day period of eligibility, and on an annual basis thereafter, the employer must advise the Department of Labor in writing of the intention to employ or continue to employ such individuals at the training wage, identify the names and addresses of the establishments where such individuals are or will be employed, and include in such correspondence a copy of the notice required by paragraph (g) of this section. Such correspondence should be directed to:

Regional Director, Wage and Hour Division, Employment Standards Administration, U.S. Department of Labor.

The lower left hand corner of the envelope should state: "Training Wage Report." This correspondence should be mailed to the appropriate address from the list that follows:

*Region I—Boston* (Connecticut, Maine, Massachusetts, New Hampshire, Rhode Island, Vermont)
JFK Federal Building, Government Center, Room 1612C, Boston, Massachusetts 02203

*Region II—New York* (New Jersey, New York, Puerto Rico, Virgin Islands)
201 Varick Street, Room 750, New York, New York 10014

*Region III—Philadelphia* (Delaware, District of Columbia, Maryland, Pennsylvania, Virginia, West Virginia)
Gateway Building, Room 15210, 3535 Market Street, Philadelphia, Pennsylvania 19104

*Region IV—Atlanta* (Alabama, Florida, Georgia, Kentucky, Mississippi, North Carolina, South Carolina, Tennessee)
1375 Peachtree Street, NE., Room 662, Atlanta, Georgia 30367

*Region V—Chicago* (Illinois, Indiana, Michigan, Minnesota, Ohio, Wisconsin)
230 South Dearborn Street, Room 562-A, Chicago, Illinois 60604-1591

*Region VI—Dallas* (Arkansas, Louisiana, New Mexico, Oklahoma, Texas)

Federal Building, Room 858, 525 Griffin Street, Dallas, Texas 75202

*Region VII—Kansas City* (Iowa, Kansas, Missouri, Nebraska)

Federal Office Building, Room 2000, 911 Walnut Street, Kansas City, Missouri 64106

*Region VIII—Denver* (Colorado, Montana, North Dakota, South Dakota, Utah, Wyoming)

Federal Office Building, Room 1490, 1961 Stout Street, Denver, Colorado 80294

*Region IX—San Francisco* (Arizona, California, Hawaii, Nevada, Guam, American Samoa)

71 Stevenson Street, Suite 905, San Francisco, California 94105

*Region X—Seattle* (Alaska, Idaho, Oregon, Washington)

1111 Third Avenue, Suite 600, Seattle, Washington 98101-3212

Where employers intend to employ individuals at the training wage in establishments located in the jurisdiction of more than one Regional Office, the information for all such establishments should be sent to the Regional Director whose jurisdiction includes the location of the employer's main office or corporate headquarters.

[Approved by the Office of Management and Budget under control number 1215-0172]

### Sec. 517.207 Child labor restrictions.

(a) Employment which violates Federal, State, or local child labor laws or ordinances is not eligible for the training wage provisions. For example, under the statute itself and regulations promulgated under the FLSA, certain non-agricultural occupations are prohibited for minors who are less than 18 years of age. (See 29 CFR part 570, subpart E.) In addition, Child Labor Regulation No. 3 (29 CFR part 570, Subpart C) sets forth the permissible industries and occupations in which 14- and 15-year olds may be employed under conditions which do not interfere with their schooling, health, or well-being, as required by section 3(l) of the FLSA. Child Labor Regulation No. 3 also specifies the number of hours in a day and in a week, and the time periods within a day that such minors may be employed in compliance with the FLSA.

(b) During any workweek in which a minor is employed in violation of any Federal, State, or local child labor restriction, that minor may not be paid less than the full minimum wage set forth in section 6(a) of the FLSA for any hours worked.

(c) Violations of these child labor provisions (or any other applicable child labor restrictions prescribed by Federal, State or local law or ordinance) are subject to the remedies in sections 16 and 17 of the FLSA with respect to back wages (i.e., the difference between the training wage and the applicable statutory minimum wage in section 6 of the FLSA), as well as civil money penalties under the FLSA and regulations issued pursuant thereto.

### Subpart D—On-the-job Training

### Sec. 517.300 On-the-job training.

(a) Section 6(h)(2) of the 1989 Amendments provides that in order for an employer to pay the training wage to an individual during any portion of his or her second 90-day period, in addition to meeting all the other statutory requirements as set forth in this Part, on-the-job training must be provided which meets the general criteria contained in regulations issued by the Secretary.

(b) As required by sec. 6(h)(3) of the Amendments, the on-the-job training program must be in writing and a copy retained in accordance with Sec. 517.206 of this Part. In addition, as set forth in Sec. 517.206, section 6(h)(4) of the Amendments requires that a copy of the training program be furnished to each employee who is to be employed at the training wage in a position to which it applies.

(c) In order to qualify as bona fide training under this provision of law, an on-the-job training program must provide for the development of job-specific skills and personal skills.

(1) Job-specific training means development of skills and knowledge necessary for full and adequate performance of the specific job to be performed by the individual paid the training wage. The training shall provide knowledge and skills beyond those customarily learned by observation and incidental work exposure. The kinds of job activities for

which on-the-job training is appropriate are too numerous and varied to permit an exhaustive lisiting. Examples of the types of job-related skills and knowledge for which such training could be provided include:

(i) Telephone techniques such as answering phones, responding to questions, taking messages;

(ii) Office etiquette and interpersonal skills, such as office relationships, handling of customers or visitors;

(iii) Skills such as typing, proofreading, copying, ordering—stocking — inventorying of supplies and equipment, computer keyboarding;

(iv) Operation of a cash register and making change;

(v) Opening and closing of a store or establishment;

(vi) Preparation and cooking of food;

(vii) Packaging of products for serving, delivery, shipping, etc.;

(viii) Cleaning or maintenance of building or office space and equipment; and

(ix) Familiarity with and use of set-up procedures, safety measures, work-related terminology, recordkeeping and paperwork formats, tools, equipment and materials, and breakdown and clean-up routines.

(2) Personal skills are skills other than specific job-related skills that affect an individual's employability and satisfactory work adjustment to any job. Examples of such skills include:

(i) Courteous behavior;

(ii) Customer relations/service;

(iii) Punctuality;

(iv) Oral and, where appropriate, written communications skills, reading and arithmetic, listening skills, and problem-solving skills;

(v) Personal hygiene, grooming, neatness, and appearance;

(vi) Appropriate dress;

(vii) Taking responsibility for one's work;

(viii) Finishing assigned tasks;

(ix) Taking direction and following instructions;

(x) Regular work attendance;

(xi) Cooperation/teamwork;

(xii) Personal management (self esteem, goal setting, motivation, personal and career development);

(xiii) Positive work habits, attitudes, and behavior;

(xiv) Substance abuse prevention training; and

(xv) Safety and health training.

(d) Nothing in this regulation shall be construed to require any employer to provide training in any particular one of the specific activities identified in (c) of this section.

(e) It is recognized that not all of the job specific skills acquired in the training program may be immediately applicable to the current position the employee occupies. Any additional skills which the employer wishes to teach should be applicable to other positions in the firm for which the individual may later qualify. For example, a grocery stockperson may receive training in the operation of a cash register, a messenger may receive training in computer keyboarding, or a shipping packer may receive training in operation of a fork-lift truck (provided, in accordance with Hazardous Occupations Order No. 7 (29 CFR 570.58, the packer is not under 18 years of age). Nothing in this subpart would preclude an employer from including training in such skills in the on-the-job training program.

(f) The training program must specify the job(s) covered by the plan, provide for planned instruction and include a schedule for the completion of the training program covering specific skills necessary for the particular job for which the individual is being trained, personal skills, and any additional skills for which training will be provided. In addition, the training program must provide for some kind of oral or written review of an employee's performance. As prescribed in section 6(a)(1) (B) of the Amendments, payment of the training wage is permitted in the second 90-day period only while the employee is engaged in on-the-job training.

(g) Nothing in this subpart precludes an employer from developing a training program which is based on a period longer than 90 days, so long as the training provided for the 90-day period complies with the requirements stated above, and any hours worked after the 90-day (maximum) period are compensated at not less than the minimum wage otherwise required by the FLSA. Also, an existing training program that is generally utilized may be used for training wage employees provided all other requirements in this part are met.

## Subpart E—Wage Conditions and Prohibitions

### Sec. 517.400 Prohibited actions.

Employers are prohibited by the Act from employing any individual at the training wage when any other employee has been laid off from the position to be filled at the training wage, or from any substantially equivalent position. Employers are also prohibited from displacing employees for purposes of employing individuals at the training wage. If an employer has unlawfully displaced any employee for such purpose, that employer shall thereafter be disqualified from employing any individuals at the training wage.

### Sec. 517.401 Prohibited layoffs.

(a) No person may be hired for any position at the training wage if, in the previous six months, the employer has laid off any employee (including an employee paid the training wage) from the position to be filled at the training wage, or from any substantially equivalent position in the same locality. This prohibition shall apply unless and until the employer offers the laid off employee(s) employment in the position which the employer proposes to fill at the training

wage, or in the position from which the layoff took place; or if the employer has been unable to locate the laid-off employee(s), until the employer makes a good faith effort to locate such employee(s).

(b) For purposes of this subsection, "layoff" shall mean any involuntary temporary or permanent discontinuance of an employee's employment for reasons not related to the employee's conduct or performance on the job.

(c) For purposes of this subsection, "locality" shall mean the geographic area from which the labor force of the community is predominantly drawn.

(d) For purposes of this subsection, "substantially equivalent position" shall mean a position in which the work is substantially similar in terms of skill, qualifications and responsibility.

### Sec. 517.402 Prohibited displacements.

(a) No employer may terminate any employee (including any employee paid the training wage) or otherwise reduce the number of employees with the intention of filling the vacancy with an employee to be paid the training wage. Furthermore, no employer may take any action to displace any employee (including any employee paid the training wage) for purposes of employing the same employee or any other individual at the training wage, whether or not such displacement creates a vacancy to be filled by such individual.

(b) For purposes of this subsection, "displacement" shall mean a discharge, or any reduction or other change in an employee's hours, wages, benefits or other conditions of employment which may be reasonably viewed as having an adverse effect on the employee.

(c) Examples of prohibited displacements include (but are not limited to) the following:

(1) Termination of employment;

(2) Reduction in wages or benefits;

(3) Reduction in hours of employment;

(4) Demotion;

(5) Reassignment, whether within one establishment or from one establishment to another;

(6) Change in working hours, days or shifts;

(7) Adverse change in established employment practices, such as annual bonuses, wage increases, or promotional opportunities.

### Sec. 517.403 Disqualification and enforcement.

(a) Any employer who violates the provision of this subpart shall be considered to have violated section 15(a)(3) of the Fair Labor Standards Act.

(b) Whenever the Secretary determines that an employer has taken any action to displace employees for purposes of employing individuals at the training wage, the Secretary shall issue an order disqualifying such employer from employing any individual at the training wage.

(c) Employees who are laid off or displaced in violation of section 6 (c) or (d) of the 1989 Amendments may bring an action under section 16(b) of the Act for the payment of wages lost and an additional amount as liquidated damages, and other such legal and equitable relief as may be appropriate, including without limitation employment, reinstatement, or promotion.

(d) Employees who are paid the training wage in violation of the conditions or other requirements of the 1989 Amendments, including the layoff and displacement provisions of sections 6(c), and 6(d)(2)(A), may bring an action under section 16(b) of the Act to recover unpaid minimum wages and unpaid overtime compensation, and an additional amount as liquidated damages.

(e) The Secretary may bring action under section 16(c) or section 17 for such legal or equitable relief as may be appropriate, including relief with respect to employees who are laid off or displaced in violation of the 1989 Amendments, as well as employees who are paid the training wage in violation of the conditions or other requirements set forth in this part.

## Subpart F—Administrative Proceedings

### General

### Sec. 517.500 Applicability of procedures and rules.

The procedures and rules contained in this subpart prescribe the administrative process for disqualification of an employer from employment of an individual eligible for the training wage when the employer has violated the provisions of section 6(d)(2)(A) of the 1989 Amendments, as set forth in Sec. 517.402 of this part.

### Procedures Relating to Hearing

### Sec. 517.501 Written notice of determination required.

Whenever the Administrator determines, on the basis of evidence resulting from an investigation pursuant to Subpart E above, or on the basis of a determination of a court of competent jurisdiction, or otherwise, that an employer has violated the provisions of section 6(d)(2)(A) of the 1989 Amendments, the Administrator shall issue an order proposing to disqualify the employer from employment of any employees at the training wage. The employer against whom such order is proposed shall be notified in writing of such determination. Such notice shall be served in person or by certified mail.

### Sec. 517.502 Contents of notice.

(a) The notice required by Sec. 517.501 of this subpart shall:

(1) Set forth the determination of the Administrator and the reason or reasons therefor;

(2) Except as provided in paragraph (d) of this section, set forth the right to request a hearing on such determination and inform any affected person or persons that in the absence of a timely request for a hearing postmarked or received within 30 days of the date of the notice, the determination of the Administrator shall become final and unappealable; and

(3) Set forth the time and method for requesting a hearing, and the procedures relating thereto, as set forth in Sec. 517.503 of this subpart.

(b) If the Administrator's order is based on a final determination of a court of competent jurisdiction that the employer has displaced an employee in violation of this subpart, the notice shall state that the Administrator's order of disqualification shall be final and is not appealable.

### Sec. 517.503 Request for hearing.

(a) Any person desiring to request an administrative hearing on an order of disqualification pursuant to this subpart shall make such request in writing to the Administrator of the Wage and Hour Division, Employment Standards Administration, U.S. Department of Labor, 200 Constitution Avenue, NW., Washington, DC 20210, postmarked or received no later than thirty (30) days after the date of the notice referred to in Sec. 517.501 of this subpart.

(b) No particular form is prescribed for any request for hearing permitted by this subpart. However, any such request shall:

(1) Be dated;

(2) Be typewritten or legibly written;

(3) Specify the issue or issues stated in the notice of determination giving rise to such request;

(4) State the specific reason or reasons why the person requesting the hearing believes such determination is in error;

(5) Be signed by the person making the request or by an authorized representative of such person; and

(6) Include the address at which such person or authorized representative desires to receive further communications relating thereto.

(c) No hearing shall be afforded to an employer when the Administrator's order is based on a final determination of a court of competent jurisdiction.

### Rules of Practice

### Sec. 517.504 General.

(a) Except as specifically provided in this subpart, and to the extent they do not conflict with the provisions of this subpart, the "Rules of Practice and Procedure for Administrative Hearings Before the Office of Administrative Law Judges" established by the Secretary at 29 CFR part 18 shall apply to administrative proceedings under this subpart.

(b) As provided in the Administrative Procedure Act, 5 U.S.C. 556, any oral or documentary evidence may be received in proceedings under this part. The Federal Rules of Evidence or other rules of evidence shall not apply, but principles designed to ensure production of relevant and probative evidence shall guide the admission of evidence. The Administrative Law Judge may exclude evidence which is immaterial, irrelevant, or unduly repetitive.

### Sec. 517.505 Service and computation of time.

(a) Service of documents under this subpart shall be made by personal service to the individual, an officer of a corporation, or attorney of record or by mailing the determination to the last known address of the individual, officer, or attorney. If done by certified mail, service is complete upon mailing. If done by regular mail or in person, service is complete upon receipt by the addressee or the addressee's agent.

(b) Two (2) copies of all pleadings and other documents required for any administrative proceeding provided by this subpart shall be served on the attorneys for the Department of Labor. One copy shall be served on the Associate Solicitor, Division of Fair Labor Standards, Office of the Solicitor, U.S. Department of Labor, 200 Constitution Avenue NW., Washington, DC 20210, and one copy on the Attorney representing the Department in the proceeding.

(c) Time will be computed beginning with the day following the action and includes the last day of the period unless it is a Saturday, Sunday, or federally-observed holiday, in which case the time period includes the next business day.

### Sec. 517.506 Commencement of proceeding.

Each administrative proceeding permitted under the Act and these regulations shall be commenced upon receipt of a timely request for hearing filed in accordance with Sec. 517.503 of this subpart.

### Referral for Hearing

### Sec. 517.507 Referral to Administrative Law Judge.

(a) Upon receipt of a timely request for a hearing filed pursuant to and in accordance with Sec. 517.503 of this subpart, the Administrator, by the Associate Solicitor for the Division of Fair Labor Standards or by the Regional Solicitor for the Region in which the action arose, shall, by Order of Reference, refer a copy of the notice of administrative determination, and a duplicate copy of the request for hearing, to the Chief Administrative Law Judge, for a determination in an administrative proceeding as provided herein. The notice of administrative determination and request for hearing shall be filed of record in the Office of the Chief Administrative Law Judge and shall, respectively, be given the effect of a complaint and answer thereto for purposes of the administrative proceeding, subject to any amendment that may be permitted under this subpart and 29 CFR part 18.

(b) A copy of the Order of Reference, together with a copy of this part, shall be served by counsel for the Administrator upon the person requesting the hearing, in the manner provided in Sec. 517.505 of this subpart.

### Sec. 517.508 Appointment of Administrative Law Judge and notification of prehearing conference and hearing date.

Upon receipt from the Administrator of an Order of Reference, notice to the parties, attachments and certificate of service, the Chief Administrative Law Judge shall appoint an Administrative Law Judge to hear the case. The Administrative Law Judge shall notify all interested parties of the time and place of a prehearing conference and of the hearing, which shall be held immediately upon the completion of prehearing conference. The date of the prehearing conference and hearing shall be not less than 60 days and not more than 120 days from the date on which the certificate of service indicates the Order of Reference was mailed.

### Sec. 517.509 Decision and Order of Administrative Law Judge.

(a) The Administrative Law Judge shall render, within 120 days after receipt of the transcript of the hearing, a decision on the issues referred by the Administrator.

(b) The decision of the Administrative Law Judge shall be limited to a determination whether the respondent has violated section 6(d)(2)(A) of the 1989 Amendments. The Administrative Law Judge shall not render determinations on the legality of a regulatory provision or the constitutionality of a statutory provision.

(c) The decision of the Administrative Law Judge shall include a statement of findings and conclusions, with reasons and basis therefor, upon each material issue presented on the record. The decision shall also include an appropriate order which may affirm, deny, reverse, or modify, in whole or in part, the determination of the Administrator. If the Administrative Law Judge finds that the Administrator has established by a preponderance of the evidence that the employer has violated the provisions of section 6(d)(2)(A) of the 1989 Amendments, as set forth in Sec. 517.402 of this part, the Administrative Law Judge shall issue an order disqualifying the respondent from employment of any employee at the training wage, effective the date of the employer's violation.

(d) The Administrative Law Judge shall serve copies of the decision on each of the parties.

(e) If any party desires review of the decision of the Administrative Law Judge, a petition for review shall be filed in accordance with Sec. 517.511 of this subpart.

(f) The decision of the Administrative Law Judge shall constitute the final order of the Secretary unless the Secretary, pursuant to Sec. 517.512 of this subpart, issues a notice of intent to review the decision.

### Sec. 517.510 Non-Applicability of the Equal Access to Justice Act.

Proceedings under this part are not subject to the provisions of the Equal Access Justice Act, as amended, 5 U.S.C. 504. In any hearing conducted pursuant to the provisions of this Part, Administrative Law Judges shall have no power or authority to award attorney fees and/or other litigation expenses pursuant to the provisions of the Equal Access to Justice Act.

### Appeals to the Secretary

### Sec. 517.511 Procedures for initiating and undertaking review.

Any party desiring review of the decision of the Administrative Law Judge may petition the Secretary to review the decision. To be effective, such petition must be received by the Secretary within 45 days of the date of the decision of the Administrative Law Judge. Copies of the petition shall be served on all parties and on the Chief Administrative Law Judge. If no timely petition for review has been filed, or where a timely petition has been filed and the Secretary does not issue a notice accepting such a petition for review within 30 days after receipt, the decision of the Administrative Law Judge shall be deemed the final agency action.

### Sec. 517.512 Notice of the Secretary to review decision.

Whenever the Secretary determines to review the decision and order of an Administrative Law Judge, the Secretary shall notify each party of the issue or issues raised; the form in which submission shall be made (i.e., briefs, oral argument, etc.); and the time within which such presentation shall be submitted.

### Sec. 517.513 Final decision of the Secretary.

The Secretary's final decision shall be issued within 120 days of the notice of intent to review the decision and order of the Administrative Law Judge and shall be served upon all parties and the Administrative Law Judge, in person or by certified mail.

### Sec. 517.514 Filing and service.

(a) *Filing.* All documents submitted to the Secretary shall be filed with the Secretary of Labor, U.S. Department of Labor, Washington, DC 20210.

(b) *Number of copies.* An original and two copies of all documents shall be filed.

(c) *Computation of time for delivery by mail.* Documents are not deemed filed with the Secretary until actually received by the Secretary. All documents, including documents filed by mail, must be received by the Secretary either on or before the due date. No additional time shall be added where service of a document requiring action within a prescribed time thereafter was made by mail.

(d) *Manner and proof of service.* A copy of all documents filed with the Secretary shall be served upon all other parties involved in the proceeding. Service under this section shall be by personal delivery or by mail or telefax. Service by mail is deemed effected at the time of mailing to the last known address. Service by telefax is effected when the telefax is received.

### Sec. 517.515 Responsibility of the Office of Administrative Law Judges.

Upon receipt of a petition seeking review of the Decision and Order of an Administrative Law Judge, the Chief Administrative Law Judge shall, within fifteen (15) days, forward a copy of the complete hearing record to the Secretary.

### Record

### Sec. 517.516 Retention of official record.

The official record of every completed administrative hearing provided by this part shall be maintained and filed under the custody and control of the Chief Administrative Law Judge.

### Sec. 517.517 Certification of official record.

Upon receipt of a complaint seeking review by a United States District Court of a Decision and Order issued under this part, the Chief Administrative Law Judge shall promptly certify and file with the appropriate United States District Court, a full, true, and correct copy of the entire record, including the transcript of proceedings.

### Appendix A—Notice to Employees About the Training Wage

The 1989 Amendments to the Fair Labor Standards Act (FLSA) include a provision permitting covered employers to pay eligible workers at a training wage under certain specified conditions. The law requires that you be furnished with a copy of this written notice.

1. The FLSA generally requires that employees receive at least the minimum wage of $3.80 per hour beginning April 1, 1990, and $4.25 per hour beginning April 1, 1991. (Special rates apply to some industries in Puerto Rico and American Samoa.) Unless an exemption in the law applies to you, you are also entitled to one and one-half times your regular rate of pay for hours worked over 40 in a workweek.

2. If you are under the age of 20, your employer may be eligible to employ you for up to 90 days at a training wage of 85 percent of the FLSA's minimum wage or $3.35 per hour, whichever, is greater, under the following conditions:

(a) You are provided this notice.

(b) No other employee has been laid off from the position or a substantially equivalent position.

(c) No other employee has been terminated, or had his or her hours of work or wages, benefits or employment conditions reduced or changed for the purpose of hiring you or any other individual at the training wage.

(d) You are not a migrant or seasonal agricultural worker or a nonimmigrant agricultural worker admitted to the United States under the H-2A program.

(e) You have not previously been employed at the training wage for 90 days.

(f) You have furnished your employer with proof of your age and a signed statement (or documentation) about the starting and ending dates of your previous employment since January 1, 1990, and the hourly wage(s) you earned or, if none, a signed written statement to that effect.

(g) Your hours of work and the type of work you do are permitted under Federal, State, and local child labor laws.

(h) The total number of hours worked by all employees paid at the training wage in any month does not exceed 25 percent of the total number of hours worked by all employees in the establishment.

3. If you are under the age of 20 and you have been employed for 90 calendar days at the training wage, you may be employed at the training wage for up to an additional 90 calendar days provided all of the conditions above are met and, in addition:

(a) Your employer is *not* an employer who employed you during any portion of the initial 90-day period.

(b) Your employer provides on-the-job training in accordance with regulations issued by the Department of Labor.

(c) Your employer provides you with a copy of the training program, and retains a file copy of the training program.

(d) Your employer posts in the establishment a notice of the types of jobs (including yours) for which on-the-job training is being provided and sends the Department of Labor a copy of the notice annually.

4. Unless your employer follows the above rules, you must be paid the full minimum wage.

5. Violations of the training wage provisions by employers can result in the following:

(a) Any employee (or the Department of Labor on his or her behalf) who is terminated, laid off, or has hours, wages, benefits or conditions of employment reduced or changed for purposes of employing an individual at the training wage can file a lawsuit for wages lost and an equal amount as liquidated damages, or equitable relief, including employment, reinstatement or promotion. In addition, the Department of Labor can issue an order disqualifying an employer fom employing anyone at the training wage.

(b) Any employee (or the Department of Labor on his or her behalf) who has not received proper minimum or overtime wages (including proper training wages) can file a lawsuit to recover the amount of such wages plus an equal amount as liquidated damages.

(c) The Department of Labor can seek an injunction to restrain violations by employers, including an injunction requiring the payment of proper wages under the FLSA.

(d) Child labor violations and willful or repeated minimum wage or overtime pay violations by employers can result in the Department of Labor assessing a civil money penalty of up to $1,000 per violation.

(e) In the case of criminal violations by employers, the FLSA provides for penalties of up to $10,000, and, in the case of a second conviction, imprisonment of up to six months, or both.

# TABLE OF CASES

## A

A-AN-E Mfg. Corp., In re, 6 WH Cases 1175 (1946)  80

Aarid Van Lines, In re, 22 WH Cases 1189 (1976)  97

Abbott v. Virginia Beach, 29 WH Cases 609 (CA 4 1989)  46

Ackinclose v. Palm Beach County, 28 WH Cases 1057 (CA 11 1988)  45

Aetna Ins. Co.; EEOC v., 616 F.2d 719, 24 WH Cases 641 (CA 4 1980)  71

Allstate Constr. Co. v. Durkin, 345 U.S. 13, 11 WH Cases 274 (1953)  25

American Airlines; Donovan v., 514 F. Supp. 526, 24 WH Cases 1377 (D Tex 1981), aff'd, 686 F.2d 267, 25 WH Cases 901 (CA 5 1982)  33

American Can Co.; Schultz v., 424 F.2d 536, 19 WH Cases 424 (CA 8 1970)  74

Anaco Reproductions, In re, ASBCA 13799, 70-1 BCA ¶ 8236 (1970)  123

Anclote Manor Found.; Hodgson v., 21 WH Cases 290 (MD Fla 1973)  72

Anderson v. Mt. Clemens Pottery Co., 328 U.S. 680, 6 WH Cases 83 (1946)  6, 48, 53

Anderson & Cristofani, In re, 9 WH Cases 86 (1949), aff'd, 9 WH Cases 596 (1950)  78

Applicability of Bargained Wages, In re, 22 WH Cases 831 (1974)  92, 93

Associated Builders v. Brennan, 21 WH Cases 1009 (DDC 1974)  27

## B

Beal, In re, 29 WH Cases 367 (US DOL 1988)  98

Belo, A.H., Corp.; Walling v., 316 U.S. 624, 2 WH Cases 39 (1942), aff'g 121 F.2d 207, 1 WH Cases 127 (CA 5 1941)  43

Berry v. Board of Supervisors, LSU, 27 WH Cases 1143 (CA 5 1986)  66

Binghamton Constr. Co.; United States v., 347 U.S. 171, 12 WH Cases 20 (1954)  108

Blanton v. Murfreesboro, 28 WH Cases 1353 (CA 6 1988)  44

Bond v. City of Jackson, 29 WH Cases 1022 (SD Miss 1989)  62

Brandon v. United States, 24 WH Cases 1261 (1981)  48

Brennan v., see name of opposing party

Bright v. Houston Northwest Medical Center Survivor, Inc. 29 WH Cases 905 (CA 5 1989)  41

Broad Ave. Laundry v. United States, 681 F.2d 746, 25 WH Cases 918 (Ct Clms 1982), denied attorney's fees, 693 F.2d 1387, 25 WH Cases 1048 (CA FC 1982)  93, 100

Brock v., see name of opposing party

Brookhaven Gen. Hosp.; Hodgson v., 436 F.2d 719, 19 WH Cases 822 (CA 5 1970)  72

Brunner; Marshall v., 668 F.2d 748, 25 WH Cases 313 (CA 3 1982)  24

Building & Constr. Trades v. Donovan, 543 F. Supp. 1282, 25 WH Cases 820 and 553 F. Supp. 352, 25 WH Cases 1078 (DDC 1982), aff'd in part, rev'd in part, 712 F.2d 611, 26 WH Cases 404 (CA DC), cert. denied, 464 U.S. 1069, 26 WH Cases 932 (1983)  108

Burch; Walling v., 5 WH Cases 323 (SD Ga 1945)  18

Burnett Constr. Co. v. United States, 18

WH Cases 698 (Ct Clms 1968), *aff'd*, 413 F.2d 563, 19 WH Cases 185 (1969)　109

Burris v. Mahaney, 29 WH Cases 760 (MD Tenn 1989)　127

Bushman Constr. Co. v. United States, 164 F. Supp. 239, 13 WH Cases 728 (Ct Clms 1968)　110

## C

C. & P. Shoe Corp.; Wirtz v., 336 F.2d 21, 16 WH Cases 624 (CA 5 1964)　27

Calaf v. Gonzalez, 127 F.2d 934, 2 WH Cases 154 (CA 1 1942)　26

Caldwell; Mitchell v., 12 WH Cases 469 (CA 10 1957)　33

Carrasco dba J.C. Liquid Waste Disposal; Brennan v., 540 F.2d 454, 22 WH Cases 1243 (CA 9 1976)　25

Caryk v. Coupe, 663 F. Supp. 1243, 27 WH Cases 1665 (DDC 1987)　34, 51

Charleston Coca-Cola Bottling Co.; Wirtz v., 237 F. Supp. 857, 16 WH Cases 857 (DSC 1965), *rev'd and remanded*, 356 F.2d 428, 17 WH Cases 230 (CA 4 1966)　21

Citicorp Indus. Credit v. Brock, 107 S.Ct. 2694, 28 WH Cases 141 (1987)　18

Claridge Hotel & Casino; Brock v., 664 F. Supp. 899, 28 WH Cases 577 (DNJ 1987)　34

Clark v. Unified Servs., 659 F.2d 49, 25 WH Cases 145 (CA 5 1981)　93

Clothing & Textile Workers, Baltimore Regional Joint Bd.; Hodgson v., 462 F.2d 180, 20 WH Cases 697 (CA 4 1972)　73

Coast Van Lines v. Armstrong, 7 WH Cases 969 (CA 9 1948)　26

Cobra Constr. Co. v. United States, 28 WH Cases 1552 (US ClmsCt 1988)　122

Coleman v. Jiffy June Farms, 458 F.2d 1139, 20 WH Cases 321 (CA 5 1971), *reh'g denied*, 458 F.2d 1142, 20 WH Cases 630 (CA 5), *cert. denied*, 409 U.S. 948, 20 WH Cases 937 (1972)　6, 50, 57

Commercial Index Bureau; Brock v., 27 WH Cases 1384 (D Md 1986)　21

Cooper Gen. Contractor, Inc. v. United States, 28 WH Cases 1135 (CA FC 1988)　122, 131

Copper Plumbing & Heating Co. v. Campbell, 290 F.2d 368, 15 WH Cases 34 (CA DC 1961)　124

Corning Glass Works v. Brennan, 417 U.S. 188, 21 WH Cases 767 (1974)　74

## D

Dallas Indep. School Dist.; Usery v., 421 F. Supp. 111, 22 WH Cases 1377 (ND Tex 1976)　69

Darby, F.W., Lumber Co.; United States v., 312 U.S. 100, 1 WH Cases 17 (1941)　18

Davis v. Food Lion, 27 WH Cases 1214 (CA 4 1986)　33

Davison Fuel & Dock Co.; United States v., 371 F.2d 705, 17 WH Cases 622 (CA 4 1967)　79

Delaware State College v. Ricks, 449 U.S. 250, 24 FEP Cases 827 (1980)　51

Deluxe Cleaners & Laundry; United States v., 511 F.2d 926, 22 WH Cases 159 (CA 4 1975)　98

Descomp, Inc. v. Sampson, 377 F. Supp. 254, 21 WH Cases 999 (D Del 1974)　92

Dokken, In re, 25 WH Cases 700 (1981)　99

Dole v.; *see* name of opposing party

Donovan v., *see* name of opposing party

Duchon v. Cajon Co., 27 WH Cases 1077 (CA 6 1986)　48

Durham Sandwich Co.; Wirtz v., 367 F.2d 810, 17 WH Cases 474 (CA 4 1966)　47

Dynamic Enters., In re, 22 WH Cases 1163 (1976)　100

## E

Eastern Serv. Mgmt. Co., In re, 22 WH Cases 796 (1975)　92–93

Ebert v. Lamar Truck Plaza, 29 WH Cases 814 (CA 10 1989)　73

EEOC v., *see* name of opposing party

El Paso Natural Gas Co.; Brock v., 826 F.2d 369, 28 WH Cases 629 (CA 5 1987)　34

Electric City Linoleum, Inc., In re, 22 WH Cases 987 (1976)　100

Electrical Workers (IBEW) Local 5 v. United States Dep't of Housing & Urban Dev., 28 WH Cases 1215 (CA 3 1988)　115

Emerald Maintenance, In re, 20 WH
Cases 1174 (1972) *and* 21 WH Cases
10 (1973)   96, 99

# F

Facchiano v. Brock, 28 WH Cases 1529
(CA 3 1988)   117
Fallon v. Illinois, 29 WH Cases 733 (CA
7 1989)   72
Filardo v. Foley Bros., Inc., 297 NY 217,
78 N.E.2d 484, 7 WH Cases 811
(CtApps 1948), *cert. denied*, 336 U.S.
281, 8 WH Cases 576 (1949)   121
Finnan v. Elmhurst Contracting Co.,
107 N.Y.S.2d 497, 9 WH Cases 686
(1950)   123
Firefighters Local 2203 v. West Adams
County, 29 WH Cases 542 (CA 10
1989)   46
First State Abstract & Ins. Co.; Wirtz v.,
362 F.2d 83, 17 WH Cases 358 (CA 8
1966)   47
First Victoria Nat'l Bank; Hodgson v.,
446 F.2d 47, 20 WH Cases 132 (CA 5
1971)   72
Foster v. Parker Transfer Co., 528 F.
Supp. 906, 25 WH Cases 848 (WD Pa
1981)   97
Framlau Corp. v. Dembling, 21 WH
Cases 1024 (ED Pa 1973)   108
Friedman v. Weiner, 515 F. Supp. 563,
25 WH Cases 38 (D Colo 1981)   68

# G

Garcia v. San Antonio Metropolitan
Transit Auth., 469 U.S. 528, 27 WH
Cases 65 (1985)   4, 15, 43, 69
Gilioz v. Webb, 99 F.2d 585, 1 WH
Cases 210 (CA 5 1938)   108
Glenn Elec. Co. v. Donovan, 755 F.2d
1028, 27 WH Cases 97 (CA 11
1985)   51, 59
Glover dba Safe Bldg. Maintenance Co.,
In re, 22 WH Cases 702 (1974),
*recommendation for relief from penalty*, 22
WH Cases 705 (1975)   99
Griffin & Brand of McAllen, Inc.;
Hodgson v., 471 F.2d 235, 20 WH
Cases 1051 (CA 5 1973)   32
Griffith Co., In re, 17 WH Cases 49
(1965)   103
Guess v. Montague, 140 F.2d 500, 3
WH Cases 590 (CA 4 1943)   17

# H

Hardin & Co.; Wirtz v., 359 F.2d 792,
17 WH Cases 331 (CA 5 1966)   21
Hay Assocs.; EEOC v., 545 F. Supp.
1064, 25 WH Cases 858 (ED Pa
1982)   71
Hill v. J.C. Penney Co., 688 F.2d 370,
25 WH Cases 974 (CA 5 1982)   74
Ho Fat Seto; McLaughlin v., 28 WH
Cases 1225 (CA 9 1988)   55
Hodgson v., *see* name of opposing
party
Home Improvement Corp. v. Brennan,
22 WH Cases 295 (ND Ohio
1974)   116
Home of Economy, Inc.; EEOC v., 539
F. Supp. 507, 25 WH Cases 675 (DND
1982), *rev'd*, 712 F.2d 356, 26 WH
Cases 481 (CA 8 1983)   67
Hudgins-Dize Co.; United States v., 83
F. Supp. 593, 8 WH Cases 592 (ED
Va 1949)   80

# I

Inland Serv. Corp. v. United States, 25
WH Cases 1017 (Ct Clms 1982)   123

# J

Jacksonville Terminal Co.; Walling v.,
148 F.2d 768, 5 WH Cases 269 (CA 5
1945)   32
Janik Paving & Constr. v. Brock, 828
F.2d 84, 28 WH Cases 417 (CA 2
1987)   124
Janitorial Servs. Inc.; Donovan v., 672
F.2d 528, 25 WH Cases 487 (CA 5
1982)   21
Jen-Beck Assocs., In re, 28 WH Cases
1162 (US DOL 1987)   117
Jewell Ridge Coal Corp. v. Mine
Workers Local 6167, 325 U.S. 161, 5
WH Cases 301 (1945)   54

# K

Kane, John J., Hosp.; Usery v., 544
F.2d 148, 22 WH Cases 1382 (CA 3
1976)   69
Keziah v. W.M. Brown & Son, 29 WH
Cases 862 (CA 4 1989)   73
Kirchdorfer v. McLaughlin, 29 WH
Cases 426 (WD Ky 1989)   100

## L

Labor Department v.; *see* name of opposing party

Laborers' Pension Trust Fund v. Safeco Ins. Co. of Am., 29 WH Cases 61 (ED Mich 1988)　131

Laffey v. Northwest Airlines, 567 F.2d 429, 22 WH Cases 1320 (CA DC 1976), *cert. denied*, 434 U.S. 1086 (1978)　58

Lauritzen Farms; Brock v., 27 WH Cases 930 (ED Wis 1985)　32

Le Vick v. Skaggs Co., 701 F.2d 777, 26 WH Cases 72 (CA 9 1983)　127

Lease of Space for Outpatient Clinic, Crown Point, Ind., In re, WAB No. 86-33 (1987)　89

Legg v. Rock Prods. Mfg. Corp., 309 F.2d 172, 15 WH Cases 671 (CA 10 1962)　28

Lewis v. News World Communications, Inc., 28 WH Cases 473 (DDC 1987)　29

Lyon & Borah, Inc., In re, 8 WH Cases 566 (1949)　80

## M

Mabee v. White Plains Publishing Co., 327 U.S. 178, 5 WH Cases 877 (1946)　18

Mack Farland & Sons Roofing Co.; Schultz v., 413 F.2d 1296, 19 WH Cases 49 (CA 5 1969)　21

Maguire v. Trans World Airlines, 535 F. Supp. 1283, 25 WH Cases 529 (SD NY 1982)　66, 70

Marshall v., *see* name of opposing party

Martinez v. Phillips Petroleum Co., 283 F. Supp. 514, 18 WH Cases 573 (D Idaho 1968), *aff'd*, 424 F.2d 547, 19 WH Cases 587 (CA 9 1970)　120

McDaniel v. Brown & Root, Inc., 7 WH Cases 978 (ED Okla 1948), *aff'd*, 172 F.2d 466, 8 WH Cases 487 (CA 10 1949)　121

McDaniel v. University of Chicago, 548 F.2d 689, 23 WH Cases 43 (CA 7), *cert. denied*, 434 U.S. 1033, 23 WH Cases 556 (1977)　114

McGee Bros. Co.; McLaughlin v., 28 WH Cases 808 (1988)　48

McLaughlin v., *see* name of opposing party

McLaughlin Storage, Inc., In re, 22 WH Cases 711 (1975)　99

Mechmet v. Four Seasons Hotels, 825 F.2d 1173, 28 WH Cases 441 (CA 7 1987)　42

Melos Constr. Corp.; Wirtz v., 408 F.2d 626, 18 WH Cases 794 (CA 2 1969)　21

Military Housing, Ft. Drum, In re (WAB 1985)　109

Miree Constr. Corp., In re, 29 WH Cases 286 (WAB 1989)　112

Mitchell v., *see* name of opposing party

Molinari v. McNeil Pharmaceutical, 27 WH Cases 1236 (ED Pa 1986)　29

Mullens v. Howard County, 29 WH Cases 1081 (D Md 1990)　47

Myers & Myers, Inc., In re, 22 WH Cases 961 (1975)　99

## N

National Electro-Coatings, Inc. v. Brock, 28 WH Cases 1289 (ND Ohio 1988)　88, 119

National League of Cities v. Usery, 426 U.S. 833, 22 WH Cases 1064 (1976)　4, 15, 68

Negri, In re, 9 WH Cases 139 (1949), *aff'd*, 9 WH Cases 578 (1950)　79

New England Coal & Coke Co.; United States v., 318 F.2d 138, 16 WH Cases 11 (CA 1 1963)　80

Norris, Inc., In re, 8 WH Cases 643 (1949)　79

Northwest Airlines v. Transport Workers, 451 U.S. 77, 24 WH Cases 1302 (1981)　73

## O

Oil Workers Local 2-652 v. EG & G Idaho, Inc., 29 WH Cases 255 (Idaho SupCt 1989)　113

Operating Eng'rs Local 3 v. Bohn, 541 F. Supp. 486, 25 WH Cases 740 (D Utah 1982), *aff'd*, 737 F.2d 860, 26 WH Cases 1314 (CA 10 1984)　110

Ortiz v. San Juan Dock Co., 5 WH Cases 662 (DPR 1945)　107

Overstreet v. North Shore Corp., 318 U.S. 125, 2 WH Cases 68 (1943)　17

Ozmer; United States v., 8 WH Cases 789 (ND Ga 1949), *aff'd*, 181 F.2d 508, 9 WH Cases 360 (CA 5 1950)　79

# P

Painters Local 419 v. Brown, 656 F.2d 564, 25 WH Cases 22 (CA 10 1981)   116

Palardy v. Horner, 29 WH Cases 393 (D Mass 1989)   61

Patel v. Quality Inn South, 28 WH Cases 1105 (CA 11 1988)   24

Patton-Tulley Transp. Co.; Walling v., 134 F.2d 945, 3 WH Cases 225 (CA 6 1943)   107

Pelham's, In re, 7 WH Cases 966 (1948)   79

Pilgrim Equip. Co.; Usery v., 527 F.2d 1308, 22 WH Cases 783 (CA 5 1976)   32

Poirier & McLane Corp. v. United States, 120 F. Supp. 209, 12 WH Cases 73 (Ct Clms 1954)   109

Portland Terminal Co.; Walling v., 330 U.S. 148, 6 WH Cases 611 (1947)   31

Powell v., *see* name of opposing party

Powers Bldg. Maintenance Co.; United States v., 336 F. Supp. 819, 20 WH Cases 434 (WD Okla 1972)   98

# Q

Quality Maintenance Co., In re, 20 WH Cases 1010 (1972) *and* 21 WH Cases 303 (1973)   94, 99

# R

Real v. Driscoll Strawberry Assocs., 603 F.2d 748, 24 WH Cases 279 (CA 9 1979)   32

Rhinebarger v. Orr, 28 WH Cases 1424 (CA 7 1988)   45

Richland Shoe Co.; McLaughlin v., 799 F.2d 80, 28 WH Cases 1017 (1988)   7, 57

Roman, In re, 22 WH Cases 764 (1975)   94, 95

Rutherford Food Corp. v. McComb, 331 U.S. 722, 6 WH Cases 990 (1947)   21

# S

Sagner, Inc.; Hodgson v., 326 F. Supp. 371, 20 WH Cases 49 (D Md 1971), *aff'd*, 462 F.2d 180, 20 WH Cases 697 (CA 4 1972)   73

Sansone Co. v. California Dep't of Transp., 22 WH Cases 1008 (Cal CtApps 1976)   103

Savannah Bank & Trust Co. of Savannah; Wirtz v., 362 F.2d 857, 17 WH Cases 374 (CA 5 1966)   21

Schultz v., *see* name of opposing party

Shenandoah Baptist Church; Dole v., 899 F.2d 1389, 29 WH Cases 1209 (CA 4 1990)   22

Sherwood v. Washington Post, 29 WH Cases 399 (CA DC 1989)   29

Sideris; Donovan v., 524 F. Supp. 521 (D Neb 1981), *rev'd*, 688 F.2d 74, 25 WH Cases 922 (CA 8 1982)   21

Skipper v. Superior Dairies, Inc., 512 F.2d 409, 22 WH Cases 272 (CA 5 1975)   47

Sniadach v. Family Finance Corp., 395 U.S. 337, 19 WH Cases 5 (1969)   128

South Davis Community Hosp.; Brennan v., 22 WH Cases 177 (D Utah 1974), *aff'd*, 538 F.2d 859, 22 WH Cases 1153 (CA 10 1976)   71

Southern Packaging & Storage Co. v. United States, 458 F. Supp. 726, 23 WH Cases 1085 (DSC 1978), *aff'd*, 618 F.2d 1093, 24 WH Cases 701 (CA 4 1980)   92

Southwest Eng'g Corp. v. United States, 21 WH Cases 1069 (Ct Clms 1974)   108

Stafford's Might Maid, Inc.; Department of Labor v., 29 WH Cases 94 (US DOL 1988)   124

Steele v. L.F. Rothschild & Co., 29 WH Cases 259 (CA 2 1988), *dismissing* 29 WH Cases 258 (SDNY 1988)   67

Steuart & Bros. v. Bowles, 322 U.S. 398 (1944)   124

# T

Taskpower Int'l, In re, 22 WH Cases 802, *on remand*, 22 WH Cases 807 (1975)   99

Teamsters Local 427 v. Philco-Ford Corp., 661 F.2d 776, 25 WH Cases 185 (CA 9 1981)   97

Tennessee Coal, Iron & RR v. Muscoda Local 123, 321 U.S. 590, 4 WH Cases 293 (1944), *aff'g* 135 F.2d 320, 3 WH Cases 142 (CA 5 1943)   54

Tierra Vista, Inc.; Donovan v., 27 WH Cases 1222 (CA 10 1986)   43

Townsend v. Mercy Hosp. of
Pittsburgh, 29 WH Cases 68 (CA 3
1988)   41
Trans World Airlines v. Thurston, 469
U.S. 111, 36 FEP Cases 977 (1985)   58
Trent v. Adria Laboratories, Inc., 25
WH Cases 373 (ND Ga 1982)   72
Trinity Servs., Inc. v. Usery, 428 F.
Supp. 318, 22 WH Cases 1452 (DDC
1976), *rev'd*, 593 F.2d 1250, 24 WH
Cases 216 (CA DC 1978)   96

## U

United Cal. Discount Corp., 29 WH
Cases 1086 (1990)   93
United States v., *see* name of opposing
party
Universities Research Ass'n v. Coutu,
450 U.S. 754, 24 WH Cases 1273
(1981)   115
U.S. Cartridge Co.; Powell v., 339 U.S.
497, 9 WH Cases 362 (1950)   24, 85
Usery v., *see* name of opposing party

## V

Van Elk, In re, 22 WH Cases 708
(1975)   99
Veader v. Bay State Dredging &
Contracting Co., 79 F. Supp. 837, 8
WH Cases 71 (D Mass 1948)   116
Verticare, In re, 29 WH Cases 265 (DOL
1988)   125
Veterans Admin., In re, 28 WH Cases
435 (WAB 1987)   112
Veterans Cleaning Serv., Inc.; Brennan
v. 21 WH Cases 218 (CA 5 1973)   40

Victoria Bank & Trust Co.; Brennan v.,
493 F.2d 896, 21 WH Cases 798 (CA 5
1974)   72

## W

Walling v., *see* name of opposing party
West Coast Hotel Co. v. Parrish, 300
U.S. 379, 1 WH Cases 38 (1937)   3
Western Union Tel. Co. v. Lenroot, 323
U.S. 490, 4 WH Cases 951 (1945)   24
White Glove-Building Maintenance v.
Brennan, 518 F.2d 1271, 22 WH Cases
319 (CA 9 1975)   96
White Glove-Building Maintenance, Inc.
v. Hodgson, 459 F.2d 179, 20 WH
Cases 539 (CA 9 1972)   96
Wilamowsky; Brock v., 833 F.2d 11, 28
WH Cases 608 (CA 2 1987)   42
Williams dba Williams Sand & Gravel
Co.; Wirtz v., 369 F.2d 783, 17 WH
Cases 526 (CA 5 1966)   27
Wilson v. City of Charlotte, 29 WH
Cases 132 (WDNC 1988)   46
Wirtz v., *see* name of opposing party
Woodside Village, In re, 22 WH Cases
1115 (1976)   116
Wright v. City of Jackson, 29 WH Cases
1025 (SD Miss 1989)   63

## Z

Zachry, H.B., Co.; Mitchell v., 362 U.S.
310, 14 WH Cases 525 (1960)   25
Zachry Co. v. United States, 16 WH
Cases 926 (Ct Clms 1965)   103

# INDEX

## A

Abatement; OSHA   128–130
Administrative employee   28–29
  directly related test   28
Administrative Procedure Act   108
Affiliated persons   40
Age Discrimination in Employment Act
      of 1967 (ADEA)   64, 130
Airline trainees   33
Anti-Kickback Law   126
Apprentices   31
  appenticeship agreements   31
Arbitration
  Davis-Bacon Act   113
  Equal Pay Act   67
Area Redevelopment Act of 1961   130
Armed Services Board of Contract
      Appeals   100
Attorney's fees
  Davis-Bacon Act   110
  FLSA   50, 51

## B

Bankruptcy   126–127
Basic rate of pay; CWHSSA   118
Belo plans (see also Fluctuating
      workweek)   43, 118
Blacklist (see Debarment)

## C

Cause of action
  accrual of   56
Certificate of exemption   37
Child Labor   48
Child Support Enforcement Act (CSEA)
  in general   12, 128

notice   12, 128
penalties   12
prohibitions   12, 128
wage withholding   12, 128
Closely related standard   68
Compensatory (comp) time   15–16, 43,
      45–46
Conciliation; Equal Pay Act
  EEOC duty   67
Consumer Credit Protection Act (CCPA)
  bankruptcy   126–127
  disposable earnings   11, 127
  enforcement   11, 127
  garnishment   11, 127
  in general   11–12, 126–128
  penalties   12, 127
  prohibitions   11, 127
  state sovereignty   12, 127–128
Continuing violation theory   56
Contract Work-Hours and Safety
      Standards Act (Work-Hours
      Act; CWHSSA)
  basic rate of pay   118
  blacklist   119, 121, 124
  conflict with other laws   120
  coverage
    contracts   119–120
    employees   120
  criminal sanctions   121
  debarment   119, 121, 124, 125
  dollar-volume standard   125
  in general   10–11, 77, 92, 102, 108,
      118–125
  health & safety   120–121
  limitations   122–123
  liquidated damages   122–123
  open-market contracts   120
  overtime   10–11, 92, 118
  penalties   11, 109, 119, 121, 124

willful violations   11, 119, 121
withholding of payments   11, 122, 124
Copeland Act   126
Criminal penalties; OSHA   130
Criminal sanctions; CWHSSA   121

# D

Davis-Bacon Act
  actions against U.S.
    government   115–116
  1965 amendments   112
  attorney's fees   110
  conflict with other laws   106–107
  coverage   102–106
  debarment   10, 116–117
  dollar-volume test   102
  employee actions   114–115
  enforcement   113–116
  fringe benefits   112
    mix formula of fringe/wage
      pay   112
  in general   9–10, 55, 59, 77, 83, 102–117, 123
  helpers   107
  initial construction standard   103
  integral part standard   104, 105–106
  limitations   114
  locality   107
  materialmen   102
  prevailing party   110
  prevailing wages   9–10, 92, 107–112, 115
  reimbursement   109–110, 113
  willful violations   10, 117
  withholding of payments   10, 109
De minimis rule   48, 54–55
Debarment
  CWHSSA   119, 121, 124
  Davis-Bacon Act   116
  Service Contract Act   98
Deductions from wages   39–40
Department of Defense Authorization
    Act of 1986
  affecting Contract Work-Hours
    Act   10–11, 118
  affecting Walsh-Healey Act   8, 75
Directly essential standard   68
Directly related test (*see also*
    Administrative employee)   28
Disposable earnings; CCPA   127
Dollar-volume test
  CWHSSA   125
  FLSA   18–19, 69–70

Service Contract Act   88, 89
Walsh-Healey Act   78–79

# E

Economic realities test   5, 32
Eight-Hour Law   3, 118, 123
Employee; Service Contract Act
    definition   91
Employee coverage
  Equal Pay Act   67–68
  FLSA
    engaged in commerce test   22–24
    fringe production employees   24–25
    production for commerce test   24
Employee exemptions; FLSA
  administrative employee   28–29
  executive employee   26–28
  in general   25–33
  independent contractors   31–32
  nonemployees   31–33
  professional employee   29
    directly related standard   28
    long test   30
    primary duty standard   26–31
    short test   30–31
    sole charge standard   28
    salary tests   27, 30–31
    white-collar exemptions   26–31, 91
Employee exemptions; Walsh-
    Healey   78
Employee protection provisions   130–132
Employee Retirement Income Security
    Act of 1974 (ERISA)   130
Energy Reorganization Act   130
Enterprise   5, 20–22
Equal Access to Justice Act   100–101
Equal Employment Opportunity
    Commission (EEOC)   64, 66–67, 92
Equal Pay Act
  enterprise   7, 66, 69–70
  enforcement   66–67
    conciliation   67
  employee coverage   67–68
  employer coverage   68–69
  establishment   7, 66, 70
  exemptions   65, 70–73
  factor other than sex   65–66, 70–73
  in general   6–7, 14–15, 64–74
  good-faith defense   64–65
  limitations   74
  penalties   74

prejudgment interest 74
remedies 74
Equivalent combination of fringes & wages; SCA 87
Executive employee 26–28
sole charge standard 28
Executive Order 12144 64

## F

Fair Labor Standards Act (FLSA)
1949 amendments 68
1961 amendments 49, 69
1963 amendments 14
1966 amendments 3, 14–15, 56
1974 amendments 3–4, 15, 70
1985 amendments 4, 15–16, 43–44
1986 amendments 37
1989 amendments 34–37
commerce 13
congressional policy 13
coverage
employees 13–14, 22–25
employers 13, 18–20
dollar-volume test 18–19
enforcement 49–50
engaged in production of goods for commerce 13
enterprise 13–14, 20–22
in general 2–6, 13–52, 92, 98, 107, 118, 123
injunctions 49
Interstate Commerce requirement 17–18
investigations 50
limitations (*see* Limitations)
liquidated damages 51–52
minimum wages 34–40, 91
overtime 40–43
compensatory time (*see* Compensatory time)
penalties 50
posters 48
report to Congress 50
white-collar exemptions 26–31
Fluctuating workweek (*see also* Belo plans) 42–43, 118
Fringe benefits
Davis-Bacon Act 112
Service Contract Act
in geneal 95–96
offsets 96–97
Fringe production employees 24–25, 68

## G

Garnishment; CCPA 127
Good-faith defense
Equal Pay Act 64–65
Portal Act 6, 51, 60–63, 123
Government employees (*see* State and local government employees)

## H

*Handbook of Blue-Collar Occupational Families and Series* 91
Handicapped workers 37
Health and safety
CWHSSA 120–121
Walsh-Healey Act 85
Helpers; Davis-Bacon Act 107
Hours of work 33

## I

Immigration Reform & Control Act 21
In the picture standard 6, 50, 57–58
Independent contractors 31–32
test 32
Initial construction standard; Davis-Bacon Act 103
Injunctions; FLSA 49
Integral part standard; Davis-Bacon Act 104, 105–106
Interest
prejudgment 74
Service Contract Act 98
Interpretative Bulletin; Wage-Hour Administrator's 60, 61–62
Investigations; FLSA 50
Irregular hours 43

## J

Joint employer 5

## K

Kickbacks 39

## L

Limitations
CWHSSA 122–123
Davis-Bacon Act 114
FLSA 50–51, 98
general six-year period 48

Portal Act requirements   51, 58–59
Service Contract Act   98
Liquidated damages
  CWHSSA   122–133
  FLSA   51–52
Locality
  Davis-Bacon Act   107
  Service Contract Act   92
Long test (*see also* Employee
      exemptions)   30

# M

Market-force theory   72
Materialmen; Davis-Bacon Act   102
McNamara-O'Hara Service Contract Act
      (Service Contract Act)
  attorney's fees   100–101
  blacklist   9, 87–88, 98–100
  coverage
    contracts   88–90
    employees   90–91
    exemptions   89–90
    in general   88–91
  debarment   9, 87, 98–100
  dollar-volume standard   88, 89
  employee; defined   91
  enforcement   97–98
  in general   9, 77, 87–101, 123
  limitations   98
  locality   92
  overtime   92
  penalties   87–88, 97–98, 98–100
    unusual circumstances   87–88,
        99–100
  prevailing wages   91–92
  principal purpose   88
  recordkeeping   94–95, 97
  service employees   90
  Standard Metropolitan Statistical
        Area   92
  statistics   92
  successors   92–93
  underpayments   87, 97–98
  United States; as contracting
        party   90
  unusual circumstances   87–88,
        99–100
  variance proceedings   93
  wages   9, 87, 91–92, 95–96
    deductions   94
    fringe benefits   87, 91–93, 95–96
      equivalent combination   87
    payments   94–95

  wage determinations   91–92
  willful violation   99
  withholding of payments   9, 87, 94,
        97–98
Meals, lodgings and other facilities   39
Merit system exemption; Equal Pay
        Act   65–66, 70, 71
Migrant farmworkers   32
Migrant & Seasonal Agricultural
        Workers Protection Act
        (MSAWPA)   130
Miller Act   114, 130, 131
Mineral Land Act   130
Minimum wages
  certificate of exemption   37
  in general   34–40
  handicapped workers   37
  sheltered workshops   37
Mix formula; wage-fringe payments
        under Davis-Bacon Act   112
Motor Carrier Act   130

# N

National Defense Contracts Act of
        1958   111
National Foundation on the Arts and
        Humanities Act   130
National Institute of Occupational
        Safety and Health
        (NIOSH)   129
Nonemployees   31–33
  apprentices   31
  independent contractors   31–32
  trainees   32–33

# O

Occupational Safety and Health Act
        (OSHA)
  abatement   129
  in general   128–130
  NIOSH   129
  penalties   130
  prohibitions   130
  rulemaking   129
Off-the-road employees   25
Open-market agreements   77, 81
Overtime
  comp time   43
  in general   40–43
  maximum hours   40
  recordkeeping   47–48
  regular rate of pay   41–42

Service Contract Act 92
Walsh-Healey Act 8, 76

## P

Penalties
  CCPA 127
  CWHSSA 11, 109, 119, 121, 124
  FLSA 50
  OSHA 130
Personal liability; Walsh-Healey 80
Portal-to-Portal Act (Portal Act)
  1966 amendments 56–57, 58
  accrual of action 56
  area of production 60
  continuing violation theory 56
  in general 6–7, 51–52, 53–63, 114, 123
  good-faith belief; defense of 6, 51, 59, 60–63, 123
  Interpretative Bulletin; Wage-Hour Admin. 60–62
  limitations (*see* Limitations)
  liquidated damages (*see* Liquidated damages)
  in the picture standard 6, 50, 57–58
  postliminary activities 54–55, 56, 59
  preliminary activities 53–55, 56, 59
  principal activities 55–56
  representative actions 56, 59
  willful violations 56–59
Posters; FLSA provisions 48
Postliminary activities 54–55, 56, 59
Prejudgment interest
  Equal Pay Act 74
  Service Contract Act 98
Preliminary activities 53–55, 56, 59
Prevailing party; Davis-Bacon Act 110
Prevailing wages
  Davis-Bacon Act 9–10, 92, 107–112
  Service Contract Act 91–92
  Walsh-Healey Act 8, 76–77
Primary duty standard 26–31
Principal activities 55–56
Principal purpose of contract; Service Contract Act 88
Production of goods for interstate commerce 67–68
Productivity exemption; Equal Pay Act 65, 70–73
Professional employee 29, 68
Prohibitions; CCPA 127
Public safety, emergency and seasonal personnel 16, 45
Purchase-notice agreement 79

## R

Rates of pay
  in general 34–40
  hourly rate 34, 35, 36
  mixed rate 38
  piece rate 38
  regular rate 40–42
  tipped employee 37
  weekly salary 38
Recordkeeping; FLSA
  in general 47–48
  limitations; general 47–48
  limitations; Portal Act 51
  Service Contract Act 94–95, 97
  Walsh-Healey Act 84
Regular rate of pay; FLSA 40–42, 118
Rehabilitation Act of 1973 130
Reimbursement; Davis-Bacon Act 109–110, 113
Reorganization Act of 1977 64
Reorganization Plan No. 1 of 1978 64
Report to Congress; FLSA 50
Representative actions; Portal Act 56, 59
Retaliation; OSHA 130
Rule on trifles 48, 54–55
Rulemaking; OSHA 129

## S

Safety standards
  Walsh-Healey Act 85
  Work-Hours Act 120
Salary tests (*see also* White-collar exemptions) 27, 30–31
Seniority system exemption; Equal Pay Act 65, 70
Service employees; Service Contract Act 90
Sheltered workshops 37
Short test (*see also* Employee Exemptions) 30–31
Social Security Act 128
Sole charge standard (*see* Executive employee) 28
Sporadic and substitute employment 16, 43
Standard Metropolitan Statistical Area 92
State and local government employees
  comp time 43, 45–46
  exemption for small force 46
  in general 43–47
  overtime limits 46–47

police and firefighters tour of duty
    rules  45, 46–47
public safety, emergency and
    seasonal employees  45
Statistics; Service Contract Act  92
Statute of limitations (*see* Limitations)
Subcontractors; Walsh-Healey  77, 80
Substitute manufacturer  82
Successor; Walsh-Healey  81–82
Suffer or permit to work standard  32
Supply contract; Walsh-Healey  79
Surface Transportation Assistance Act
    of 1982  130

**T**

Tipped employee  37
Title VII, Civil Rights Act of 1964  7
Traditional governmental functions
    test  15
Trainees (*see* Nonemployees)
Tucker Act  130–131

**U**

Underpayments; Service Contract
    Act  87
United States
    as defendant in Davis-Bacon Act
        suits  115–116
United States as contracting party;
    Service Contract Act  90
Unusual circumstances; Service Contract
    Act  87–88, 99–100
U.S. Constitution
    Commerce Clause  15
    State sovereignty  12, 69
    Tenth Amendment  12, 69

**V**

Volunteers  16

**W**

Wage Appeals Board  108
Wage determinations; Service Contract
    Act  91–92
Wage withholding; CSEA  12, 128
Wages; Service Contract Act
    deductions  94

determinations  91–92
payments  94–95
Walsh-Healey Act
    blacklist  9, 84
    conflict with other laws  84–85, 125
    coverage
        contractors  79–80
        contracts  78–79, 83–84
        employees  77–78, 82–83
        subcontractors  77, 80, 81–82
    debarment  9, 84
    dollar-volume standard  78–79
    employees  77–78, 82–83
    enforcement  84–85
    exemptions  64–67, 78, 80–84
    in general  8–9, 55, 59, 75–86, 87,
        92, 106, 107, 114, 123, 125
    health & safety provisions  76
    open-market agreements  77, 81
    overtime  8, 76
    penalties  84
    personal liability  80
    prevailing wages  8, 76–77
    purchase–notice agreements  79
    recordkeeping  84
    regular dealers  76, 79
    successor  81–82
    supply contracts  79
    willful violation  84
Weekly salary; fixed (*see also* Rates of
    pay)  38
White-collar exemptions
    Equal Pay Act  68
    FLSA (*see also* Employee exemptions)
        administrative employee  28–29
        executive employee  26–28
        in general  5, 25–33
        long test  30
        professional employee  29
        salary tests  27, 30–31
        short test  30–31
Willful violations
    CWHSSA  119, 121
    FLSA  5–6, 50, 51, 56–59, 74
    Walsh-Healey Act  84
Withholding of payment; Service
    Contract Act  87
Work-Hours Act (*see* Contract Work-
    Hours and Safety Standards
    Act)
Workweek  38
    fluctuating  42–43

# About the Author

Joseph E. Kalet, a former cryptologist/interpreter for the U.S. Navy, is Assistant Legal Counsel for the Metropolitan Washington Airports Authority. Formerly with The Bureau of National Affairs, Inc., Washington, D.C., Mr. Kalet is an Honors Graduate from the State University of New York at Binghamton, N.Y., and an Honors Graduate from the Foreign Service Institute, Washington, D.C. He received his Juris Doctor from the George Washington University-National Law Center, Washington, D.C.

Mr. Kalet is a frequent speaker on labor law before such organizations as the National Association of Attorneys General and the National Labor Relations Board. He has written for the *American Bar Association Journal*, the *Arbitration Journal*, and other professional publications. He is a member of the National Labor Panel of the American Arbitration Association. He also is a member of the District of Columbia and Pennsylvania Bars. Mr. Kalet is also the author of *Age Discrimination in Employment Law*, Second Edition.